D1131165

FRANKLIN BARBECUE

# FRANKLIN
# BARBECUE

## • A MEAT-SMOKING MANIFESTO •

**AARON FRANKLIN**

*and*

**JORDAN MACKAY**

Photography by Wyatt McSpadden

**TEN SPEED PRESS**
Berkeley

**DEDICATION**

*To my wonderful wife, Stacy,*
*our beautiful daughter, Vivian,*
*and our little dog too!*

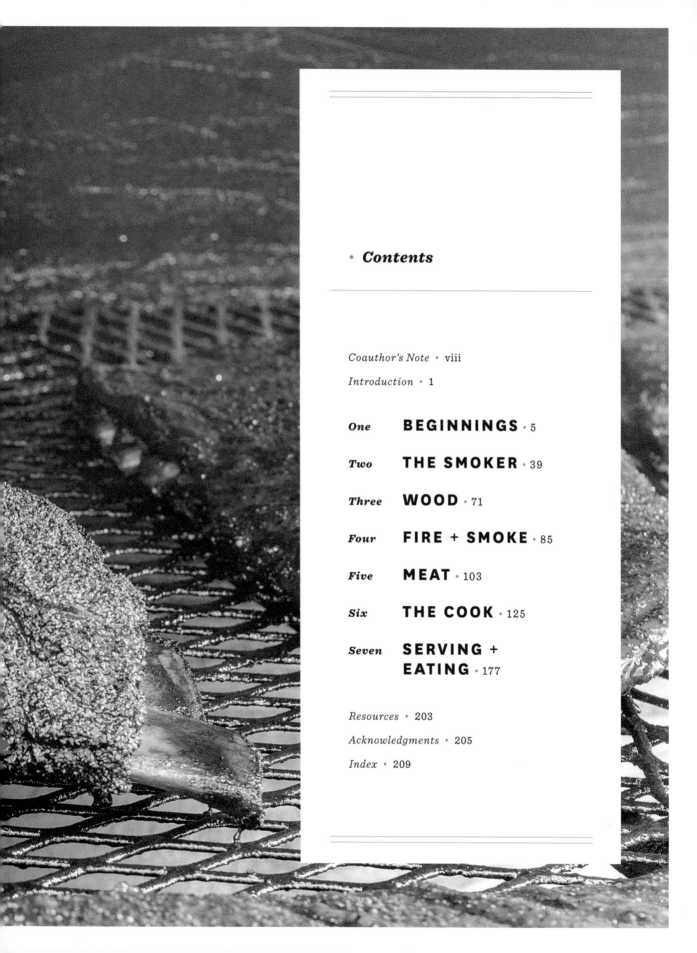

## • Contents

# Coauthor's Note

The first question people always asked when they heard I was working on a book with Aaron Franklin—the man whose Austin restaurant is as famous for its incredibly long lines as it is for its food—was, "Is it really that good? Is the barbecue that much better than everyone else's?" And, I always answered, Yep, pretty much.

The second question was always the same too. "What does he do that's so different from everyone else?" And my answer to that was always the same too: Not that much.

So what is the secret? That's what everyone really wants to know. It's true that Aaron uses more expensive and higher grade meat than almost everyone else. It's also true that he has a talent for designing and tinkering with his smokers to get the optimal smoking action he desires. And, yes, he has an almost demented attention to detail when it comes to cooking meat—every log on the fire, every rib, every brisket is treated individually and given discreet consideration as it cooks and becomes barbecue. But I can't answer the original question by describing any specific maneuvers or secret techniques I learned while working with Aaron. What I can say after having spent hours and hours cooking with him at all times of day and night is that the reason his food is so successful seems to lie in his personality, his work ethic,

and his remarkable talent for comprehending how things work.

During our time together, I jokingly referred to the latter as his ability to "think like smoke." When he constructs a smoker, burns wood in a firebox, and puts meat in the cooker, Aaron appears—in his own completely intuitive form of consideration—to calculate the way heat and smoke will curl and bounce around the insides of the smoker, around the meat, and ultimately swirl out of the stack in his desired perfect "vortices." He understands how it all works, and consequently he wraps and pulls his meats at just the right moment. It's impressive.

But even more impressive—and what I most admire about the man and what I think is his greatest asset and the greatest secret of his success—is the absolute, utter commitment he has to the customers who truly humble him every day by waiting for hours in line for his food. His obsessive dedication to the happiness and satisfaction of every person who eats at Franklin Barbecue is awe inspiring, especially given how easy it would be for him to kick back, drink some beers, and rest on his smoky laurels. I've never met anyone who, while running an overwhelmingly popular restaurant, welding, working on books, and filming television shows, also tries so hard to make sure people get what they want. And these people—diners, media, fans, amateur pitmasters—want a lot from him. He sleeps very little, and I hope he can keep it up.

Some folks may also wonder how a writer best known for his writing on wine ended up in Austin working with a modern barbecue master. Besides the fact that I grew up in Austin and went to school there (though I now live in San Francisco), wine and barbecue share several qualities that deserve observation. Both are best when made "low and slow," with wine being one of the few products that goes even lower and slower than great barbecue. With both barbecue and wine, you're never exactly sure how it's going to turn out until it's done and you open it up. Both rely on a combination of good-quality natural ingredients and the technique and skill of an experienced practitioner. Thanks to local, natural ingredients—be they beef or pork, hickory or oak, Pinot Noir or Riesling—and the techniques that have been developed to transform them, expressive, distinctive, and regional styles have

arisen in both the barbecue and the wine world. In short, at their best, both wine and barbecue have some sort of *terroir* (a great French term): give me a taste of your barbecue or a swallow of your wine, and I'll tell you who you are.

That said, very little wine was consumed during the making of this book. And happily so. While wine is wonderful, immersion in the far-more-relaxed culture of barbecue was refreshing and inspiring (though the day often starts way too early). Yes, we drank a lot of beer.

Now that I'm in, I don't think I'll ever be able to leave the barbecue world. I'm in too deep; the compulsion is there now. I'm going to continue working on keeping my fires steady, get better at knowing when to pull the ribs, and practice getting my rubs more evenly spread. And whenever I get back to Austin, I'll be putting in a few hours waiting in line at Franklin Barbecue because, yes, it's just that good.

• *Jordan Mackay*

# • *Introduction*

The notion of putting everything I know about barbecue into a book is a daunting one. Not because I know so much—I'm still learning—but because of the nature of barbecue itself. It's because the printed word—definitive, exacting, permanent—is in many ways antithetical to the process of cooking barbecue, which is, for lack of a better word, loosey-goosey.

So many people want to have a recipe, but with all of the variables in barbecue—wood, quality of fire, meat selection, type of cooker, weather, and so on—there is no "magic" recipe. It just doesn't operate with absolutes of temperature, time, and measurement. In fact, there are no rights or wrongs in barbecue (well, that may be a stretch), no "just one way," and certainly no simple "black and white." You're much better off with general knowledge of what you want and an arsenal of tricks to have up your sleeve.

So unlike most books that you may flip through a few times and then place on the shelf to display with the others, I hope this one will live a good portion of its life out in the field, be it in the kitchen or out by the smoker. These recipes aren't really recipes but more of an idea of how I go about cooking barbecue and some guidelines.

Now, this book is not a survey of barbecue traditions across the country. While I've been all over the United States and have eaten lots of great

barbecue, there's really only one tradition that I know intimately: my own. My style is steeped in the tradition of Central Texas, but it's also got some wrinkles that I discovered along the way. So, with the greatest respect to all of the other styles around the country, in this book, all I discuss is what we do. Yes, I am wedded to the tradition of great Central Texas barbecue and the principles it holds—brisket, oak, open flame—but I'm also always willing to try something new or look into new designs that might make things cook faster and better. And my hope is that by being hyperdetailed and specific about my techniques, I will help you in your cooking and in your ability to develop your own style too. At Franklin Barbecue, the only thing we've got is the dedication to make the best food we can and to keep it consistently the same every day (which itself is the biggest challenge). It's that dedication that keeps us evolving as cooks and constantly thinking about new ways to do old things.

You'll notice that there's a serious thread of do-it-yourself running through this book. That's because one of the words with which I've been known to describe myself is *cheap*. For large stretches of my life, I didn't have the cash to buy things I wanted, so I often just figured out how to make them myself. In the process, I sometimes discovered how to make them better or at least how to tailor them to my own needs. However, while I participate in DIY culture and continue to build stuff all of the time, it's by no means necessary to take this approach in order to benefit from this book. I say, use whatever equipment you've got on hand; ideally, the information I present here will help you make the best of it.

Most barbecue books I've looked at are organized around the major food groups: beef, pork, poultry, and so on. (At least, those are *my* food groups.) In this book, which isn't heavily focused on recipes, I've taken a different approach. It's a more elemental and theoretical breakdown of the barbecue process. In each chapter, I drill down into some fairly technical information with regard to how the process of barbecue works. It can get a little geeky, but I hope that in a way the geekiness keeps you engaged. I include this information because I myself love the technical details. Understanding how something works is the first step toward successfully replicating and improving it.

The first chapter is an extended telling of my own story. I include it at this length not for the purpose of vanity, but the opposite—so that everyone can see how you don't have to have much money, history, training, or even time to become proficient at barbecue. I really just want to show how a love for barbecue coupled with enthusiasm can equal really good-tasting smoked meat. If I can do this, you can too.

The second chapter is all about the smoker. In Texas, this piece of equipment might be called a smoker, cooker, and pit all in the same sentence, but whatever you call it, barbecue practitioners have no end of fascination with these clunky steel constructions. Everyone who designs and builds his or her own smoker does something

a little bit different, always looking for that tweak that will improve its performance. In this chapter, I talk about various kinds of smokers and various modifications you can make to improve the performance of an inexpensive off-the-rack smoker you might buy at an outdoors store. I also give a very basic template for how to build your own smoker from scratch. It's by no means a blueprint but rather intended to give you an idea of what to think about if you undertake such a project. While smoker construction sounds—and is—fairly ambitious, I can tell you that I've built very heavy smokers in my backyard with a cheap welder, rope, and a tree branch to hoist pieces up.

Chapter three is about wood. Wood is our sole fuel, but it's also arguably the most important seasoning in the food. Without wood, barbecue wouldn't be barbecue, so we have to take the wood we use as seriously as we would any ingredient in any dish. Just as you wouldn't sauté meats and vegetables in rancid butter, you want to use good-quality firewood in pristine condition whenever possible. In this chapter, you'll learn all about seasoning, splitting, buying, and judging wood for barbecue. After reading it, you'll definitely be wanting your own little woodpile in the backyard. Just keep it dry.

It's no big leap from wood to fire and smoke, the subjects of chapter four. Most people don't realize there are gradations of smoke and fire. But a good fire and the fine smoke it produces are two of the most fundamental elements to producing superior Central Texas barbecue. In this chapter, I get into the nitty-gritty of what good smoke and fire mean and how to produce them in various conditions. It's a bit sciencey, but it also tends to be pretty interesting, so hopefully you'll get a lot out of it.

Chapter five is about meat. One of things I do differently from most other barbecue joints is use a higher grade of meat. It makes things more expensive for everyone (including me), but I think it's worth it not only for the quality of the end product but also for the quality of life of the humans eating it and of the noble animals that were sacrificed to bring us this food. You'll learn here what certain grades of meat mean, where they come from on the animal, and how to go about selecting the best meat for your cooking.

Chapter six is a doozy. It's the one where I finally get into the actual cooking of the meat. If you buy this book and just want to dive right in, you could start here, though I recommend going back at some time to read all of the other stuff. This is the chapter where I do things like suggest temperatures and times for your cook, even though ultimately you have to figure out the fine details of these things for your own kind of cooker, your own conditions, and ultimately your own taste. But I do talk about other important stuff like trimming meats, rubbing, and wrapping—all the techniques that will help your meat turn out great. The bulk of this chapter is devoted to brisket and ribs, which are the two most popular meats, and cooked using the two basic methods of cooking we do. All of our other fare basically follows these methods, so to learn how to cook brisket and ribs in a smoker is to learn how to cook just about anything.

Lastly, we talk a little bit about sides, sauces, serving, drinking, and all of the stuff that goes hand in hand with enjoying the fruits of your labor. In Central Texas, sides and sauces are always considered secondary to the meat, if indeed necessary at all. So I don't place a huge emphasis on them, even though I will admit that our beans are really good. More important is brisket slicing technique, which is something I go into detail about here. It's hard to train people to cut brisket really well, but once you practice and repeat it, you'll be glad to have good skill in this area, since there's nothing worse than hacking up something you just spent a day coddling. And at last, beer, like day and night, is a fact of life for the pitmaster, and it's something I think about a lot! So I talk a little about what I like and what I think works best with barbecue, though beer in general gets a big fat *Yes*.

Hopefully, while you read this book, you'll find yourself chomping at the bit to get out there and throw a few racks of ribs or a big, honking brisket onto your smoker. And all I can say is, Go for it! The key to my own development—and it will be to yours—is repetition. Just as with anything, the more you do it, the better you'll get. In barbecue that's especially true, particularly if you pay close attention along the way to what you did during the cooking process and when you did it, and then you note the final results and think about how to make the next cook better. That's what I did, and my barbecue improved steadily along the way. And I didn't even have a resource like this book.

Ultimately, that's the best advice I can give. Do, and do some more. Drink beer, but not so much that you lose track of what you're doing. And pay attention. Sweat the details and you'll end up producing barbecue that would make the most seasoned of pitmasters proud.

BEGINNINGS

## *Chapter One*

It's 2 a.m. on a foggy, cold February night. I have just arrived at work and am looking everywhere for the tamper for the espresso machine. It's not where it should be, and I'm slightly annoyed. Here at Franklin Barbecue, often the very first thing new kitchen employees are trained to do is pull a good espresso shot. Very important. We have a two-group classic La Marzocco Linea espresso machine taking up good real estate back in the kitchen, and it pulls beautiful shots. Espresso is not on the menu, though, and we don't serve it to customers. It's just for us. But it's what you need when your day starts at 2 a.m.

Having no luck finding the tamper, I improvise and pull the shot anyway using the bottom of a hot sauce bottle. Good enough. Warm espresso cup cradled in my hand, I step outside into the bracing 28°F night. We're in the middle of one of the massive cold fronts that swoop down through the Midwest from Canada and plunge Austin—and all of Central Texas—into subfreezing weather. This happens several times a year. It can be tricky when it comes to barbecue, as dealing with the changing weather is one of the supreme challenges of cooking good, consistent meat. Weather this cold affects temperatures, cooking times, and the way our

smokers draw. But I'll talk a lot more about that later on.

We have many different shifts at Franklin Barbecue: cooking the ribs, putting the briskets on, meat and sides prep, pulling the briskets off, cutting lunch, and more. The 2 a.m. shift is the rib shift, and I work it a couple of times a week. When I arrive, I say good night to the late-night guy who's been tending the briskets—which went on yesterday morning around 10 a.m. and were pulled starting around 1 a.m. this morning—and get about my business.

Yes, it's the middle of the night—but there's a lot to do before dawn, before another person shows up to work, which won't be until 6:30 a.m. But first, I spend a moment with my steaming cup of espresso, which I take outside where I'll tend the fires. I pause to smell that beautiful mingling of crema with the ubiquitous but still sweet smell of the smoke from the multiple oak fires I have going right now.

Here's what I need to accomplish between now and 9 a.m.: trim and season sixty racks of ribs and get them on the smokers; get the giant cauldron of beans started while warming and breaking up the brisket trimmings from the day before, which will be added to those beans; assess and feed all of the fires we've got going; trim and season about twenty giant turkey breasts; constantly keep all of the cookers at about 275°F, taking into account the temperature variations that occur due to the whims of wood fires crackling in freezing cold weather; chat with Melissa, the pie woman, who makes all of our desserts; accept and possibly put away the thousands of pounds of meat—a day's supply— we'll receive from the delivery guys at 6:30 a.m. (though, annoyingly, they usually don't show up on time); carry shovelfuls of coals from the smoker (which we affectionately call Muchacho) to smoker Number Two to start the fires for the turkey breasts and (later) the sausages; get the turkey basting sauce together; check on and moisten the ribs multiple times; pull sixty giant sheets of foil to wrap the ribs; spray, sauce, and wrap the ribs; and get Rusty Shackleford up to temperature for tomorrow's briskets. Even though it's the wee hours of the morning and not a single person is around, I often find myself literally running from the kitchen out the back door to check temperatures and load the fires and running back in to handle my duties in the kitchen. Of course, I give myself a short break here or there for an espresso or, in this cold weather, an Americano, which allows for longer sipping. You can balance these coffees on the top of the firebox or on the handles of the heavy smoker doors and let the heat of the cookers keep them warm.

By now, it's been light for a couple of hours, though I may not have noticed the actual moment the sky changed. Also by now, the line is beginning to form and stretch around the side of the restaurant. On weekdays the first people usually show up by 8 a.m. On Saturdays it can be as early as 6 a.m.

By 9 a.m., I've completed most of the duties of my shift. I'm starving by now and can take a brief breather. It's Austin, so we eat a lot of breakfast tacos. I'll either put together some brisket breakfast tacos here at the restaurant or head out to Mi Madre's a mile away for some classic ones. I'll eat and maybe spend some time answering emails before checking in with my staff, which has been gradually arriving. I'll go over the day's preorders and consult with the person who's cutting the meat today (if it's not me). All kinds of demands will be hitting me now just about running the restaurant. And then, it's 11 a.m., and the mayhem begins. We open the doors, the line starts moving, and for the next four hours we'll serve over 1,500 pounds of brisket, all of those sixty racks of ribs, twenty turkey breasts, and 500 to 800 sausage links, not to mention gallons of beans, coleslaw, and iced tea and a lot of beer. I stick around for a good part of the day, putting out fires, checking food, busing tables, and greeting guests, which will be a mix of locals and people from all over the world. Today they waited in the cold, but much more often they may be waiting in the 90°F to 100°F temperatures that we see a lot of around here.

## A DAY IN THE LIFE
## AT FRANKLIN

**12 a.m.**
Briskets are pulled off the smoker to rest.

**2 a.m.**
Espresso! Start prepping for rib shift; trim and rub the beef ribs and build fires.

**2 to 3 a.m.**
Beef ribs on! Time to trim and rub the pork ribs.

**3 to 4 a.m.**
Pork ribs on! Continue to watch the fires.

**4 to 5 a.m.**
Prep turkey; set up mise en place.

**5 to 6 a.m.**
Turkeys on! Another espresso. Spritz and sauce the ribs; set up warmers.

**6 to 7 a.m.**
Wrap ribs; set up for line outside; start to rub tomorrow's briskets.

**7 to 8 a.m.**
Wrap turkey! Make sides; continue to rub tomorrow's briskets; start sorting cooked briskets; set up front of house; put up deliveries.

**8 to 10 a.m.**
Start checking the line; start pulling ribs. Cook sausage. Finish beef ribs and turkeys.

**10 to 11 a.m.**
Put food on warmers; put tomorrow's briskets on the smoker; cut any pre-orders.

**11 a.m. to 3 p.m.**
Lunch! Trim briskets for the next day. Do pork butts; cook potatoes; prep in kitchen; watch fires; dishes.

**3 to 6 p.m.**
Finish lunch service; clean; continue to trim briskets.

**6 p.m. to 12 a.m.**
Make sauce; tend briskets; kitchen prep.

**Rinse and repeat!**

They all have in common that they waited anywhere from three to five hours to eat the meat that I've been blessed enough to be able to prepare for them.

After lunch, I'll probably run errands around town or have some meetings. Or I might just go home and fall asleep for a while before dinner. Bedtime is usually between 9 and 10 o'clock, before it starts all over again.

## EARLY DAYS

A lot of people might tell their backstory for the sake of storytelling—for the sake of entertainment. And that's good and valuable in its own right. But when I look back on my barbecue life, I can see that where all this came from is absolutely integral to what it eventually became. What I mean is, I didn't learn how to cook barbecue just to master a craft. Its evolution in me is a true expression of who I am and where I came from. Specific places, specific times of life and states of mind, and specific people all contributed greatly to what Stacy and I and our restaurant have come to be. You'll be surprised that when we started we had absolutely nothing—no resources, no knowledge, no image of what we wanted to become. All I had were my own two hands, a work ethic, a positive attitude, a sense of humor, and a fine lady to help it all come together.

Barbecue to me is about more than just the smoke and the meat, more than trying to cook better with more flavor and more consistency (though those things are definitely important). Barbecue is also about a culture that I love. It's about the smell of smoke and meat browning and the sound of a wood fire crackling. It's about time, the slow passage of hours. It's about the people

that I hang out with, but also about the solitude of the long, solo cook. For me, it's about the look and feel and construction of not only smokers but also of buildings, cars, guitars, and other beautiful, artfully designed things. It's about service and about people relaxing and having a good time. It's about the connection I feel to a vast, time-honored cooking tradition and to all of the people practicing it across Texas and across the country every single day.

• • •

In 1996, when I moved to Austin from Bryan–College Station, Texas (100 miles northeast of Austin), it was never my intention to open a barbecue restaurant. In fact, I wasn't even into barbecue. I was nineteen years old and into rock 'n' roll. Barbecue wasn't something I even really thought about much.

It's true that when I was little, around eleven years old, my parents did own a barbecue joint in Bryan for a while. It was a cool old place with a classic brick pit from the 1920s, a fire on the floor (in barbecue, *pit* is an interchangeable term for *smoker* or *cooker* and may be an actual pit or might be something that stands on legs or wheels aboveground)—the kind of joint that just reeks of character (and that you can still find in small towns across Texas).

It did make an impression on me, but not necessarily on how I cook. Rather, it just sank into my psyche and came to kind of nestle there, associating barbecue for me with the good things in life—with family and friends and that certain sense of well-being that you have when you're a kid in a good place. Even though it didn't really occur to me until long after, I think the sense of nostalgia that I carry from my parents' restaurant sits at the heart of the passion for barbecue that I later found in myself.

But equally important was the music store that my grandparents owned. I spent a lot of time there and worked there throughout my teenage years. I did a little bit of everything—selling instruments, setting up PA systems, giving guitar lessons, repairing guitars and amps. I developed my passion for music there but also for something else: for taking things apart and fixing them—for tinkering, for disassembling objects and seeing firsthand how they work.

You might not think that that approach to things has much application to preparing great barbecue, but it does. Understanding how things are put together and how they work is the first step toward improving them. The more you do it, the better you get at it, and if you don't have any fear of getting a little dirty or of prying something open and examining how it functions, you start to develop the confidence that you can fix most anything and even make it run better than it did before. And that's basically the approach I've taken my whole barbecue career and am still taking today, working daily to improve my smokers and my restaurant in general to make it more efficient, more consistent, and more durable.

But back then, after I graduated from high school, all I wanted to do was play music. So I went to Austin and had a good time working odd jobs and playing in a couple of bands. We'd play rock shows, go on tours in vans, that kind of thing—24-inch kick drums, Marshall stacks, fists in the air, Pabst Blue Ribbon. I realize now that even playing music fed into my later endeavors. It may not seem like it, but there are many similarities between playing in a band at a show and putting on a barbecue.

• • •

My love of barbecue—my insane obsession with it—started to crop up about the same time I met Stacy, now my wife and collaborator (enabler?) in everything. It is a good thing she's patient and accepting of me because she had to tolerate a lot of barbecue talk for a long time. I'm not sure where barbecue came from exactly. It's not like it all just hit me one day. No, it was more like the way winter turns to spring slowly until one day you look up and it's green everywhere. That's how barbecue started for me, as just a little interest, before it became a full-on infatuation and ultimately, unpredictably, my life.

The whole thing really started rolling when we got our first little cooker, a New Braunfels Hondo Classic smoker, for $99 from Academy, an outdoors and recreation store here in Austin.

It's a classic offset smoker in the Texas style, with a firebox that connects to a cooking chamber on one end and a smokestack on the other. It's so cheap because it's made economically and with very thin, inexpensive metal that's not designed to last or even hold heat or smoke very well. Why did I get it? I went out to get a grill for our first place together, but I bought a smoker instead. I guess if you live in Texas long enough, barbecue starts to penetrate your consciousness. And when you get that hankering, you get a smoker, and this was what was available to me at the time.

I have a love of design and architecture overall, but especially of a certain roadside style of Americana from the 1940s, 1950s, and 1960s, which in my mind is really represented in barbecue culture. In 2003, *Texas Monthly*, our state magazine, released its second full issue devoted to barbecue (the first came out long before, in 1997), and that's when things started to hit home for me. The first time I saw Wyatt McSpadden's photos of these great old barbecue temples in Central Texas towns, I thought, *Wow, that is so cool!* I'd never been to the places Wyatt was shooting, but his photos made me think of my parents' place back when I was a little kid, and I realized that barbecue just triggered all sorts of great feelings.

Now I realize that it was about more than just the meat; it was about the character and resonance of barbecue culture. You don't go to those places just for the meat. To walk past the open fires into the smoke-blackened halls of Smitty's in Lockhart is practically a religious experience. You wouldn't want to eat barbecue—even if it was the greatest in the world—at a restaurant that felt like some sterile white box. It wouldn't taste the same without the visuals, the smells,

the smoke on the walls, the memorabilia, the pit guy lifting up the smoker lid and a plume of smoke coming out.

My relationship with Stacy was one of the main reasons I gave up the touring musician lifestyle. She supported all of my obsessions—music, carpentry, and, eventually, barbecue—but the band would go out on these tours, and I'd find that I just missed her and missed being home. I thought maybe I should just come home and get a job, but that's also when barbecue started to become a persistent presence in my mind. Stacy is from Texas too (Amarillo, way up in the Panhandle, to be exact). She wasn't *as* in love with barbecue as I was, but like me she enjoyed throwing parties and was always game to put on a cookout together. Believe it or not, a series

of casual cookouts ended up being my only real training before we opened the trailer that would eventually turn into our restaurant. So each one of those backyard parties with friends remains pretty vivid in my mind, especially as they were often tied to a particular residence we had at the time. Austin is full of funky neighborhoods and funky old rent houses, and we moved around a lot.

I cooked my very first brisket in 2002 at one of those backyard cookouts. (For those of you who are keeping track, we opened the Franklin Barbecue trailer in 2009, which means, yes, I had been cooking brisket for only seven years when we first started.) At the time we lived in a little three-plex. My band had done an in-store performance at a record shop, and we had maybe a third of a keg of Lone Star left over. So I told everyone, "Hey, I'm cooking a brisket. If anybody wants to come over tomorrow, we'll finish off this keg and eat it."

I had just gotten my New Braunfels cooker, and this would be my maiden voyage with any kind of smoker. It could hold two briskets, if they were stuffed in there, with each brisket capable of serving maybe ten people. I picked up the brisket on sale at H-E-B—our big chain of Texas grocery stores—for $0.99 a pound. It was prefrozen, commodity, probably Select-grade meat. And I had no idea what to do with it because I'd never cooked anything on an offset cooker. In fact, I'd never shown any particular aptitude for cooking with fire. Negative talent, probably. So, I went online to try to figure out how to make a brisket. Let's just say the Web in 2002 was not as robust as it is today. I called my dad and asked him how to smoke a brisket, and he said something vague like "Just cook it until it's done."

About fifteen of us—the band and some friends—convened the next day. My brisket was flavorless—tough and dry—but everyone was terribly nice about it. They all said it was good. Maybe they really thought that, but I knew it was not true. In hindsight, I didn't wrap it, and I pulled it off right when it was at 165°F internal temperature, smack in the middle of the stall. (We'll talk much more about that later, but at the time I didn't even know what that was.) That was my first brisket: $0.99 a pound on a cheap cooker I'd bought for $99.

Shortly after, Stacy and I moved to Bryan–College Station with the plan to save some money and eventually move to Philadelphia, a city I adore, for a while. Only, we were so miserable to be back in a small town that we found ourselves driving to Austin all the time for work, to be with our friends, and to play music. But it was in Bryan that I did my second cook.

We had a small two-bedroom wood-frame house from the 1950s. It had a pretty nice little backyard. So we had a few people over on a Sunday, just like everyone does. I was itching pretty badly to smoke another brisket, which, again, I purchased on sale for an incredibly low price, and I cooked it on the same little cooker. I still didn't know what I was doing, but I do believe this one turned out slightly better.

I also decided to take things to the next level by making a bunch of barbecue sauces. As a test, I also bought a bunch of crappy commercial ones. We composed a grid and asked everyone to pick their favorite sauces and to offer some tasting notes. I didn't realize it at the time, but I was clearly behaving in a way that suggested I might think of doing this in some kind of official capacity. The sauce test was pretty much the moment when I learned to stop asking for opinions and to listen to my own judgment. People chose the worst ones as their favorites. I believe Kraft actually won. The few commercial ones that I really liked didn't place very high, while the couple I made from scratch placed somewhere in the middle. As it was, our experiment of living in Bryan to save money didn't last long. We missed our friends and our lives in Austin and were spending lots of our time there anyway. Ultimately, we gave up the Philly idea and decided to head back to Austin, where our futures clearly lay.

• • •

Still, Stacy and I were incredibly poor, and when I say poor, I mean well below the poverty line. The kind of poor where you're writing your rent check before you get your paycheck and just hoping it works out. After your paycheck goes through, you realize you have $8 to last you a week before you get your next one. I remember going down to H-E-B to cash in a jar full of change so I could go out and buy a little barbecue.

But we weren't terribly stressed about this. Austin was like that back then. It was a good time and a simpler one. You could pass on jobs to friends, just as you could houses or apartments. You could live cheaply off minimum wage and tips. It was a city full of people like me—people not doing the stereotypical thing of going to college just to get out and find a job, but trying to figure out and do something they really enjoy, like playing music for not much money. People like to say that Austin was a town full of slackers, and I guess on the surface I could have fallen under that category. But I was never a slack worker. I've always had various jobs and always worked hard. I just can't easily work for other people or do work that I don't care for.

Stacy had a job—she waited tables. She was the breadwinner for years, though I always had

something I was doing, something to bring in some money. For years, I did random stuff—more often than not, I worked for free on projects for friends. Someone would ask me for help, and I'd think, *Well, I don't have a job right now, so, sure, I'll help you build that.* There were times when Stacy was definitely frustrated with me.

And, yes, in those years, my interest in barbecue was still percolating—it was kind of a constant buzz in the back of my mind. I did a small tour with my friend Big Jeff Keyton, a terrific local musician, and his band, and on those long drives we realized that both of us were really into barbecue. So he started taking me out on occasional day trips to visit local barbecue joints—heading 30 miles south down to Lockhart for Smitty's and Kreuz, or 20 miles farther to Luling's City Market, and especially 40 miles northeast to Taylor to the great Louie Mueller. I'd save and save to scrounge together a few bucks just to be able to go out and taste some barbecue.

I remember that first morsel at Louie Mueller. The place has great counter service— really nice and friendly—and the staff traditionally cuts customers a little taste of beef when they get through the line and up to the counter to order. When I got to the front of the line, Bobby Mueller gave me one bite that turned out to be a whole end cut. I don't know why he gave me that gigantic piece. My eyes must have been bulging, and I might have cried a little bit, but it was so, so good. Sooooooo good! And it started to change me.

It was maybe another year before my next cook, in 2004. This cook signaled another small step in my development, as I prepared the sides as well as the meat, and learned I could put it all together myself. A friend wanted to have a party and said, "Hey, I'll buy the briskets if you want to cook them."

I said, "Hell yeah," because any chance I could get to learn how to cook these things was a boon. And so I cooked the briskets in the front yard of our house and took them to his house while they were resting. And I remember that was the first time people recognized me and said, "Man, that's Aaron, the barbecue guy."

For that party, I had saved up my money and bought a $20 knife. Friggin' sad. I saved up $20! But it's true. I had gone to Ace Mart and bought a cheap Dexter-Russell knife. Still have it. It's at the restaurant, though we don't use it anymore. It just goes to show that you don't need fancy equipment to do most any task in barbecue.

Our next residence was an incredibly dumpy house. There was no real backyard, as the house was on a quarter lot and it took up almost the whole property. It was a one-bedroom, 480-square-foot house, probably around $500 a month in rent. We had one barbecue while we lived there. That was the fifth cook, and the year was 2005.

I had played a show somewhere that night, packed up my drums and left the show early, and got back to the house feeling very gung-ho. The prospect of cooking a brisket was just the most exhilarating thing. Months had gone by, with me trying to scrape together enough cash to put this one puny barbecue on. And, man, I was so excited. I remember firing up that little New Braunfels cooker. I had bought two briskets from H-E-B on sale for $0.99 a pound. I recall feeling like a badass walking out of H-E-B with a shopping cart filled with a whopping two briskets.

I got home from that show probably around 2:30 a.m. I remember just sitting in this small hammock in our tiny, 10-foot-wide backyard, getting the fire going. Our place was at a four-way stop, and there was this streetlamp that would

cast its light down into our yard. I just stared at it, thinking it was the coolest thing to see that smoke start wafting up into the night. I was so stoked.

I dozed outside on the hammock while tending the fire. By the next morning, things were going smoothly. I'd pulled the briskets and we were getting the yard ready. Just when it all seemed perfect and twenty to thirty people were about to show up, go figure, the plumbing backed up. A root had cracked a pipe from the toilet, and there was sewage floating up into the yard. Gross! The owner of the house was in prison, so we couldn't really call anyone. And I had bought all of this food with what was, as usual, my last few dollars, so we couldn't call it off. It was a Sunday, and I remember finding a piece of plywood and just covering up the swamp. Stacy and I were looking at each other saying, *Oh my God, oh my God, oh my God. The bathroom doesn't work. This is terrible!*

But, somehow, no one noticed, except that we couldn't use the house's one bathroom. I remember not being really happy with the brisket. For one thing, I may not have realized that cooking two briskets at the same time would alter the process. But I might have also been disappointed that I wasn't improving by leaps and bounds every time I managed to cook a brisket. Now I know that progress doesn't always flow in a steady stream. You have to give yourself some slack, because learning how to make barbecue takes time, and not everything's going to be a big success.

Not that this was by any means a failure. The brisket just wasn't appreciably better than what I'd done the last time. (Of course, what do you expect when you take months and months off in between cooks?) And I didn't know if my sauce would come out really bad, so I bought a gallon of some really crappy stuff that I could doctor up

just in case my own efforts were inedible. But my sauce was fine, and everyone seemed to have a great time. The next day I fixed the pipe. We got out of that house pretty darn quick.

•  •  •

I was still working various jobs that didn't pay too well. I worked at a van place, fitting out and customizing vans. I worked in various restaurants. But there were two jobs that ended up having the greatest impact on me: at a coffee shop called Little City, where I worked in the back making sandwiches and doing maintenance, and where I started developing my love of coffee; and the Austin barbecue joint of John Mueller, grandson of the legendary Louie Mueller.

Somewhere around that fifth cook—yes, the one with the septic disaster—I caught myself daydreaming about opening my own barbecue place. (Of course, now that I have my own restaurant, bathroom disasters are an ever-looming threat!) I'd hardly ever been that excited about anything other than music. So I started applying to a bunch of Austin barbecue joints, some of them several times. I wanted to work at a place that barbecued with a real fire, not gas ovens, and there weren't many of these in Austin at the time. I wanted to learn barbecue from the inside out; I want to live it.

I got the job at Mueller and worked a lot, even though I was making only $6 or so an hour. I was constantly observing and soaking up whatever lessons I could. (I should interrupt myself here and offer a little backstory for anyone who doesn't know John Mueller. Here is how *Texas Monthly* describes him: "If there's a dark prince of Texas barbecue, it's probably John Mueller, the famously irascible, hugely talented, at times erratic master

of meat who left his family's legendary joint—Louie Mueller Barbecue, in Taylor—and set out on his own in 2001." That place is the one I worked at. It developed a big following, but for various reasons he closed it in 2006 and disappeared from the scene for a while. He opened a new place in 2011 with his sister, but a fallout there led to him departing again. Now he has his own place once more. He and I appeared on the cover of *Texas Monthly* together in 2012.) When I worked at John Mueller's, I didn't cook anything. But I got good at chopping cabbage and onions. I could cut 50 pounds of onions without shedding a tear. I started rubbing briskets in the afternoons and watched how John handled the meats. I ended up getting to cut the brisket for the customers, which turned out to be a valuable skill. Often at night, the owner would leave, and I would just be left there on my own, which was great. People would come in, and I'd greet them warmly, take their order, and cut their meat for them. At those times, I would sort of treat that place with care and a friendly spirit as if it were my own. That kind of amiable, hospitable spirit is important, something that we've always emphasized at Franklin Barbecue.

It helped that I love cutting brisket, and I love talking to people. To this day, people who used to eat at that defunct restaurant still come into Franklin every now and then and remember me from when I was working behind the counter. Even more than I care to admit, that short-term job probably led to much of what I do now. But it wasn't because I received any mentoring. It was because I found myself doing something I really loved. Eventually, when I could see that writing on the wall that its days were numbered, I quit.

•  •  •

## LEGENDARY CENTRAL TEXAS BARBECUE

Before I ever cooked a brisket, I was taking day trips out to visit the various pillars of Central Texas barbecue. In those days, there wasn't really any good barbecue in Austin; it all lived in the small towns outside of the city in every direction. There are barbecue joints everywhere in Central Texas, but there have always been a few places that have stood above the rest. It's worthwhile to visit these temples because in their old buildings and time-honored ways, they provide a window into barbecue history, not to mention a taste. These days quality can be up and down, but they all do something really well, and when they're on, the food can be as good as it gets.

**SMITTY'S MARKET, LOCKHART** • Just 30 miles southeast of Austin, Lockhart is a historic barbecue town, and Smitty's is a glorious living relic of the way things used to be. The building itself is a must-see place that all barbecue fans should visit. You enter through the back and walk right past a roaring fire literally at your feet, even if it's 100°F outside. • **FAVE DISH:** the best sausage!

**KREUZ MARKET, LOCKHART** • Just down the street from Smitty's is the massive redbrick food hall known as Kreuz. Smitty's used to be called Kreuz, but due to a familial disagreement, one sibling took the name while the other kept the original building. So here you have a new building, but with the original name and techniques. Mutton-chopped, soft-spoken Roy Perez is the pitmaster and a barbecue celebrity. It's always heartening to stop in and see him tending his pits. No forks or sauce here, following the old ways. Lots of good food is on offer, but the true specialties are the smoked-to-perfection pork chop and the snappy, spicy sausage links. • **FAVE DISHES:** end-cut prime rib, pork chop, jalapeño-cheese sausage.

**CITY MARKET, LULING** • Luling is a little town 15 miles past Lockhart and is home to yet another Central Texas barbecue great: City Market. Under the pitmastership (yes, I just coined that term) of hard hat–sporting Joe Capello, City Market is one cool spot. You enter a little smoke-filled room in the back of the restaurant where the meat is cut. Then you step back out into the dining room to find a table. There's great people-watching at City Market, and the sausage and ribs are great! • **FAVE DISHES:** sausage, crackers, cheddar cheese, great sauce.

**LOUIE MUELLER BARBECUE, TAYLOR** • An hour to Austin's northeast is the little town of Taylor, which is probably most famous for the epic Louie Mueller Barbecue. Founded as a grocery store in 1946, with barbecue coming a few years later, the building itself is a beautiful shrine, with smoke-blackened walls and heavenly light streaming in through the fog. The food here has had its ups and downs over the years, but when it's good, there's almost nothing better. And it's been on a hot streak for a while. While the dipping sauce is sort of thin and watery, the meat's so good it doesn't need it, led by super-peppery brisket and a beef rib that will blow you away. Do not miss this place. • **FAVE DISH:** beef rib.

**SOUTHSIDE MARKET, ELGIN** • Elgin is the sausage capital of Central Texas in large part because of the Southside Market. Started in 1882, this place oozes amazing tradition, much in the same way its famous Hot Guts sausages ooze deliciously meaty juices. In the past Hot Guts were spicier than they are today, but they're still darn good. Just a 30 minute drive from downtown Austin, this place is always worth a visit. • **FAVE DISH:** sausage, obviously.

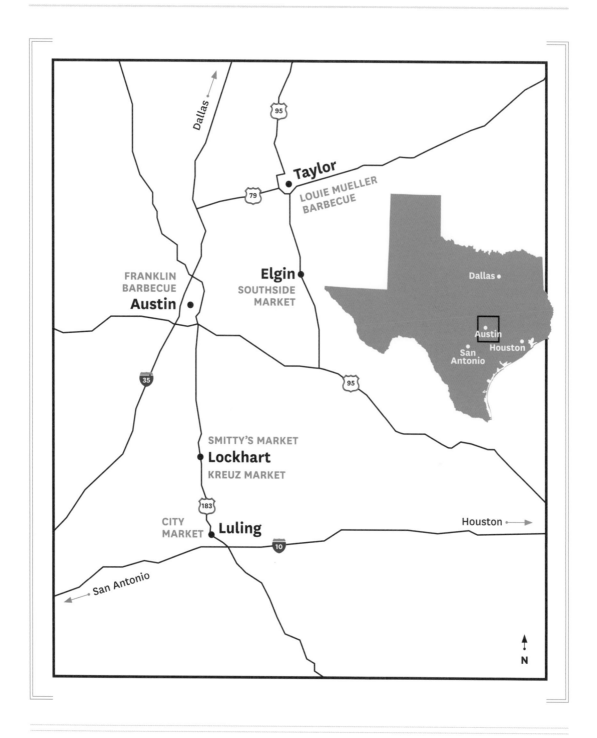

It was now 2007, and I had it in my head that I wanted just a lazy little lunchtime spot that I could design, decorate, and cook for on my own. I was trying as hard as I could to figure out some way to get my hands on or make a cooker that was big enough to cook multiple briskets. I had a dream but no real idea of how to get there except for sheer desire.

More and more, I saw entertaining as practicing for the big time when I would have my own place. I'd be calculating in my head, *This is the time I'd put the meat on; this is the amount of time I'd have to make the sides.* I knew I wanted my restaurant to be as authentic and old-school as possible, with a personal touch—*I'll never cut the brisket in advance and put it out for people to pick at. I'm going to slice each and every piece individually for each customer because that is how it's done.*

Looking back on it now, I know I probably seemed naïve. And I was. But I'm also proud that we made it happen with just ourselves and the help of our friends and family. Sure, I was poor. But barbecue has never been a rich man's pleasure. It's always been a culture of thrift. It's a poor, rural cuisine based on the leanest, throwaway cuts of the animal being cooked until edible with a fuel that can be picked up off the ground (at least it used to be).

And that's what I loved about it. How many other things can you start from nothing? There aren't a lot. In barbecue, you sell something that you bought and prepared on the same day, which gives you a little bit of positive cash flow to buy the next day's raw ingredients. You add value to the ingredients through cooking, and then do it all over again. That's how this entire thing has happened and is in fact still happening. This restaurant has not accrued one cent of debt. And that's because you can build something out of nothing if you're just willing to work at it.

And that's where all of this isn't that different from playing in a rock 'n' roll band. I didn't know it at the time, but it's all kind of the same. You get in a van, you hit the road, and you play and play and play as much as you can to get better and earn a little money. That's punk rock. That's DIY. That's the spirit. You make something with your own two hands. I run the restaurant the same way I'd run a band. It's the same thing, just a different venue.

## ALMOST THERE

When it came time to rent a new house, I definitely, without question, had cookouts on the brain. So we went with a place with a huge backyard, almost a third of an acre. I was looking at this backyard and seeing barbecues. Like a party house. It was still inexpensive, but it was a step up.

Our next cook was on the Fourth of July. We'd always had barbecues on Sundays because Stacy and I worked on Saturday nights. That meant I'd be out pretty much all night on Saturday, get home at 2 a.m., and start cooking for the next day. People would come at 5 p.m. the following evening, and we'd start serving at 7 p.m. But we scheduled this Fourth of July barbecue for a Saturday instead of a Sunday because of the holiday weekend. What a mistake. People drink a lot more on Saturdays and stay too late. Still, I was feeling good about the brisket; it was definitely improving from one cook to the next. Lesson learned: don't have barbecues on a Saturday night, because you're just asking for trouble.

I still had the one, original New Braunfels (which, by the way, is still around; I loaned it to a friend with the instruction that he could never get rid of it without asking me, as it's a sentimental piece with serious mojo, even though it's just a crappy little cooker that's probably rusted out on the bottom by now). But after we had gotten rid of the last guests—wiping the sweat off our brows and feeling lucky that we'd dodged a bullet at this rowdy party—I went online. We had dial-up Internet on one of those old clear iMac computers. Pretty much every day I looked on Craigslist under the searches "Free" and "BBQ." I'd check the Free section for anything that I could possibly use to make a smoker: old refrigerators, old water tanks, an old oven that was getting thrown away. I even tried to figure out a way to turn an old bathtub into a smoker (real classy!). Anything of substance that was free and I thought might come in handy, I considered.

That night I typed in "BBQ." To my surprise, as it had never happened before, a listing for a cooker came up, the second or third item in the list. The ad said something that amounted to "free smoker, used twice, stinks at bbq, come get this piece of junk."

And I went out of my head. I yelled to Stacy, "Oh my God, I've got to go get this thing! Somebody's probably already got it!" I ran to the truck. It was late at night. As I drove I could imagine the scenario: someone had a disastrous experience cooking some meat earlier that day, got so frustrated that he wheeled it out to the driveway, went inside and put the thing up on Craigslist that very night, and swore to themselves that they'd never do it again.

I've hardly been that excited about anything in my whole life. Thoughts raced in my head as I drove: *Must get there as fast as possible. It's heavy, how will I get it in the truck? I don't care, I'll push it home if I have to. How could somebody put something that valuable ($100) on the street? What if somebody's already grabbed it?!*

I remember turning onto the corner, heart pounding. Then I saw something—just a little black dot at the end of the street. It's getting bigger, it's getting bigger, and there it was. I probably started sobbing in the truck. I rolled up, turned off my headlights so as not to disturb the neighborhood, and took a look at the smoker. A New Braunfels Hondo. *Oh my God, it's just like the one I have! I can double my capacity!* Now I'll have two really crappy cookers that aren't worth anything. But I can do four—count them, four—briskets. That doubles my capacity and thus the number of people I can feed. I had certainly come to realize that cooking briskets on these things was hard because of their thin, heat-leaking construction and other inefficiencies. Later I'd have the opportunity to transcend those ills with better cookers. So I wheeled the thing into the street. It rattled loudly, like a shopping cart on a cracked parking lot, and I loaded it up myself. It was heavy, and a full-size truck is pretty high up there. But I got it in and drove off with what until then was my greatest-ever find.

. . .

Something changed in me when I got that second smoker—something clicked, and I started to feel as if maybe owning my own place wasn't so crazy or far-fetched after all. So I decided to start saving up some money in earnest. I was doing good, making about $11 in tips a day at Little City. Stacy worked every Friday night waiting tables. At that time, on Fridays I'd spend the money I'd saved up all week at Half Price Books, just a few dollars on whatever cool cookbooks I could find, as well as books on architecture, anything barbecue of course, roadside stuff—especially Route 66 Americana—1950s design, and old diners. I was gathering information and inspiration like so many nuts packed into a squirrel's cheeks.

After procuring the new smoker, we had our next Sunday-night cook. I think we hosted seventy-five people or so, and to accommodate them all, we collected tables and chairs from Craigslist that we mixed and matched out in the yard (thank you, Free) and strung Christmas lights overhead. I moved an old, cheesy 1960s-style bar from our living room outside and set it up to cut brisket on. I borrowed a friend's little tiny cooker to add to my two and did a record five briskets that night. The food turned out pretty good, and it was one of the most fun barbecues we ever had—and the first one where something novel happened that also helped me along the way. There I was, drinking, cutting brisket in the dark. It was kind of like a block party, way bigger than we thought it was going to be. A line of hungry people extended around the yard, and we ran out of food. Little did we know that we were really ramping up here. Big party, lots of food, major service operation. I had designed a little service area just as I'd do it in a restaurant, really paying attention to *mise en place*, ergonomics, and flow. And the meat seemed to be getting a little better. I was learning how to cook multiple briskets at the same time, learning that each one required its own attention and own program. The idea that so much of this was about attention to detail was really becoming a massive part of the way I looked at barbecue.

Toward the end of that night, Big Jeff, my great friend who's been a part of my barbecue journey since close to the beginning, came up and said, "Hey, I got this for you," and handed me a manila envelope. In it was a roll of ones, fives, and maybe some tens.

"What's this?"

"I took donations for you tonight," he said, taking a slug of whiskey. "You need it."

I didn't know he'd been asking people for money, and I got a little choked up because it was the most thoughtful thing. Throwing that cook probably cost us the equivalent of our rent. The money he raised might not have completely covered our expenses, but it helped a lot. I just couldn't believe it, because I'd worked so hard and had so much fun and then at the end of the night I got paid, which I never expected. It was like playing the best show of your life and then getting paid and realizing the venue gave you some extra and thinking, *Man, we can stay in a hotel tonight!*

I shut the bedroom door and sat on the bed and counted the money and thought to myself, *Wow, maybe I can do this*. And that was the first time it ever truly seemed real to me.

## THE FINAL PIECE

I was really conquering something that had felt unattainable. It must be like when people finally run their first marathon. I was on cloud nine by the end of that last cook. This was the first time we had a barbecue where I cut everything to order and had a stack of plates on the table and could ask people if they wanted lean or fatty, just like at a real restaurant. This is what

I still do every day when I cut lunch. I honestly believe that one of the reasons our restaurant is successful is because we take the time to talk to people, to get to know them and what they want to eat—same as if we were hosting them in our own backyard.

Not long after that fifth cook, in 2006, I volunteered to remodel a house for the brother-in-law of my best friend, Benji (who today is an essential part of the restaurant—Benji is the GM, "the Dude"). I'd never remodeled a house in my life, never even really worked on a house. I was just kind of handy with tools, and I'd done some maintenance. On restaurants. Nevertheless, I knew I could figure it out, and I worked on that house day and night.

My final pay was maybe around $6,000 and change. When I deposited it, the bank probably thought I was doing something illegal, because my account had never seen more than $300. It was the most money I'd ever had in my entire life. What did I do with it? I bought a barbecue pit (what we call a smoker in Texas), the one that is today known simply as Number One. How I got it is yet another story of luck, thrift, and perseverance.

I invested $5,000 of the money I'd made into a new house that Benji bought and where Stacy and I would be living with him. That left $1,000 or so for my next big purchase.

Number One was the very same smoker that John Mueller was cooking on when I worked for him. It was made from a 500-gallon tank procured from the side of the highway (to put that in perspective, my New Braunfels smoker had a capacity of maybe thirty gallons. As I saw coming, Mueller's restaurant had failed, and Stacy's old boss had taken over the space and gotten the smoker.

When I found out they had it, I asked them if they wanted to sell it. They said they were going to but mentioned that they thought it was worth about $5,000. *No way*, I thought, *no way.* I told them I thought it was worth about $1,000. Obviously we were far from a deal, but they said they'd get in touch when they were ready to part with it.

That cooker never left my mind, but I went on working my various jobs, doing my thing. And one day, as was my habit, I was searching Craigslist and saw a listing for a cooker. It was the same one. So I connected with the guys and they said, "Sorry, we forgot to call you."

That thing was in terrible condition, but they were holding their price. I countered that it was way too much, as I'd seen it in action a year previously and it was just an ordinary smoker with many flaws. Again, no deal, but I said that if no one bought it, I'd take it.

They called back a little later and agreed to sell it to me for my offer of $1,000. And I thought, *Oh my God, another one!* I was dancing around like a new contestant on *The Price Is Right*, because the price was right. I said, "I'll be there in five minutes," cash in hand.

This thing was huge—14 feet long, solid metal, mounted on a trailer you could pull with a truck. I figured I could put twelve briskets in there—enough to serve more than a hundred people. After all, that's all Mueller cooked with for that whole restaurant.

It didn't look anything like it does now. It had three little doors; a real crappy axle; a solid piece of pipe, probably 3 inches in diameter; two plates to make a cradle for the smoke chamber to sit on; a 500-gallon tank; and then other plates with spindles welded onto them for the legs and tires.

It had one flat tire, and its other tire was from a car. In chapter two I'll explain all of the things that make a good smoker good and what I look for in all of the smokers I buy or build. But for now, suffice it to say, when I bought it, Number One needed some work.

When I got it home, I saw what a disaster it really was. Inside, undrained grease had accumulated all of the way up to the grate, about 18 inches deep. There were still crusts of burned meat stuck to the grates. The thing hadn't been touched in well over a year, and it stank. Opening the firebox, I found it was almost completely full of ash that had hardened and become as tough as concrete. (At the restaurant we clean out the firebox constantly.) It never had a grease drain on it, so the grease oozed into the firebox, which by then had piled up layers of ash, coals, wood chunks, and then a steady trickle of animal fat. It was all rancid and hardened, like sedimentary rock with little pockets of fossil fuels dripping out.

So I went to Home Depot and bought a cheap grinder with a wire wheel (a brush with bristles for removing corrosion and gunk), a grinding disk (for grinding through metal and rust), a rock hammer (for chipping stone), and a $3 pair of goggles. Then I started the excavation, Shawshanking my way through that whole firebox, which is about 40 inches long. It's got this little back door, and eventually I crawled inside the cooker like a miner to access the back end. Chipping away at this ashy concrete, I would encounter disgusting little pockets of rancid fat. Every day for a couple of weeks, I'd grit my teeth and force myself to go back in there. It was gross, but where else would I get a huge cooker for $1,000?

Finally I got it all cleaned out. It was summertime—the sweaty months of June or July—and Stacy was at work. I think it was a Friday night, and I bought a gallon jug of vegetable oil and a spray bottle and a wheelbarrow full of wood for $25. Treating the cooker like a cast-iron skillet, I sprayed it all over inside and out, rubbed it down with towels, and got it looking like new. That was love. Then I packed the thing full of wood and built a raging fire to burn it out, season the smoker, incinerate any remnants of the cleaning process, and seal up the pores in the metal that I'd exposed through cleaning. That was probably a 500°F or 600°F inferno with flames coming out the door. I let it slow down a bit, choked off the fire with the door, and then went to H-E-B to find whatever was on sale. I just didn't want to waste the fire. What was on sale was pork ribs, which became the first rack of ribs I ever cooked in my life.

After that, Number One sat around for quite a while. I would have loved to fire it up again, but what business did I have hosting a huge barbecue when Stacy was really paying the bills? She and I were both working a lot, only she was working for money, and I was working on houses for friends with some vague faith that it would all pay off. In the meantime, the friends I was working for were covering my expenses, and I was amassing a good collection of tools that would eventually come in handy when it came time to open my own joint.

We did smoke a couple of delicious turkeys for Thanksgiving one year. But other than that, Number One just sat in the driveway. We were working and trying to save money, because by now I was fully committed to opening a place. I spent most of my time mapping out the process of somehow opening a place someday. But money had gotten a bit tight, because apparently one guy (me) building a house takes a really long time.

Consequently it had been about a year since we'd last had a barbecue, and I was really jonesing at this point to have the mother of all barbecues. Eventually, we took some money and really did it up. If I thought I was a badass the last time I walked out of H-E-B with two briskets, think about how I felt pushing out a cart carrying six! Total baller. We had sawhorses in the backyard that we used to support a sheet of plywood for the cutting table. We really thought out the flow of service, with everything I needed to cut the brisket easily at hand, all the sides and garnishes lined up after the brisket station, drinks in the back of a defunct 1966 Chevy truck whose bed we filled with ice.

We even made little handbills to pass out to friends with directions to our place. I stayed up all night working on the meat; making potato salad, coleslaw, and beans; and keeping the fires. The previous day Stacy had said, "People are really going to show up today. I think this is going to be bigger than you expect."

## A WORD ON
## TEXAS BARBECUE

Making barbecue from pig is not as common in Texas as it is in many other states. The other major barbecue styles in the United States are largely pork-derived. Kansas City is famous for pork ribs and burnt ends, Memphis for its wet (sauced) and dry (rubbed) pork ribs, and North Carolina for its whole hog barbecue and pulled pork.

Texas is mostly associated with beef, though we cook our share of pork too. But really, the state is notable for its diversity. Most folks who travel through Texas for the first time are surprised by what they see. People, especially if they're from other continents, expect the state to look like the desert backdrop of a Road Runner cartoon. But when you live here, you know that this massive state has a diverse landscape, from the lush bayou of the east, to the plains of the panhandle, to the coastal flats of the south, to the Road Runner–esque desert mountains of West Texas. Texas barbecue is just as diverse as its terrain and, indeed, is heavily influenced by that terrain. Classic West Texas style, sometimes known as "cowboy style," involves simply slow-cooking meat directly over mesquite coals. (Mesquite is one of the few trees that grow plentifully out there.) Bordering Mexico, South Texas boasts a barbecue influenced by Mexican *barbacoa*, which is all about smoking goat and lamb and cow heads wrapped in leaves and buried in a pit in the ground. East Texas is next to Arkansas and Louisiana and takes its cues from the cooking style of the Deep South, so you see more pork here, and the wood of choice is hickory and pecan. Central Texas barbecue, which is the style I mainly adhere to, is all about slow cooking in offset smokers on post oak, which grows plentifully in a large part of Central Texas. Meats are brisket and ribs, and every restaurant tends to have its signature sausage recipe too, thanks to the large German and Czech heritage around here, which is also why we have a *kolache* culture in many small towns in these parts.

Which is best? They're all delicious, of course, so long as the person cooking knows what he or she is doing.

I didn't agree, but then on the day of, we started to get call after call from people all planning to come, asking if they could bring friends. It suddenly hit us that we were in big trouble, so we ran out and rented some tables and chairs. We strung lights and hung flood lamps from the huge pecan trees in our backyard. Plugged in a stereo. Made sure we had enough ice to chill the beer that people were asked to bring.

Before I knew it, there were 130 people ambling into the backyard. I got distracted and kind of overcooked the brisket—or so I thought. In fact, it turned out incredibly, the best I'd ever made up to this point, and I took note: brisket needs to cook a lot longer than you'd think to get tender. The guests all formed a line that wrapped around the backyard and down the driveway, and I was there at the cutting board cutting for each and every one of them.

And that's when I hit some sort of stride on this barbecue thing. Something just clicked and it felt so incredibly natural, so good. And it must have seemed that way to others too, because they kept asking me, "So when are you going to open up a place?"

I said, "I don't know, but I really want to someday." Little did I know that, encouraged by the success of this massive party, it was going to be sooner than I thought.

## THE TRAILER

In 2008, the now-overgrown food truck scene in Austin was just getting started. Stacy and I knew—had known for some time—that we wanted to open a barbecue restaurant of our own. The only question was how: we were still poor, still just working to get by.

Then Stacy found the trailer. It was posted to Craigslist, a 1971 Aristocrat Lo-Liner. I've been talking a lot about my love of Americana, roadside attractions, and the like—well, this trailer fit the mold *perfectly*.

Now, I hadn't really intended to join the "mobile kitchen" movement—but hey, the Artistocrat cost $300, and we figured we should make a go of it.

"It's a piece of junk," Stacy said, looking up from the computer.

I said, "That's great. That's all we can afford."

Stacy was right; the trailer didn't look like much. But I was already envisioning its future as a mini-restaurant: parked somewhere, with Stacy and me inside, her taking orders and running the register, me cutting meat to order and running out back to check on the smokers when necessary. If we set up some picnic benches out front, people could enjoy their barbecue on-site. It could be perfect.

So we drove out to the property where this trailer was marooned, welded to a boat dock. Inside, it had old beer cozies from the Yellow Rose, a local gentleman's club, and a couple of active wasp nests. The thing needed to go to the dump, but instead it was going to our house. The trailer was in such bad condition that I didn't feel comfortable towing it home, so we actually paid to have the thing brought to our house on a platform truck.

It sat in our backyard, resting on bricks, for a long time. We were still busy, working on other things, and I was trying to decide what to do with it. I sat in it quite a bit, drank beers in there while trying to visualize how it could eventually be configured.

One of the things I was doing at the time was helping my friend Travis Kizer renovate and build out his coffee roastery. He had this place, an old, late 1940s–early 1950s derelict gas station in the heart of Austin on the access road to Interstate 35, not far from the University of Texas campus, not far from where we lived. We'd work on it every night (because we had other work during the day) sometimes until 3 or 4 in the morning. I was really into it, because Travis is one of the best people I know and because I love old gas stations. (It was thrilling to discover that this one, underneath all sorts of horrible paint and ruin, was a Texaco station from 1951. These stations, which were masterworks of art deco, were designed by Walter Dorwin Teague, who also designed some of the popular Kodak Brownie camera models. But I digress . . . )

I remember one night sitting on the tailgate of Travis's truck, drinking a beer, talking about roadside America, since we were right on the side of a highway. He said, "You've got that trailer at your place, right?"

"Yeah, had it for a while. I just want to open up a barbecue truck so bad." I was just too busy, too short of funds, and didn't know how to get the thing started.

Then Travis said, "You should renovate that thing and just park it here. If you ever make money, you can give me some rent."

I looked at him and said, "Are you serious? Has the beer gotten to you?"

I called Stacy at about 4 a.m. on my way home, even though I was only two minutes away. "Stacy! Guess what? I got a place for the trailer!"

I couldn't sleep a wink that night, my mind was exploding with ideas. Somehow, Travis offering a space was the equivalent of the light turning green for me. It had been yellow, but now it was green. I suppose I was waiting for it to

happen when it was naturally meant to happen. And, amazingly, it's analogous to the very nature of barbecue: you never know exactly what's going to happen. You know how you want it to turn out, but you can't force it, and you can't make it happen on your schedule or in your time frame . . . you can only guide it. Same thing with a little dream of opening a place: I knew it was going to happen and what it was going to look like, but it would be ready only when it was ready. After this moment, I threw myself into getting the barbecue trailer going with greater energy than I'd ever thrown into anything.

I called my mom the next day. "I think I've got a place for the trailer."

"Oh, that's nice, sweetie."

"No, seriously! I have a place!" Yes, it was going to be inside a chain-link fence behind a run-down building with no sign, on the side of a major interstate between a strip club and an adult bookstore. But we had a place!

My grandmother had died recently and left my parents some money. They knew my ambitions well and decided to help me out. As they got money, they would transfer it to my account, and I'd go buy a counter or a sink. I was so grateful.

We started gutting the trailer, and every day I'd take it apart, cut holes, install things. We continued to scour Craigslist for everything we possibly could. We found a used sink, a cash register, a food warmer, a refrigerator, a little stove. Just the cheapest things I could find. Our backyard, littered with junk, looked like Sanford and Son.

So, piece by piece, I started to put it all together. And the trailer was beautifully designed, if I do say so myself. It was outfitted like the cabin of a boat or a submarine—the most ergonomic, tight-fitting, efficient use of tiny space you could imagine.

Everything inside was either from Craigslist or scavenged. I started pulling out pieces of wood and other bits of shelving and metal I'd saved from my various construction jobs. (I'd been working these for a couple of years now, always with the trailer in mind. If we tore off the panel from a kitchen door or a good piece of wood, I'd save it. The backyard looked like it belonged to hoarders.)

The food truck permit we were getting stipulated that all of our food had to be served from the trailer, and all the sides we served had to be made in the trailer—I couldn't make stuff in our home kitchen and just bring it over. So we wired up the whole thing for electricity. I converted a little old stove to propane. Overhead and down below, I built tight, round-edged shelves for spices, plates, cups, lids, bus tubs, side dishes, bread, butcher paper. There was a neat little pocket for a slide-in trash can I could pull out with my foot when I needed to sweep something off the cutting board. I installed an 11-foot countertop, measured precisely for my dimensions: I took into account how far beneath it my toes would hit the baseboard, and I lowered the counters from standard 36-inch serving height to compensate for both the 1½-inch cutting block and the towel beneath it.

In December 2009, we put a used marquee up by the I-35 frontage road that said **FRANKLIN BBQ OPEN**. We'd festooned the freshly outfitted and ready-for-business camper and the trailer housing Number One with white, orange, and red lantern lights for as festive a vibe as you could muster in such a weird location.

It was cold—in the mid-40s, overcast—and I was a bundle of nerves. My stomach was in knots. It was heartening then that my first customers were Big Jeff Keyton and his wife, Sarah. There were probably twenty-five customers that day, and they were all friends. But it was a good day. And every day thereafter got a little bit better, although the weather wasn't great and we were heading into the holidays. As it got busier and busier, I could see how tough it was going to be. Benji came around and helped as much as he could. And Stacy worked with me on the weekends, when she wasn't at her other job.

At first, everything was cooked on Number One. The briskets were pretty darn good right out of the gate. The ribs were a little shaky. The pulled pork was fine. This was when I really started learning. I kind of thought I had a handle on things before I opened the trailer, but I quickly realized that I did not. It's when you start doing something multiple times a day, every day, that you really start to get better.

Early on, it was a real cool vibe. I could put a brisket on after lunch and watch it until 8 or 9 o'clock at night while drinking a beer. In the evenings, I'd fire up a huge pot of potatoes, which I'd peel for an hour and half each day, dicing them all by hand because it was cheaper to buy cases of whole potatoes. After I shut down, I still had the fires going. I'd of course have to run various errands, get dinner, go home. But I'd always rush back, throw a log on, wait by the fires for a little while. At some point in the night, I'd get the fires going and then head home to sleep for a few hours before speeding back to stoke up the fires again and finish things off.

But it was pretty insane in there when it got busy. (At that time, a long line was ten people.) During the week, when I was all alone, I had to bounce between cutting, register, and fire. I'd be waiting inside my little camper for someone to show up. I'd open the window and ask what they wanted. I'd cut the meat and scoop the sides. Then I'd wash my hands, take their money and give them their change, wash my hands again, and go back to serve the next customer. The trailer with Number One in it was positioned such that I could look out and read the gauges. When I saw the temperature starting to dip, I'd ask the customer to excuse me and I'd go out to throw a new log on the fire.

Within a month or so, as we got busier, I got a guy to help out a few days a week. That's how fast things were moving. Quickly, the stove inside became too small for cooking the amount of beans and sauce we needed. We outgrew that and had to start using a turkey fryer. At first, I would pick up one or two briskets every morning, but we started having them delivered instead. We had no place to put them, however. We couldn't use a commissary kitchen, because I had to be there watching fires. You can't leave and then transport things, because you can't be in two places at once, which has been a common theme for the last four years.

I also needed additional space to cook more and more meat, and I had to figure out how to find enough space on the cooker for all the meats that had to be smoked. That's how we created the little systems we have now of cooking the briskets all day and getting them off to rest in time to get the ribs going for that day's service. Even then I didn't have the room. Of course, that all became ancient history the day after we got our first review.

The review was by Daniel Vaughn, who then had a barbecue blog called *Full Custom Gospel BBQ*. He went around Texas and the country rating barbecue joints. It's worked out well for him. Now he's the barbecue editor for *Texas Monthly* magazine. The review was stunning. "It's been a while since I've found an honest 'sugar cookie' on my brisket," he wrote, "but as I waited for my order to be filled, owner and pitmaster Aaron Franklin handed me a preview morsel from the fatty end of the brisket and the flavor was transcendent. If I lived in Austin, I would go here every day if I could be guaranteed a bite like that one."

That came out at the end of January, only our second month, and that's when people started showing up before we opened. Every time I hear the song "Alex Chilton" by the Replacements (big fan), I think of this. It was a Saturday morning, beautiful, and "Alex Chilton" came on. I was drinking a coffee and the line was down the fence getting close to I-35. And we were so exhausted, but I just remember that moment, looking at this line thinking, *What have we done? This is the craziest thing ever. When is this going to stop?* Well, it hasn't yet.

By the time the South by Southwest music festival, Austin's most insane week of the year, rolled around in March, we were already rocking and rolling, serving at capacity to a line most of the time. Lines were stretching around the corner, and the wait was longer than an hour. I realized, *Oh my goodness, I'm going to need another smoker*, and somehow I found some time over six months to build Number Two, which joined Number One in producing our meat. In June 2010, Stacy quit her job to come work with me. (First two weeks: pretty rough trying to figure out how to work together. After that it got smoother.) By that fall, we just couldn't handle the traffic out of our little makeshift restaurant in a parking lot. So we started looking for a real space. And that's when we found the restaurant.

## FRANKLIN BARBECUE: THE RESTAURANT

In a lot of ways, our restaurant-opening story is similar to all the other restaurant stories out there. So I won't spend too much time telling it. After running the trailer for about eleven months, we just couldn't handle the amount of business anymore, and we knew that we needed to look for a real place.

We started looking at spaces, but there was one barbecue place that I'd been scoping out for a long time. It was clearly failing, and coincidentally went out of business right about the same time we were looking for a place. I had a commercial real estate buddy get in touch with the owner; he said the last tenants hadn't paid rent in a while.

The guy who owned the business ended up quitting. I think he'd been doing one cook a week and then cutting cold brisket and microwaving it for individual plates. After he left we walked in, and I'm surprised that we didn't get E. coli just from inhaling the smell of this place when we opened the door. The cutting board still had bits of meat on it, the knife was sitting where the previous guy had left it, and there was an apron hanging on the light switch. You could tell that one day he was cutting lunch and just said "screw this" and left. The utilities had been shut off for weeks, but he had chickens in the fridge. There were crumbs all over the counter from his cookies and all of the sinks were full of standing water.

For us, the timing couldn't have been better. We signed the lease on the restaurant almost a year to the day after we opened the trailer. It took three months to build it. Benji and I and Braun and Stacy, we gutted it all, worked our fingers to the bone, did all the carpentry ourselves. When we opened for business in this location on East 11th Street on the first day of SXSW (a famous Austin music, film, and interactive conference/festival), some of our more devoted fans slept outside overnight, determined to be the first in line.

Since then, we've sold out of meat every single day of our existence. We get visitors from all over the world; if you stand in line on any given day, you might meet some kids from Japan who are in the middle of a Texas road trip, a family from Colorado who drove all through the night to get in line at 9 a.m., or some students from the nearby University of Texas who decided to claim a bit of brisket before their afternoon classes. We even got a visit from the President of the United States. In the summer of 2014, we renovated for the first time since opening and built a smokehouse to make things run more efficiently. So far, so good. Since opening the trailer in 2009, it's been an eventful and exhausting haul to get this far. And I don't regret one second of it.

## WHY DO BARBECUE JOINTS KEEP THESE ODD HOURS? IT'S HISTORY.

Yes, I realize that my restaurant is technically open for only about four hours a day. People ask sometimes, "Why aren't you open longer?" or "Why don't you open for dinner?"

To answer the first question, we're open for only those short hours because we close when we run out of meat. And we run out every day because supply is less than demand—for the simple reason that we don't have enough real estate on the smokers. Between briskets and ribs, not to mention pork butts, turkeys, and sausages, the smokers are running at pretty much max capacity twenty-four hours a day. In the summer of 2014, we added a new smoker to the lineup, which increased our capacity slightly. But each of our smokers is incredibly heavy and over 20 feet long. I don't want to sound as though I'm making excuses, but the bottom line is that "increasing production" isn't as easy as it might sound.

As for that second question, why we don't open for dinner: it's a good one, and one I often ask myself. After all, there are things about a dinner service that make sense. For instance, I (or who-ever is cooking them that day) wouldn't have to get to work at 2 a.m. to put on the day's ribs. If we were open for dinner instead of lunch, techni-cally, I'd have to get to work at only 10 or 11 a.m. to get the ribs going. What a nice, relaxing day!

But barbecue in Central Texas is traditionally a midday—or even morning—meal. For instance, the excellent Snow's BBQ of Lexington, Texas, an hour east of Austin, is famously open from 8 a.m. until *they* run out of meat, which can often be

10:30 or 11 that morning. So be prepared to eat barbecue for breakfast if you go out there. Smitty's Market in Lockhart (a half hour south of Austin) is open from 7 a.m. to 6 p.m. during the week, which are pretty classic hours.

To understand why Central Texas barbecue joints aren't open for dinner, you have to understand the history. They didn't start out as restaurants. Rather, they began as meat markets and grocery stores. People often describe the Central Texas style as "meat market" style. The style takes its cue from the large number of German and Czech immigrants who came to this part of the state, as described by Robert F. Moss in his scholarly book, *Barbecue: The History of an American Institution*. They arrived in the mid to late nineteenth century and became farmers, craftsmen, and merchants, bringing with them many traditions, including butchery, sausage making, and smoking meat. A number of these immigrants opened meat markets. In those days, meat markets were butcher shops, where vendors would break down whole animals and sell the meat. Lacking refrigeration, the butchers would preserve the less popular cuts of meat by smoking them or grinding them up for sausages, which they'd then sell as a ready-made meal on butcher paper, just as we still do today. These places weren't restaurants, so they didn't even offer silverware, sides, or sauce, just pickles and onions, a tradition some of the more famous places in Lockhart upheld until fairly recently.

The cotton industry boomed in Central Texas in the latter part of the 1800s, and before automated harvesting, migrant cotton pickers would swarm through the area for work. According to Moss, "an estimated 600,000 workers were needed for the 1938 crop . . . and many went to local grocery stores and meat markets for takeout barbecue and sausages." Given the hours agricultural hands worked in the Texas summer, they'd come in to eat barbecue throughout standard market hours, from 7 a.m. to 6 p.m. Over time, with barbecue proving so popular and supermarkets taking over the niches of the little specialty stores, the meat markets evolved into restaurants, which they remain today, though we tend to keep some semblance of the traditional hours while we serve up this cuisine whose history in these parts goes back 150 years.

But I have another theory as to why barbecue has continued as lunchtime fare: it's just too rich and heavy to eat at night. I wouldn't really want to eat it for dinner, letting it sit ponderously in my stomach as I go to bed (and I go to bed early). Rather, it's much better to eat in the middle of the day, when you've still got a lot of moving around and digesting to do.

THE SMOKER

## *Chapter Two*

At the restaurant, occasionally we show our most enthusiastic guests around the backyard where we cook the meat. Now, in most restaurants, people who are invited into the kitchen by the chef usually don't make a big point about seeing the stoves or inquire about every last detail of the ovens. Yet, here at Franklin Barbecue, every single person who comes back wants to know about the smokers—how long have I had them, which ones did I make myself, what are the differences among them. What is it about the barbecue smoker that inspires such curiosity and scrutiny?

I'm not sure I can answer that question, except that meat smokers, whether they're little backyard fixtures or massive hunks of welded steel sitting on the back of a trailer, are where the magic happens. It's the slowest, least-guarded magic trick in the world, yet it never fails to amaze people how a raw hunk of meat can be transformed into juicy deliciousness by such a simple apparatus. Thanks, thermodynamics!

With so few ingredients and tools needed to make superlative Central Texas–style barbecue, each one is obviously of crucial importance. Yet, of course, every choice you make is fraught with its own complexities. What kind of smoker to buy or build and in what dimensions are puzzling questions that make for hours of agonizing inquiry for anyone interested in barbecuing.

Although I occasionally find myself having to cook on other people's smokers and using styles of cooker I'm not accustomed to (usually when I'm invited to cook at various events around the country), for the most part I just stick to what I know: the classic horizontal offset smoker.

Now, an experienced pitmaster should be able to produce good results on any cooker, but obviously the best chances for success are when you're working with tools you're comfortable with and that have delivered good results in the past.

To learn how to smoke meat in the Central Texas style, you don't need to spend several thousand dollars on a fancy custom rig or even build your own. Although the quality of materials and construction of a smoker are indeed important to producing large quantities of great meat over a long period with high levels of consistency, many beginners will want to start off with a smaller investment in time and money. Whether you're an aspiring professional pitmaster or just someone who likes to cook at home, this chapter is intended to teach you how to buy the best cooker for your needs, some useful hacks to make it work better, some tips on how to care for it, and for other DIY fanatics like me, even some thoughts on how to weld one yourself. I'm not into bells and whistles and am certainly into getting a good deal, so I'm the last person who'll tell you to run out and buy the biggest, most expensive cooker you can get your hands on.

Does equipment really matter? Yes and no. Any barbecue situation is about simply knowing how to deal with and get the best results from the conditions you've got. I've got six cookers at the restaurant right now. They're all pretty much identical, yet they all cook differently, changing throughout the season. In some weather conditions, one will be more consistent or provide a more thorough, even temperature and smoke, while another might cook more slowly or unevenly than usual.

I graduated to these smokers because I needed more capacity. We were having backyard barbecues for an ever-expanding bunch of guests, and I needed to be able to cook more than one or two briskets at a time. If you've read the previous chapter of this book, you'll know that I started off with an entry-level New Braunfels smoker that I bought on sale for $100 at an outdoors store here in Austin. Its weaknesses were . . . well, it had mostly weaknesses. Its strengths were that it was cheap and that it used real wood: the first and primary requirement for making proper Texas

barbecue. Was it a great-quality smoker? No, but then neither was I, and as you'd expect, the barbecue I produced from it wasn't that good either.

But you've got to crawl before you can walk, and even though I didn't know what I was doing on that thing at the time, I suppose I learned something from every cook I did on it.

It wasn't until a little further down the road when I started building my own smokers that my cooking got more dialed in. (And, by the way, it's still getting there. I've always got a lot to learn.) Built in early 2014, the sixth cooker I added to the restaurant—Nikki Six, it's called—is so far the best of them all. Little tweaks here and there (and I mean little) to the design seem to have had a sizable impact, and meats on Nikki Six finish faster and just as well as on my veteran cookers like Muchacho and Rusty Shackleford.

So why the offset smoker? For one thing, it's what we do here in Central Texas: old-school barbecue, as opposed to the smokehouses of Carolina or the gas-fired commercial smokers you find almost everywhere. I've been surrounded with this kind of barbecuing my entire life. Two, I love the offset cooker because it's such a simple, primal vessel for smoking meat. Three, it's ideal for cooking with a wood fire, which is a huge key to the great flavors we're after. (That's why one of the monikers of these types of cookers is "stick burner.") It's just a massively simple device for converting fire and air into smoke and heat, which are focused on a path in a chamber and then allowed to exit through an exhaust pipe on the opposite end of the cooker from the firebox. The only moving parts are a few doors on hinges. Couldn't be more fundamental.

However, a basic sailboat is a simple and primal vessel too, yet it still requires competent handling to both avoid disaster and ensure a graceful and elegant ride.

As with a sailboat, much of the expertise in handling a smoker comes in dealing with the elements. In this case, it has to do with the wood you choose, the airflow to the fire, and the weather of the day. But when you've set yourself up well and the fire is effortlessly crackling, a clear, blue smoke is swirling out of the stack, and your meat is gradually browning to perfection, there are few better feelings in the world.

## PROPERTIES AND TYPES OF WOOD SMOKERS

I hold no science or other higher learning degrees of any kind. But I do think it's important to understand something about the tools you're using. Knowing how they work will help you use them more effectively.

Basically, people will make barbecue cookers out of almost anything. I've seen them built from everything from old water heaters to filing cabinets. To qualify as a smoker, all you need is a place to hold a fire and a place to put the meat so it cooks in the smoke (rather than over direct heat). In the sections that follow, I outline the different types of smokers, and the basic way they function.

### Barbecue Pits

The fact that people still call barbecue cookers "pits" suggests the origin of this style of cooking: a fire contained in a hole in the ground. In Central

Texas, the fire might still be slightly dug into the ground, as it is at Smitty's (see page 18 and the photo below), where the "pits" are big brick boxes taking smoke and heat up through an opening from an adjacent wood fire that burns in a shallow indented pit in the floor of the restaurant.

This is smoke collecting at its most basic. You could just as easily dig a hole in the ground, build a fire in it, construct a cinder-block structure next to it and a chimney at the other end, and smoke something successfully, if you could get convection to pull the heat and smoke in. All basic offset cookers are advancements of that ancient concept.

## Offset Cookers

The style of "pit" I use likely originates from a different tradition, one that's welding intensive. Offset smokers, like the ones at Franklin, owe their popularity to the deep connection in Texas between the oil and barbecue industries. You'll often hear of the supposed affinity oilmen had for smoked meat, what with so many people finding work in Texas oilfields during the twentieth century. Oil extraction and refinement require a lot of metalwork, and so it's quite common to see barbecue smokers cut from old oil drums or welded from sections of heavy steel pipe. There are stories that in down times for the oil industry, bosses had their welders build barbecue pits to keep them busy.

My smokers don't come from oil drums or pipeline but from used propane tanks. We take long 1,000-gallon propane tanks and cut four doors, each up to 3 feet long, along the length of them to make our cook chambers. At one end, we attach a smaller tank of 250 gallons, cut in half, for the firebox, and at the other end, we affix a tall, wide smokestack made from pipe. Clearly, acquiring and welding a 1,000-gallon tank isn't practical for most home cooks, so I've suggested a couple of tips for adapting your own, appropriately sized smoker in the section "Modifying a Cheap Store-Bought Smoker" (page 62).

### Reverse Flow Smokers and Tuning Plate Smokers

The offset smokers I build are as simple as they come. However, there are many tricked-out versions of offset smokers that are available to home cooks. One example is the reverse flow smoker. In the reverse flow, the smokestack is located on the same side of the rig as the firebox, with the intent that the heat and smoke will travel to the far end of the smoker under a plate beneath the grates and, unable to escape there, will be pulled back to the smokestack, thus making a complete tour of the cook chamber and smoking the meat more efficiently and evenly.

Another option is an offset smoker outfitted with what are called tuning plates: heavy metal plates suspended in the bottom of the cook chamber to balance the differences in temperature that inevitably occur along the length of the chamber. Typically, the plates are laid snugly next to one another at the firebox end to form a buffer against the powerful direct heat coming from the fire. Farther away from the fire, small gaps are left between the plates to allow more heat to rise into the chamber holding the meat.

I don't really care too much for either design, but that's maybe because I've learned to cook my way on a simple, unmodified cooker. I don't feel that I get my preferred amount of convection pulling heat and smoke through the cooker with the reverse flow, and frankly, it just changes the dynamic I'm used to. As for tuning plates, I haven't worried about those things at all, instead just relying on knowing my smoker and using experience to cook on it properly. A lot of people believe in plates and reverse flow, but my feeling is that I don't want anything restricting airflow in the smoker. Ultimately, you need to figure out what works best for your style of cooking and follow that road with confidence.

## The So-Called Cheap Offset Cooker

If you read around, you'll find that a good deal of antipathy exists for what is called the cheap offset smoker. This is the kind of horizontal smoker with a low price tag that sits chained up outside a Home Depot. Of course, that's exactly what I started with—my New Braunfels Hondo was nothing if not a cheap offset.

I began with one of those because I didn't know any better and because that's all the money I could scrounge together. But the cheap offset smoker is in many ways set up for failure, especially for people who are just learning. It is inconsistent and porous and because the metal

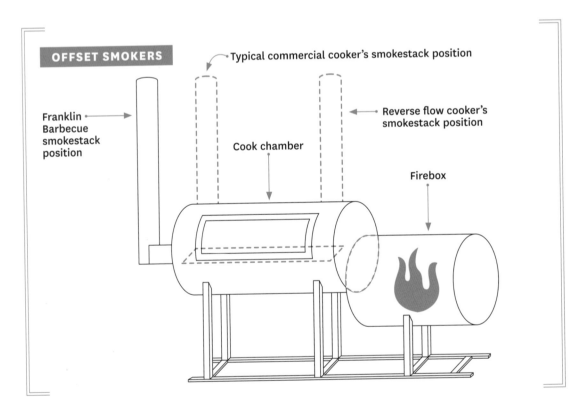

OFFSET SMOKERS

Typical commercial cooker's smokestack position

Franklin Barbecue smokestack position

Reverse flow cooker's smokestack position

Cook chamber

Firebox

is so thin, it doesn't retain heat well. When I picked up my second cheap smoker, which was abandoned at the curb and advertised in the Free section of Craigslist, I couldn't believe my good fortune. Today I can easily imagine its owner screwing up yet another brisket and simply wanting the thing out of sight. And, no, owning two cheap smokers does not improve your odds of success. But I do think that my cooking inevitably got slightly better as I continued to cook on them. So if a cheap offset smoker is all you can afford—and you'll know it's a "cheap" one not only because of the price tag but also because of its use of very thin metal and rickety design (see "What to Look for When Buying a Smoker," page 49)—I say buy it. A cheap offset is better than no smoker at all, and you can always modify it a bit to somewhat mitigate its feebleness. You might not be able to achieve greatness, but you'll be able to learn, as I did.

## Upright Drum Smoker

The only smoker that is more basic than the offset is the upright drum smoker. This design uses a single barrel or drum with the fire built at the bottom and the heat and smoke rising vertically through a shelf or series of shelves containing your meat. Since what you are cooking will be sitting above the heat source, it's necessary to position it high above the fire. Also, since you can't burn wood, which produces flames that will burn the meat, you'll be relying on charcoal and wood chips, which don't give the same flavor as burning wood.

This is a similar technique to what you'd use if you were smoking on a basic Weber kettle grill or on a Big Green Egg or other *kamado*-style cooker. You place the coals on one side and the meat on the other, cover, and get the smoke and heat you need. Again, the drawbacks are relying on smoke from smoldering—not burning—wood and the difficulty of regulating temperature and airflow. Big Green Eggs and company are a better choice than a flimsy Weber kettle, because their thick ceramic sides allow them to stabilize and hold a temperature more efficiently, which is what you need for long cooks. They're basically naturally fired outdoor ovens with smoke.

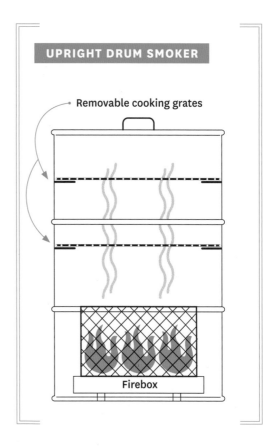

**UPRIGHT DRUM SMOKER**

Removable cooking grates

Firebox

## THE COOKERS OF FRANKLIN BARBECUE

I've gone through quite a number of smokers in my day, but here's the roster we're playing right now at the restaurant.

**NUMBER TWO** · This smoker, which I built during the heyday of the barbecue truck, now sits on a trailer in my driveway and gets pulled out occasionally for a mobile cook. It is made of a 500-gallon tank, has an insulated firebox with an 8-inch stack, and is the model all my 1,000-gallon smokers are based on. It is my favorite!

**MUCHACHO** · Built just after we moved into the restaurant space to satisfy still-rising demand for barbecue, I made Muchacho in my standard design of a 1,000-gallon propane tank, with a firebox made from a 250-gallon tank cut in half and insulated with a 24-inch liner. We use him for brisket, ribs, and turkey.

**RUSTY SHACKLEFORD, AKA SHORTY** · Demand continued to rise and rise, so a couple of months after Muchacho, I built Rusty with the same design. Rusty has since been renamed "Shorty" because we had to take 20 inches off him to fit him into the new covered smokehouse we built in the summer of 2014. Shorty helps us out with brisket, beef ribs, turkey, pork butts, and sausage.

**MC5** · The line kept growing, so I just kept building smokers. A good, solid cooker, MC5 is my least favorite mostly because the grate is ¾ inch lower. That's the way it goes—every cooker is different, even if it basically looks the same. MC5 does its service with briskets and ribs.

**NIKKI SIX** · My favorite 1,000-gallon cooker! Nikki cooks ribs and briskets faster and better than all of the others.

**BETHESDA** · The most ambitious cooker I've ever built, Bethesda is a big, bad mama. She is a rotisserie, which means she has sturdy racks that rotate around, cooking ribs and briskets more evenly and in less space than in long, horizontal smokers. Bethesda can handle seventy-two racks of ribs at once, cooking them evenly and deliciously, and unlike all commercial rotisseries (which rely on gas for heat), Bethesda is completely wood fired. My favorite part? Some badass local dudes who design motors for drag racers built the motor that drives her.

## HOW SMOKERS WORK

With any new smoker I see, the most important consideration is airflow. It's the airflow that dictates how evenly, quickly, and effectively the smoker cooks.

You probably understand the principles of airflow intuitively, but it always helps to be able to visualize the mechanics. It's fairly basic thermodynamics. Cooler air is drawn in through the firebox door by the fire, which is ravenously consuming oxygen to keep itself going. With the cool air pulled into the fire from one direction, the rapidly expanding hot air is pushed off from the fire in the opposite direction—into the cook chamber. We know that, due to the expansion of gases when heated, hot air rises because it is less dense than

cool air. (Scientists would tell you that what's happening is that cooler air is falling because it is denser and thus more affected by gravity.) Anyway, this movement of air is convection.

For offset cookers, the action of the fire is not the only force driving the movement, however. The smokestack is another part of the engine, working in tandem with the fire. Thanks to something called the stack or chimney effect, columns have a way of focusing the energies of convection. As the hot air is sucked into the cook chamber, an imbalance of air pressure from the cooler air outside can create tremendous airflow that will in turn create convection inside the cooker, and, when everything's right, the heat and smoke will move continuously and vigorously from the fire out through the

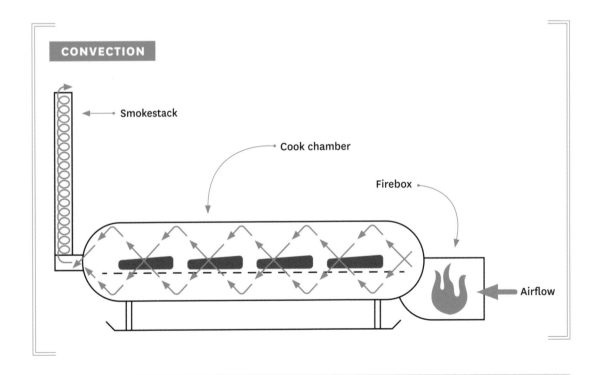

**CONVECTION**

Smokestack

Cook chamber

Firebox

Airflow

stack. Hot air that's moving cooks things faster and more evenly than stale warm air (which is continuously being cooled by the thing being cooked), thus crucially speeding up cooking times. The smokestack is an essential part of getting the hot air flowing.

Smokestacks and chimneys need to have the right proportions with regard to the cook chamber and firebox so they vent the heat and smoke properly. Too tall a smokestack and the cooler outside air will exert more pressure on the dwindling heat, which will back your smoker up and ultimately extinguish your fire. Too big an opening on the cook chamber will cause the smoke and heat to evacuate too quickly and you won't have enough heat or smoke for cooking.

A science book covering combustion and convection might have formulas that describe all of this and might lead you to a reasonable ratio of firebox volume to cook chamber volume to smokestack height and diameter. But when I'm building a smoker, I just tend to eyeball it. I can offer some advice, however: longer smokestacks tend to pull harder. And it's easier to make a stack shorter than it is to make it longer (I've done both). In other words, you can always dampen a stack that works too well, but it's much harder to make a stack "pull harder." The best thing to do is to get a measure of your smoker's draw and be willing to lengthen the stack somewhat if you think it might help or shorten it if you think things are getting bogged down. There's no better way to discover this than by simply learning your cooker.

Ultimately, repetition is the key to cooking well on any cooker, but especially a standard offset cooker. Experience, patience, and attention are going to be the keys to successful cooks. I've talked to many people who've screwed up a brisket because they left the cooker for too long, weren't watching their temperatures, fell asleep, and so on. Heck, I've done the same things myself. There's nothing worse than ruining a big expensive piece of meat into which you've already put hours.

But the more you use your cooker, the better you'll understand its airflow, the needs of its fire, the draw out through the smokestack, the high and low temperature points within the cook chamber, and more. And as you get to know this simple machine, your cooking will get better and better.

Of course, at the end of the day, if you're buying a new smoker, you still want something that makes your job as easy as possible. Yes, practice *does* make perfect, but better still would be to buy or build a smoker that sets you up for success. I've worked with many of the varieties of commercial offset cookers out there and can offer you the following tips when you're looking to make your next smoker purchase.

## WHAT TO LOOK FOR WHEN BUYING A SMOKER

Because barbecue is so popular these days, you'll find a huge variety of smokers in a wide range of prices on the market. In some cases you get what you pay for; in others not so much. As with any significant purchase, you should avoid an impulse buy and take a while to consider a number of factors before you choose. Some of these factors may seem obvious, but I think it's good to be reminded of them, if nothing else than for the sake of due diligence.

## Do You Have a Place to Put It?

This may seem like a foolishly basic point, but it's worth considering. People can become infatuated with barbecues the way kids get about puppies. They want one real bad, but after a month of scooping up poop and having to walk the animal twice a day, suddenly they're foisting those chores off on their parents. Likewise with great barbecue. After having tasty brisket somewhere, people become inspired, and in the excitement of the moment, they rush out to the store to buy a smoker. It's when they get it home that they realize it takes up a third of their yard or that they'll have to stow it in the garage behind all of that other stuff. They'll have to clean it and take care of it too. Suddenly it's wasting away. Don't let your cooker become a neglected puppy!

My advice is to figure out exactly where you're going to put it before you buy it. Some of these smokers have a big footprint, so take a measurement and really visualize the space. Also consider that you'll need to access the firebox with enough space to throw in another piece of wood. You'll want to be able to get around this thing. And it must be freestanding, not leaning up against a wooden fence or a side of the house. (That's obvious, I know, but every year some three thousand homes burn down because of barbecue and grill fires, according to the National Fire Protection Association.)

And if it's a smaller backyard cooker, it's better not to stow it in the back of the garden shed or garage. Chances are that you'll use it less often than you would if it's placed in plain sight and you see it every day. Consider these simple things before laying down your money.

## What and How Much Do You Plan on Cooking?

I was so excited when I got my first smoker. It could hold one, maybe two briskets comfortably— enough to serve ten to twenty people. But it wasn't long after my first cook that I was invited to cook for a friend's birthday and then a wedding party, and then our backyard barbecues started to expand. In effect, I'd outgrown my smoker after just a couple of cooks. So you need to think about how you'll use your cooker, especially if you're planning to buy something that costs more than a couple of hundred dollars.

For how many people will you usually be cooking? If it's just you and a couple of friends, you might not need too much space on the grill. But if you often daydream about being referred to as "the barbecue guy" and cooking for big parties, you'll probably want to start off with something that can handle more volume.

Volume is important, because the slow part of "low and slow" cooking is very real. It's not like a steak, where you can just throw another one on and it's done in 5 to 10 minutes. In fact, with barbecue you get significantly less than what you started with. Over 12 hours, 25 pounds of brisket gradually becomes 15, and you can't "throw another one on" when your cousin decides to invite her neighbors. Slowness and capacity have continuously challenged us at the restaurant— how to find enough grill space to do the volume we want to do when we need it done. As it is, our smokers are in use 24 hours a day. We are literally at maximum capacity. So, if you're firing up the smoker for a big party and doing a couple of briskets, you have to remember that those things will occupy the entire surface of a small smoker

## TO INSULATE YOUR
## FIREBOX OR NOT

Some fireboxes are insulated, using everything from multiple layers of metal, fire bricks, and fiberglass insulation to mineral wool. Ultimately, the question of whether to have an insulated firebox or not depends on the nature of the cooker you use and where you're cooking.

The main reason to insulate your firebox is to improve heat retention. Once up to temperature, an insulated firebox will hold its temperature much better than an uninsulated one, even if you'll be going in and out of the cook chamber a bit, which always costs you heat. Other advantages to insulation are much more efficient fires and therefore lower fuel costs. (My first smoker, Number One, doesn't have an insulated firebox, and it uses almost twice as much wood as Number Two, which does.)

Insulated fireboxes are a must for people who live in cold climates and want to cook in winter. You'll want a well-insulated firebox so you're not constantly battling to keep your temperatures up.

There are corollary disadvantages too. If the firebox is insulated with rock or with an extra layer of metal, the cooker will be heavier and consequently more difficult to move around. If logistics are a concern, this is something to think about. Also, too much insulation can generate too much heat for a smaller cooker. If the firebox is too well insulated, it will keep its coals warm for really long periods, hardly requiring

wood fuel to keep its temperature up. This way, without smoke, the cooker is basically an oven. We do want a smoker to exhaust its fuel at a fast-enough rate that we can keep adding wood to maintain a continuous supply of smoke. A certain amount of inefficiency can be a good thing. It's important to be able to balance the power of the heat source with the cooking vessel—a giant bonfire is counterproductive if you're just trying to scramble a single egg.

That sense of proportion is why I think an insulated firebox is really important for a large-scale cooker, but not as critical on a smaller one, as long as the smaller one is still constructed out of reasonably thick ¼- or ⅜-inch steel. For really long cooks in which you've got anywhere from five to twenty-five briskets going, you're going to need that steady, powerful source of heat from an insulated box. If you're just doing one or a handful of briskets, you can manage fine without.

My large cookers' fireboxes are two concentric cylinders with a small pocket of air between them. They're round instead of the more common square firebox because the round firebox allows me to build up a nice deep bed of coals at the base of the circle. Wood stacked across the arc of the circle gets natural airflow between it and the coal bed. I also like the way the flames rise in the round firebox and are forced to curl around the edges. I feel (no hard science here) this helps create a certain amount of vorticity that propels the air, heat, and smoke with great velocity and chaos into the cook chamber.

for 12 to 18 hours. You won't have a chance to cook anything else on there before the party starts, so it had better be enough.

Speaking of brisket, before you buy your smoker, take a look at how big a full 12-pound brisket measures and then think about how many you can get on the cooker you're looking at. And you don't want the meat smushed up against the edges either. It needs to have space around it for airflow. Now visualize a couple of racks of ribs, which can measure between 12 and 18 inches in length. Also consider height, such as the stature of a whole turkey, which you will quite likely want to smoke some Thanksgiving.

## Quality of the Build

Now you're in a hardware or outdoors shop looking at the various models of offset smokers they have. As with anything you're buying—a car, a jacket, a puppy—you're going to want to consider the quality of the materials and workmanship. If you've never bought a smoker before, how will you know what's good or not? First and foremost, trust your instincts: you'll be surprised to what degree rickety construction—and, likewise, really good craftsmanship—will stand out to even unpracticed eyes. But there are also some other details to consider.

If you're cooking with wood—and, after all, that is what we're talking about here—there are some important qualities you should be looking for. Wood fires are more inconsistent and variable than those fueled by gas, charcoal, or electricity. Therefore, heat retention is key, and good heat retention is a feature of thicker metal. At the low end of the price spectrum,

you'll definitely see a number of cookers whose cook chamber and firebox are built out of thin, stamped sheet metal. You'll want to avoid those, as the heat will spike or escape quickly, leading to terribly uneven cooking. Likewise, it will be hard to achieve and hold decent temperatures in colder weather. Thicker metal is more expensive and unwieldy to transport, but it will save a ton of aggravation during your cooks. Acceptably thick metal will run anywhere from $1/8$ to $3/8$ inch thick. You'll know metal that's too thin, because it's not much thicker than sheet metal.

Durability is also a significant question. If you buy a new smoker, season it, modify it, and spend months discovering its inner habits and quirks, you won't be too happy if its doors don't fit, its screws buckle, or it burns through in a year or two. Of course, this is a particular worry with cookers made of thinner metal. Rust is an inevitability with anything made from metal, but thin fireboxes can rust through within a couple of years of moderate usage. Best to look for a solid, well-constructed or insulated firebox. Especially with cookers made of thinner metal, good maintenance means dealing with rust as it occurs: take a wire brush, sandpaper, or steel wool and scour rust out when you see it pop up.

Along the same lines, you need to examine the quality of the closures, seals, and of the insulation, if there is any (see "To Insulate Your Firebox or Not," page 51). Doors lacking seals or outfitted with flimsy ones will leak heat and smoke copiously, which makes a cook uncontrollable and unpredictable. Seals should be tight and completely cover the gap between the door and the body of the cooker, usually from the outside. If at the store you see a smoker with a door that seems to fit so perfectly and snugly that you're convinced it's well sealed, don't be convinced. Just wait until you get it home and get it fired up at 300°F for 10 hours. You'll see even thicker metals twist and shift when heated, and suddenly a seemingly well-made smoker of dainty metal becomes a contorted, ill-fitting heat sieve.

## DETAILS AND ACCESSORIES

Good, simple offset smokers have few moving parts, but the ones they do sport should be of good quality and soundly integrated.

Thermometers are important. While making good barbecue requires touch and instinct, I refer to temperature gauges dozens of times every hour. I'd go as far as saying that great barbecue is impossible without them. So, two things that you want to look for in your prospective smoker are thermometer placement and quality. The gauge should be located down at grill height. If it's not, but rather placed up at the top of the chamber, make sure that it won't be too hard to install a new thermometer yourself, as I discuss later in this chapter.

Also, check to make sure that it's a good-quality, heavy-duty thermometer. The probe will be sitting for long periods of time in a hot environment filled with soot, tar, smoke, and grease. Chances are the included thermometer won't be of the greatest pedigree, so make sure that you can replace it with one of your own purchased down the road.

A baffle is a device (such as a wall or screen) that is used to control the flow of something (such as a fluid, light, or sound). In a cooker, it's a plate used to redirect heat and smoke as they enter the cook chamber from the firebox. It's often welded right above the opening between these two spaces, so it redirects the heat from the fire down and disperses it into the cooker, instead of letting it rise up and out through the top. It also adds to that chaotic effect, getting heat and air bouncing around, reducing unevenness in the cooking. I think it's important to have one of these in pretty much every offset smoker design.

I use the firebox door to control airflow to the fire (more on that in the fire chapter), but a damper on the smokestack can be a handy tool to further control the rate of draw. It's also handy for closing off the stack if your smoker's not going to be in use for a while, to keep the critters out. However, if you do leave a smoker completely closed up, it can eventually get moldy inside. So, if you're not going to be using it for a long time, always leave it cracked.

Other things to consider include the handles of the cooker and firebox doors. Are they made of a less conductive material so that you can grab them without melting the skin on your hands? Are they sturdy and well attached?

Finally, is there an outlet for drippings? Over a 12-hour or longer cook, a brisket might lose half its weight. Most of that is just going to drip down into the bottom of the cooker in the form of grease and rendered fat which, incidentally, is a fire hazard. You'll want to get it out of there rather than just letting it pile up and turn rancid. It's much easier to have some sort of drain or valve to let it pour out than to have to remove the grates, lean in, and scoop it out by hand. I'd look for a cooker that has a drip pan, a place for a drip pan in the bottom, or a drain at one end from which grease can run out.

## BUILDING A SMOKER

I started our business back in the trailer with a smoker that I bought from someone else. But since then, for the barbecue we sell at the restaurant, we haven't cooked on a smoker that I didn't build or design myself.

Building a smoker might sound like a daunting task, but if you have the right tools and some common sense, it's not as hard as you might think. It helps to be drawn to taking things apart, tinkering, and building stuff, which I am. Since I was kid, I've liked deconstructing things just to figure out how they work. If I didn't know how to use a tool, I just taught myself. It's that simple. And building a smoker can be too.

You'll need elementary metalworking skills. If you read that last sentence and thought, *Yeah right, buddy*, just skip ahead to "Modifying a Cheap Store-Bought Smoker" on page 62, where there are some more entry-level projects laid out. But welding big, stupid hunks of metal is not as hard as it might look. Welding complicated, delicate things like jet engines—now that's another story. But I started welding when my parents gave me a rig, and I basically taught myself. The more I welded, the better—and faster—I got.

Building smokers got a lot easier for me when I rented a basic workshop space in a small industrial park on the outskirts of Austin and stopped doing it in the sweltering heat and uneven ground of my backyard. Now it's just the sweltering heat of the shop. But it was indeed the backyard where I started the hot, grimy activity of welding together large pieces of heavy steel. It also got easier when I procured an old, 1970s Komatsu forklift. But by then we were well into business at the restaurant, and I needed to add cooking capacity and speed as quickly as possible. I spent many, many brutal days cooking from 2 a.m. at the restaurant, working through lunch, then heading off to weld for a few hours before grabbing a quick bite to eat and collapsing.

In this section of the book, I want to take you through some of the basic decisions and processes you'll want to consider if you go the route of building your own smoker. This is by no means a manual, and I'm offering no schematics or measurements. Indeed, I never started with any of those myself for any of the many smokers I've built. Rather, I've just employed my eyeballs and good judgment when designing and figuring out proportions. As I said, it's not rocket science—just effort, commitment, and a small degree of handiness.

Speaking of which, here's a look at some tools you'll need. I own these tools because I do a lot of welding. But if you don't see yourself getting grimy and breathing slag on a regular basis and still want to try your hand on a one-time project, I'm sure you can find hardware shops that will rent the tools for the few days that you'll need them.

**Welder** • I recommend a MIG welder over a stick, which, in my opinion, is not as easy to use. A MIG you can just plug in and go. A 140-amp wire-feed MIG should be sufficient for light jobs and plugs into a standard home outlet.

**Welding helmet** • I have an auto-darkening one; it's neat.

**Angle (disc) grinder** • I have a big one and a smaller one from DeWalt. You use these to grind down your welds, smooth sharp and jagged edges, cut thinner pieces of metal, and the like.

***Dry-cut metal saw*** • This speeds up cutting of thinner metal rods, pipes, and tubes, but you could also get by without one.

***Assorted measuring tools and clamps*** • These are what you'd need for any building project: levels, measuring tape, soapstone pencil (for marking steel), magnetic welding angles, gloves, and a range of vice clamps for holding pieces together before you apply the weld.

## Choose Your Material for the Body and Firebox

A simple horizontal offset smoker is really just two cylinders welded together with legs and a smokestack or some fundamental variation of that. Most homemade smokers I've seen are made of scrap metal, a detail that brings the satisfaction of creating something for cheap or for free with your own ingenuity, which, as you can tell from chapter one, is what I'm all about.

The first thing you'll need to do is figure out what you want to make your main body out of. As noted earlier, I use old propane tanks for my big smokers. These are 1,000-gallon tanks that are 16 feet long. The fireboxes are made from a 250-gallon tank, cut in half. I like propane tanks for their ready-made cylindrical shapes, their rounded ends, and their heavy but manageable 5/16-inch steel walls.

Before I proceed, I must offer a disclaimer: I am in no way recommending you procure and cut into a used propane tank. In industrial zones you can often find whole yards full of used propane tanks just sitting there, rusting in the dirt. They sit because they're difficult to recycle, as some propane outfits won't sell them for scrap because there's a chance they'll blow up upon deconstruction. It's said that working propane tanks are never completely empty and that even the metal used to fashion them is porous and can absorb potentially explosive propane traces. Resale of used propane tanks might be illegal in your area, or you may find that some shops will refuse to sell them because of liability. I've been stymied on many occasions, yet I've also found businesses that will gladly sell.

So, now that my disclaimer is out of the way, I will say that these propane graveyards often have used tanks with open or busted valves that would almost certainly not have any gas left in them. Also, before using the tanks, people often fill them with water and lots of dish soap to force out any remaining gas and the stinky mercaptans added to propane to give it an odor (so we will notice when there's a leak).

Alternatives to propane tanks include finding two pieces of used big steel pipe from a discount store or a scrap metal operation and fusing them together. Diameters of 20 or 24 inches will work well for this purpose. Or you can always buy plate steel and have a machine shop roll it for you to a length and diameter of your choosing.

Typically, if your firebox is insulated, it doesn't have to be quite as big as an uninsulated firebox.

## Notes on Building the Stand

Once I've determined the dimensions of the smoker's body and firebox, I set out to making the legs and the stand. For smaller smokers I'd use 1-inch square steel tubing that comes in 12-foot lengths. For bigger ones, I've used 2-inch square steel tubing. Determine and cut the lengths of tube for the two pieces that make up the base. These look like skis. I prefer these to freestanding legs on casters because they offer more reinforcement. I choose a length a couple of inches longer on each side than the entire assembly is going to be, including the cook chamber and firebox. Position these parallel to each other as far apart as the diameter of the pipe or tank and weld a couple of crossbars in between them (see **"A" ON FIGURE 1**, page 58).

Next, build the leg assemblies. For this, consider what is a comfortable height for the actual grill that will hold the meat. After all, this will be your cooker, so you might as well design it to fit your own body. I'm 5 feet 10, and for me, the ideal (waist) height is 36 inches off the ground (see **"B" ON FIGURE 1**, page 58).

There's no need to get fancy when shaping the ends of the legs that will attach to the tank. Cutting a 45° angle on these ends will allow it to fit the cylinder pretty closely, and you can fill in the gaps through welding.

After you've cut and fused the leg pieces together and perhaps reinforced them with their own crossbar, you can weld them to the base skids to create the whole stand. Then you've got to lower your tank or pipe onto the stand. I can do this easily with a forklift now, but in the old days of backyard builds, I'd have to use ropes and pulleys and a tree branch to lift the metal cylinder onto the shafts of the legs. Once that's done, however, all the parts are easy to fuse together. By this point it's starting to take shape, though you will probably want to attach tires or casters for easier movement of something that will end up weighing several hundred pounds. I recommend good, strong casters. Estimate how much your assembly will weigh and buy casters that are rated appropriately.

The most important thing in building the stand is this: Don't cut corners. Don't have flimsy welds; use strong-enough materials.

## Cutting the Doors

Figure out how many doors you'll need to be able to access every section of your cooking area. Doors are pretty easy to design and cut. Things to remember about the cook chamber doors is that they should extend right down to the height of the grill itself (which should be located at the midpoint of the circle) and extend up close to the apex of the circle (see **"C" ON FIGURE 1**, page 58). Make sure to give yourself room to work. When you need to reach in there to place or turn heavy pieces of meat, you'll realize that the cook chamber doors need to be fairly wide and pretty much span the entire length of the chamber.

One tip I can offer: don't cut the entire piece of the door completely out after marking it on the side of the cylinder. Rather, I leave the corners just barely attached. That allows me to weld on the hinges before cutting out the last connecting bits of the door, saving a lot of trouble in trying to realign what ends up being a very heavy piece of metal.

For the firebox, just weld a piece of plate metal to cover the end of the cylinder and mark a pretty good-size door, one that's long enough to get decent-size logs in and then to be able to shift those around with a shovel or poker.

I spend way too much time making my own hinges from steel rods and tubes. A much easier solution is to buy some heavy-duty ones at a welding supply store.

The final step is to weld the strips of flat bar trim to the edges of the doors so they overlap the sides of the cook chamber and firebox (see **"D" ON FIGURE 1**, below), making a snug fit to ensure very little heat and smoke escape and cold air doesn't get pulled in.

## Attaching the Firebox and Smokestack

If your firebox and cook chamber are both made out of pipe or other cylindrical metal, when you attach them, the opening will resemble a football, an oval-shaped aperture existing in the zone where the two circles of pipe overlap each other. The bigger the opening, the more heat you'll get flowing directly into the cook chamber. You'll need to install a small plate (see page 53)

to prevent grease from entering the firebox. Try to position the top of firebox to meet the cook chamber at grate level; that should give you a good-size aperture (see **"E" ON FIGURE 1**, below). Remember, grate level should be waist high for you, the eventual pitmaster. Fireboxes that are set too low won't draw as well.

You'll see lots of commercial cookers with the smokestack coming out of the top of the cook chamber at the opposite end from the firebox. But I do things differently: my chimneys are attached at about grate level, which means I weld it to the side of the cook chamber rather than the top (see **"F" ON FIGURE 1**, below). This is because I want the smoke and heat to flow across the meat thoroughly and evenly rather than be on a rush

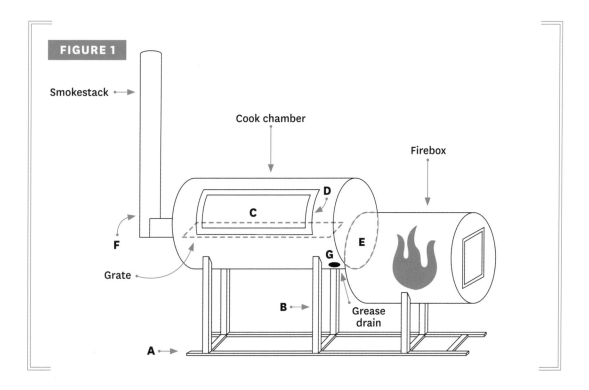

**FIGURE 1**

Smokestack

Cook chamber

Firebox

D

C

F

E

G

Grate

B

A

Grease drain

to rise out of the cooker. You can attach the stack any way you prefer. You can buy prefabricated 90° exhaust elbows. I tend to buy a pipe, cut a piece out of one end, and fabricate an assembly that allows it to attach to the farthest end of the cook chamber at the midpoint. And, in general, I prefer pretty wide and tall smokestacks. I wouldn't go any smaller than a 4-inch diameter, and I like them to be as long as possible, between 3 and 4 feet for a smaller backyard smoker. I usually just determine the length in 6-inch increments. Better to have too much draw than too little. You can always install a damper to regulate airflow if you feel it's pulling too hard once you've fired the thing up.

## Last Things

Once you've got all of this built and cut, it's quite easy to go in and install the brackets that will support the grates that hold the meat. Naturally, you'll want to install several brackets for good support, since the grates will have to be in pieces to facilitate easy placement and removal. I cut the brackets out of what's called angle iron, which you can find at any metal shop. For the grates, I buy steel raised expanded metal. I put a frame on the outside of each grate, like a window screen, for structural integrity and because it makes the grate much easier to take in and out when we clean. Make sure that you construct your "screens" small enough that they can be inserted and removed through the width of your cook chamber door.

Above the opening between the firebox and cooker, below the grate inside the chamber, I like to add a small plate to deflect the direct heat that will enter from the firebox. This small but crucial step will buffer some of that intense heat and

allow you to use more of that cooking surface on the end close to the firebox.

Last but not least, don't forget to make a hole in the cook chamber, at the end closest to the firebox (see **"G" ON FIGURE 1**, left), from which grease can drain (into a bucket that you'll place underneath).

## Burn It Out

Before using any new smoker, be it store-bought or homemade, it's crucial to burn it out with a hot fire to seal up the pores of the metal and incinerate any remains and by-products—oil, grease, metal shavings, and any other gunk—of the manufacturing process. I build as big a fire as I can and let it go for an hour or so. Then treat your smoker like a cast-iron skillet and season it by rubbing vegetable oil, tallow, or lard into the metal.

## MODIFYING A CHEAP STORE-BOUGHT SMOKER

Building a smoker from scratch is, even for the most bullish barbecue enthusiast, a big—and perhaps impractical—endeavor. Even I didn't start out by building a smoker from the ground up. But that doesn't mean you're stuck using whatever smoker you can buy in a traditional outdoors or cookware store. I've found that with some relatively simple modifications (okay, I know, this *is* coming from the guy who just admitted to owning a forklift and welding for fun), you can improve practically any smoker you buy.

### Installing a Proper Temperature Gauge

One of the easiest and most essential modifications you can make is to install a decent thermometer in a smoker that doesn't have one or replace or reposition the thermometer that comes preinstalled in many entry-level smokers.

Knowing your cooking temperature and keeping it consistent are two of the most important factors in barbecue. If they even have a temperature gauge, most inexpensive smokers position it, stupidly, at the top. Perhaps this convenience is meant for lazy people who want to be able to read it without bending over, but it's a useless placement for reading the temperature at the cooking surface where the meat is. Because heat rises, the temperature of the area near the top of the smoker is going to be higher than the temperature down where the meat is, which is obviously the only place that matters. In addition, smoker companies save money by using inferior thermometers, which only com-pounds the problems of bad placement. You'll want to throw down a few bucks for a higher-quality thermometer. After that, the work is easy and takes only a few minutes, yet moves you significantly down the road toward improving your homemade barbecue.

### Equipment

• Thermometer: There are many of these on the market, at varying prices. Without question, my favorite is the Tel-Tru Barbecue Thermometer BQ300, which costs between $40 and $50. I recommend one that has a 2.5- to 4-inch stem and is made out of high-quality stainless steel, shatter-proof glass and plastic, and paint that won't fade over time. Tel-Tru makes a variety of models, and if you order on the Internet, you

might also want to throw in the Thermometer Installation Kit to ensure that you've got everything you need.

- Drill with a hole-saw attachment capable of drilling through light metal.

**Steps**

**1** • First, determine exactly where to drill the hole. The temperature gauge should be positioned between the meat and the heat, right at meat level. This means the hole you're going to drill will be near the edge of the lid, close to where the lid meets the grill top, about 1½ inches from the bottom edge of the smoker's lid because that's about where the center of a piece of meat would be. To determine the distance from the firebox opening, measure the length of a hypothetical 10- to 12-pound brisket, which is generally somewhere between 15 and 22 inches long. It's easy enough to measure this out inside the smoker and then eyeball it on the lid, where the hole needs to be drilled. On the outside of the lid, mark off with a pencil or a Sharpie where you're going to drill the hole (see **"A" ON FIGURE 2**, page 67).

**2** • Next, select the right-size hole saw. If you use a Tel-Tru, the website tells you the size of the hole you'll need for each model. Otherwise, you can measure the back of the temperature gauge to figure out the diameter of the hole needed to allow the gauge to fit securely.

**3** • Finally, time to drill. Easy enough. All it takes is a steady hand. Now, insert the temperature gauge and screw it in from the back, making sure it fits snugly but not too tight. Adjust the dial for easy reading but make sure not to turn it by the gauge, which can throw off calibration.

## Extending the Stack

When I cook on other people's smokers, one of the biggest challenges is bad airflow. Smoke may be billowing out the chimney, but often too slowly and without enough force. The solution for this is to extend the smokestack upward, which will increase the draw.

In the discussion on building a cooker (see page 53), I mentioned that I like to position the smokestack to leave from the midpoint of the back of the cook chamber, not the top, because it pulls the heat more evenly across the surface of the meat. Many store-bought smokers have the stack connecting at the top of the chamber, creating exactly this problem. The solution for this is to lengthen the smokestack *inside* the cooking chamber down to within a couple of inches of grate level.

In a pinch, to extend the smokestack upward, I've been known to collect empty soup cans, cut out the bottoms, and pinch them onto the smokestack to gain several inches or a foot. But, for a longer-term solution, you can get thin flexible sheet metal and a few screws or clamps and simply wrap it around the stack to increase the length. Likewise, extending the smokestack down to grate level is not hard.

## Equipment

- Flexible aluminum or steel hose, a foot or two, at the diameter of your smokestack (hose usually comes in 1-inch-diameter increments)

- Hose clamp to match the diameter of the hose

- Screwdriver

- Clippers to cut the metal

## Steps

1 • The smokestack will likely protrude slightly into the interior of your cook chamber. Measure the diameter to determine the width of steel hose you'll need to buy.

2 • After procuring a short length of tubing, attach it with the clamp around the edge of the smokestack, tightening the screws of the clamp.

3 • Measure the length you'll need to extend the smokestack within an inch or two of grill height and cut off the rest of the hose. This should extend the smokestack inside the cook chamber to reorient airflow closer to the grill (see **"B" ON FIGURE 2**, right).

## Heat Buffer Plate

The flow of heat from the firebox into the cook chamber is largely a good thing, except for on the side closest to the firebox, where the heat will be much greater than on the far side. And if you've got a smoker packed with meat, which retards airflow, heat has an even tougher time getting over to the far end of the chamber, creating a frustrating disparity between ends of the cook chamber.

One solution to this problem is to install a baffle (buffer plate) above the opening to the firebox, extending at a downward angle into the cooking chamber (see **"C" ON FIGURE 2**, right). In a pinch, I've even jammed an old license plate into that opening. But with more time and space, it wouldn't be hard to cut a piece of thick metal from something lying around.

## Water Pan

I'm of the mind that you should always use a water pan while cooking on an offset smoker, so this isn't a modification so much as a technique. It adds humidity (which is constantly being whisked out by convection) to the cooking environment, which is important to your success, as it helps hasten the cooking process while slowing the drying process of meat. But if the smoker you bought doesn't have a built-in place for a water pan (and it probably doesn't), you could buy a small, 4- or 6-inch-deep, narrow steam table pan at a restaurant supply store (although really, any small metal container will do), place it on the grate nearest to the firebox, and keep it filled with water while doing a cook (see **"D" ON FIGURE 2**, right).

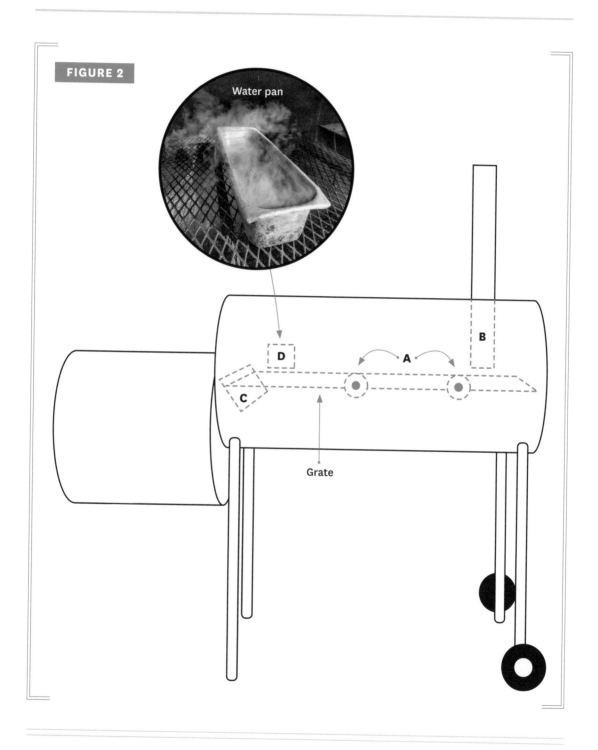

FIGURE 2

Water pan

B

A

D

C

Grate

## CARE AND MAINTENANCE

Taking good care of your cooker is crucial for both its own longevity and for the quality of what comes out of it. At the restaurant, we clean the smokers once a week, on the day we're closed to the public, and we periodically take one off duty to perform maintenance and adjustment.

Home cookers will not be running 24 hours a day as ours do, so there will be far less wear and tear. But time always takes its toll, so here are some ways to care for your smoker.

First, as mentioned earlier, make sure to burn out a new smoker. Get a vigorous wood fire going and let it rage for a good 45 minutes or an hour—as long as it takes. This is also a good thing to do if you haven't used your cooker in a long time and don't clean it regularly and the inside is covered with rancid grease or mold. The process is roughly the same as any modern, self-cleaning oven.

After burning it out, you should treat it like a cast-iron skillet. Wipe away any smoke or ash and then apply oil to the surface. I like to use tallow, which is beef fat from our brisket cooks. But any sort of vegetable oil will work just as well. You want to season the metal with the oil, as it helps form a protective layer that slows down the onset of rust.

As for regular maintenance on our cookers, once a week we use shovels to clean the bottoms thoroughly of any grease or burnt bits that have fallen down there. We take a wire brush to the grates and then hose the whole thing off. If you're cooking on your smoker only periodically, you'll want to do this after each use.

Another thing you'll want to do after each use is to shovel the ashes out of the firebox and dispose of them. (Use a shovel, don't hose it out. Do not get water in the firebox.) Leaving them in there, especially on smokers made of thin-gauge metal, greatly accelerates the rate of rust. And once your firebox has rusted out, it's hard to repair.

## LAST THOUGHTS

Building, modifying, and thinking about smokers is a big part of what I and any serious barbecue cook does. We're always looking at our cookers and thinking of ways to make them more efficient, cook more evenly, and—for the restaurant—cook faster. That said, once you get one that's in great tune, you'll know it. Then the trick is to use it over and over, every time taking note of its cooler and hotter zones, the way it cooks in different weather conditions, and always trying to get a sense of the way heat and smoke are flowing through there when the door is closed. The more you work with a smoker, the more you'll understand it. That's when you might get the hankering to modify one you've bought. And after you've reached the limits of what homemade modifications can offer, that's when you might consider building your own. In any case, you end up having a pretty intimate relationship with your smoker. You should know it well and hopefully spend many happy hours together.

WOOD

## • *Chapter Three*

Wood is king in Central Texas barbecue. We like to cook with a full-on wood fire. That is, we always like to see a flame in our smokers, convinced that this gives us the sweetest smoke. In the age of gas-fired restaurant smokers, this is not as common a thing as you might guess. But there's an art to burning wood for barbecue.

When I was just starting out and cooking barbecue out of a trailer parked on the I-35 access road not far from the University of Texas, I didn't have as good a sense for firewood as I do now. A significant yet overlooked factor in a restaurant's ability to produce good barbecue is a consistent, reliable source of quality firewood. At our little trailer restaurant, I did not have this.

In those days, I'd buy my wood from here and there and scour Craigslist for people selling firewood from their yards, deer leases, ranches, and rental properties. I'd pretty much accept what they brought me. After all, I was already pulling close to twenty-hour days, cooking all of the meat and making all of the sides by hand. It was a lot of work, and it left me little time to cultivate wood sources, even though I was probably going through about a third of a cord (128 cubic feet—in other words, *a lot*) per week.

In retrospect, I realize that I mostly lucked out with my wood sources in those early days.

I know this because, well, one time I *didn't* luck out and was delivered really green wood. I'll never forget that experience. This was about a month into our year in the trailer. Up until then, all of the logs I'd been cooking with had been relatively dry and well seasoned. But one day I got a big delivery of wood that was really green— a term used to describe wood from a tree that was recently alive—probably from a living tree that had been cut down to clear land and then sold without giving it any time to season. I just stacked it up to use later in the week.

The day I got into that wood, I had trouble getting the fire to go. All through lunch, I was completely frustrated, as I struggled to stoke the fire while simultaneously trying to cut meat for customers. I'd have to say to the person at the window, "gimme a second," and I'd run outside to look at the fire, throw a log on, and then rush back to keep cutting meat. All day, I ended up fiddling with it, trying to get the fire to work.

I was splitting the wood into smaller and smaller pieces so it would burn faster. But it was fresh, so incredibly fresh.

Up until then, I'd used only stuff that was pretty dry, and I didn't realize how nice that was. You could throw a piece of wood on, it would catch, and you would see the temperature get hotter for about 10 minutes and then cool off when the wood was spent. The green wood didn't want to catch at all. But as I found out at the end of that fateful day, not catching wasn't the green wood's only problem.

It all started around 4 p.m. the previous day, when I needed to get the briskets going. I warily watched the fire as it putzed around, haphazardly burning. I put another log on and hung out for a while, staring into and poking at the fire, trying to get a sense of its character. Finally, dead tired and having been there all friggin' day, at 10:30 p.m. I thought to myself, *Man, I've got to go home! It's okay to leave it. Going to be back here in a couple of hours anyway.* But another part of my mind cast a shadow of doubt on that, unsure whether it would manage to sustain itself while I was gone.

But part of doing barbecue is that you've got to be able to walk away. You've got to train yourself to know your fire and know your wood. If you just stand there, staring at the fire the whole time, you'll go crazy. So I convinced myself that it would be okay and went home to catch a couple of hours of sleep.

In those days, I had a different process for making briskets than we do today: I'd set a fire, put the briskets on, and let them go for about six hours of smoke time, then I'd return at the crack of dawn (before it, actually) and revive the fire and finish them off. But this time, when I came back to finish them off, I found that I didn't need

to. The green wood had more than done the job for me. Too much so.

Given that it was wood that I'd had so much trouble lighting, I naïvely didn't realize that eventually it was going to light, and that when it did, that sucker was going to burn hot and big. When I came back the next morning, I'd burned up everything. Little toasty pucks of badly burned meat—barely edible, just barely salvageable— were all that was left. And I had a line to feed, so I served them. But everyone ate for free that day—I didn't charge a soul.

That's the day I learned my lesson about green wood and also had drilled into me why it's so important to know your wood and to have a good idea of what you're going to get when you put a log on the fire. That skill clearly comes with experience, but hopefully sharing what I know will help you avoid what happened to me that day long ago.

## PROPERTIES AND TYPES OF WOOD

Chefs may value their stoves and their ovens, but they aren't an essential flavor of their dishes. How many other cuisines are there in which the heat source is a vital part of the dish?

Wood is important for two functions: providing heat and supplying smoke. The two are obviously connected but different. When you're cooking, moments will arise when you want more heat (but not necessarily more smoke), and there will be times when you're after extra smoke (but not necessarily more heat). Having a sense of your wood supply will allow you to approach your woodpile like a chef approaches his spice

rack. Well, maybe not with that much precision, but you'll see that an experienced pitmaster will have more control over cooking temperature and smoke absorption than a lot of people would believe.

Since we're going to be using so much wood, I find it empowering to have some idea about its makeup. Thanks to one of my favorite books, Harold McGee's indispensable *On Food and Cooking*, I know that all wood is composed mostly of three organic compounds: cellulose, hemicellulose, and lignin. They give the cell walls of wood its structure. Green plants are made up of cellulose, but in wood, the high percentage of lignin provides the girders that reinforce the cellulose and hemicellulose cells and gives wood its tensile strength. It also provides many of the more flavorful compounds of smoke (which is why we barbecuers care about it at all) and also burns hotter than cellulose.

Lignin content in wood varies and is pertinent to the discussion of woods for barbecue. Yet it's good to note that solidity is not what distinguishes hardwoods from soft. That distinction has to do with how the two plants reproduce: hardwoods produce seeds with covering (for example, a fruit or a nut), while softwoods like cedar and pine release their seeds uncovered. (However, it is true that on average most hardwoods are in fact harder [denser] than most softwoods. Yet wood geeks will point out that balsa—a notably soft and flexible wood—is technically a hardwood, making the whole discussion moot.)

Smoking meat is much better when done with hardwoods. They burn slower and with less heat than softwoods, and they tend to have less resin than softwoods do (which burns into a nasty soot). Incidentally, mesquite, a hardwood,

has much higher lignin content than oak, which causes it to burn hotter and faster and also have a much more pungent and distinct smoke, which some people really go for.

Along those lines, all different woods burn slightly differently and supply unique things to any smoked food. Up in the Pacific Northwest, folks use alder planks, which contribute delicate flavor to salmon. East Texas and much of the barbecue along the Eastern Seaboard rely heavily on hickory, while great swaths of Texas favor mesquite. But in this state we've also got pecan and various fruitwoods. The long and short of it is that most people use what's plentiful locally.

In Central Texas, we're lucky to have access to a lot of oak. Having played around with other woods, though, I feel lucky to be located in the middle of the Texas oak belt, since, for my style of barbecue, I feel oak is just about perfect.

Of course, there are many other hardwoods you can cook with. Each has its own contribution to make to a meat—and you should choose whatever wood is readily available where you live and that you like. Like I said, at the restaurant, all we use is oak (although the odd, unintentional log of something else might slip in occasionally). That said, I've had the opportunity to experience cooking with several other kinds of wood, and here are a few of my opinions on them.

## Oak

How can you not love oak? The very symbol of strength and persistence, it's meant so much to humanity during our brief existence on this planet. Great to build with, it's created a lot of shelters and sturdy sailing vessels that for centuries got people around the planet. It produces wine barrels, furniture, and those little shellacked coasters to put your drink on, and here in Austin tremendous live oak trees with huge, undulating branches are great for kids to climb on and provide tons of shade during our long, hot summers. And, of course, we love the fires oak makes and the sweet smoke it produces.

There are some six hundred species of oak. But the one I'm most concerned with is *Quercus stellata*, what we call post oak. A relatively small oak, post oak is classified as a white oak and, according the USDA Forest Service, "is a medium-sized tree abundant throughout the Southeastern and South Central United States where it forms pure stands in the prairie transition area." Central Texas could fall into that definition, as it transitions from the wetter forests of East Texas to the desert of West Texas. The Texas Native Plants Database adds that it occurs in "all areas of Texas except the High Plains and Trans-Pecos" and remarks that it's "a shrub or tree ranging from 20 to 75 feet tall with stout limbs and a dense rounded canopy, it grows in dry, gravelly, sandy soils and rocky ridges." Those stout limbs are classified as "very resistant to decay." That and the fact that it doesn't grow too big made it popular for use as fence posts, hence the name. But it also seems to me the perfect wood for cooking brisket.

Oak is one of the mildest woods. It burns beautifully—not too fast, not too slow. It gives fairly even and predictable moderate heat, meaning that I can control the fire pretty accurately. And it gives a mellow, smoky flavor whose presence is obvious yet at the same time sort of hovers in the background, letting the flavor of the meat itself take center stage.

Red oak and live oak are also commonly used, but both seem to have a stronger flavor and burn slower than post. Blackjack oak, *Q. marilandica*, grows in and around the groves of post oak here in Central Texas, especially toward East Texas, and is notable for the dark ring in its core. We occasionally burn a log here and there when it comes mixed in with the post oak, but I'm not a big fan. For one thing, the post oak tends to rot from the outside in. The blackjack oak tends to decay from the inside out because it is softer in the middle, which means you're not burning pristine wood when you throw it on the fire.

## Hickory

The Texas Native Plants Database recognizes many different kinds of hickory growing in Texas, most of them in East Texas, where hickory is probably the dominant wood for smoking, as it is nationwide. Hickory is a bit more powerful than oak, but I like it because it burns long and clean. The taste is strong and smoky, with a hint of sweetness. I think it's best for heavier meats like beef, but people use it all the time for chicken and pork, which can be good too. In my experience, it burns about the same as oak.

## Pecan

Actually a member of the hickory family, pecan is also plentiful throughout East and Central Texas. It doesn't burn as hot as oak, but its gentle, sweet flavor is delicious. Nor does it burn as long as oak, so I like to use it for short cooks. Fish, chicken, and especially pork take to its mildness.

## Apple, Cherry, Peach, and Other Fruitwoods

The fruitwoods are a terrific family of quality fuels. They tend to have a gentle, rounded sweetness and extremely subtle flavor impact. Because of this subtlety, these woods wouldn't do a lot for a brisket, as it's such a huge, bulky, and powerful piece of meat. But they can be really nice for fish, chicken, and pork, which might get overpowered by a bolder wood. I think fruitwoods are best when they're a little greener—barely seasoned—as they deliver a denser smoke. Because of their relatively short cook time and mild flavor, fruitwoods are better for direct cooking than long smoking.

## Mesquite

Mesquite is generally a strong-flavored wood. It burns hot and fast, but becomes more transparent the more it cooks. For this reason I like to use it best when it is burned down to coals, for direct grilling. Beyond that, it's used so ubiquitously as hardwood charcoal and on steak-house grills that its heavy flavor now seems somewhat generic. If mesquite is at all green or has some sugar left in it, it's overly aggressive for my tastes. But if it's really dry and heavily seasoned, it doesn't have its characteristic smell and it's more acceptably neutral, though it still burns fast. That said, if you're looking for some quick, smoky flavor when grilling a steak, it's a convenient and effective wood.

## SOURCING WOOD

As you know from chapter one, Craigslist has been a constant in my life. But as with any classified-ad marketplace, it's also full of charlatans, scammers, and cheats. Some of them sell wood. Plenty of firewood is available for sale on Austin's Craigslist site and probably where you live too. Folks are always needing to clear land or cut down old, inconvenient, and dangerous trees and then want to profit from it.

Over my years of buying wood, I was lucky enough to find Rod Moline through Craigslist. It was totally random, but since then, thanks to his knowledge, honesty, and reliability, he has become known simply as Rod, the Wood Guy around Franklin Barbecue. Supplying firewood is not his full-time job, however, but rather a weekend offshoot of his projects in clearing and organizing some of his land outside of Austin. But he's taken it upon himself to help organize other suppliers for us, which we really appreciate. While Rod still brings us a good bit of wood, he also got us connected with Joan Barganier, who has made selling and distributing firewood her full-time job.

For unfortunate and disturbing reasons, the availability of oak right now is high. This is because of the prolonged and dangerous drought that has been drying up Texas. The drought started in 2010, and at the time of writing, it's still going. It has been called among the five worst in the past five hundred years, according to the state climatologist. In a few short years, the desiccated soil has led to the deaths of between three hundred million and five hundred million trees across the state. And that's left a lot of landowners with thousands of dead trees across their property.

"These dead trees present a real hazard to property owners," Rod says. "They're instant fuel for raging prairie fires and they become housing for all kinds of pests, from rodents to snakes to insects."

Land needs to be cleared of dead trees quickly, only it's not possible to clear it fast enough. There's too much land and too many dead trees. A lot of ranchers will just drag the dead trees together and create massive bonfires to get rid of them. It was seeing such measures that led Joan to get into the business. "I just hated to see all that good wood going to waste," she says. "It seemed foolish to just burn it when there are plenty of people out there who want firewood." So she became entrepreneurial.

I rely on my wood suppliers not only to cut up the trees and split the logs into the sizes I can use but also to bring me good, sound wood, which requires an understanding of what I need and a sense of responsibility on the part of the supplier. They know I need high-quality logs, because part of them are going into the food.

"The drought is also influencing the quality of the wood right now," Rod says, "because these trees are not dying a natural death. They're already stressed when they die and vulnerable to beetle infestation and more."

Rod and Joan bring me the best wood they have. There are variances, of course—not every log is perfect. But for the most part, I need it cut and split to my specifications: clean, not too green, not too dry or overseasoned, not powdery and dead, and certainly not rotting or waterlogged or misshapened. I want logs with energy and some life to them that have some heft and density to give me a great burst of heat and smoke.

I'm lucky to have Rod and the other sources he finds for me. A lot of bad wood guys lurk out there behind the innocuous-seeming listings of Craigslist. People are always trying to cheat you— not everybody, of course, but in my experience about 90 percent of the people who come through here selling wood are shady (no pun intended). Indeed, I still have numbers stored in my phone labeled Bad Wood Guy #1, Bad Wood Guy #2, Guy with Messed Up Oak, and so on. This is so that every now and then, when one of those numbers rings and the fellow at the other end says, "Hey, I've got wood for you," I can instantly know that it's a scammer on the line and can tell him no thanks, that we're in good shape.

Usually, the scam involves overcharging you for the amount delivered. A cord of wood is a neatly stacked block of logs measuring 4 feet wide by 4 feet high by 8 feet long. It amounts to 128 cubic feet of wood. A true cord is a lot of wood but can be difficult to estimate since most people, including us, don't buy our wood in 4-foot-long logs.

People drive up all the time claiming they have a cord of wood, yet when you look at it, you know it's not even close. They deliberately stack it inconsistently or throw it in a big pile so that it can't really be measured. And then they'll try to charge you extra to stack it. They'll fluff it up when they stack it so it looks like more than it is, or they'll split it poorly.

My advice is be wary when people are selling "a truckload" or "a trailer full" of wood. Don't agree to buy it over the phone before you've had a chance to look at it. And when you do look at it, inspect it closely. Don't pull up only the top few logs to assess their greenness or general condition. Poke around and make sure they're not hiding a lot of bad wood just below the surface.

Another thing to watch out for is people selling what's known as a "face cord." A lot of people on Craigslist will advertise a cord when it's actually a face cord. As just noted, a full cord measures 8 by 4 by 4 feet. A face cord shares the first two dimensions but is only 16 to 18 inches deep. Don't pay for a full cord if what you are getting is a face cord.

## HOW TO BUY WOOD
## FROM A STORE

It's convenient that modern supermarkets carry firewood. Or is it? Much of the wood you see in bags or boxes in the grocery aisle between charcoal and cat litter is not suitable for barbecue. One reason is that a lot of it is kiln dried, meaning that even the most pyro-challenged among us will have no trouble starting a fire with it, but the pieces will burn so fast and with so little smoke that you won't get anywhere when you cook with them. Other times, supermarket firewood comes in a bag, so you can't pick up a log to feel whether it's been kiln dried or not.

To tell if a log has been kiln dried, measure by weight in your hand: if the log feels unnaturally light in your hand, then it's going to burn like gasoline. You're better off checking Craigslist or the classifieds for someone selling firewood that you can pick up and feel. Chances are with a little calling and driving around, you'll find someone you like and trust who can become a regular source.

## SEASONING WOOD

My perfect piece of wood to use in a smoker would come from a nice straight post oak tree that was cut down alive, split into firewood—for the size of our fireboxes, we like pieces 16 to 18 inches in length and with diameters no smaller than 3 inches and no bigger than 6 inches—and then seasoned for a year or so until the moisture content is about 20 percent. Of course, I never use my perfect piece of firewood.

That's because I don't have access to it. For one thing, I don't cut down trees for barbecue, as there's just too much dead wood already around Central Texas for me to need or want to do that. Two, being located smack in the middle of Austin and operating a young business without a big property, even if I had a lot of freshly cut wood, we don't have room to store a year's worth of it. At least not like the eye-catching stacks you find outside of the major places in Lockhart. Kreuz's infinite-seeming, all-you-can-burn wood yard out back is a thing I envy greatly. That's because it's stack after stack—worth a trip just to marvel at, if you've never been to Lockhart; *you've never been to Lockhart?*—of perfectly cured wood.

Ah, maybe someday. . . For now, I work with a mishmash of stuff: some of it is green, some is dry, a tiny bit is blackjack oak, most is post oak. With each wood delivery, we're never sure exactly what we're going to get. On one hand, this is frustrating, as even I sometimes discover that a recent delivery of wood is unusably green. On the other hand, I think the diversity of wood we use has probably made us better pitmasters. We've had to learn how to construct better fires and how to get the most from somewhat green wood.

Green wood comes from a tree that was recently alive. Living trees are full of water, which is retained in the wood after it's been felled or died of its own natural causes. The weight difference due to the water content in similar-size logs can been startling: up to 5 or 6 pounds in the dimensions we use.

Green wood presents many problems to the pitmaster. The high moisture content makes it inefficient and harder to burn. The demands of heating the water in wood steals some of the heat needed to properly burn the wood, and when heated, the evaporating water cools the combustible gases, making it harder to burn them successfully. The result is a heavier, dirtier smoke than can be useful in very small doses, but it's hardly what you want to build the flavor of your meat around.

On the other hand, wood that's too dry will burn so quickly that it may elevate the temperature of the fire beyond desirable levels and can also break down smoke into lighter, flavorless vapors that don't do you any good.

Hence, the desirability of wood that retains about 20 percent moisture. How do you recognize such a piece? That becomes a question of feel. Locate some properly seasoned wood—that is, wood that has been left to dry out for a certain period of time to lose some of its moisture—and some green wood and compare them. The weight difference and feeling of density will be obvious. Some other clues that a piece of wood is properly seasoned is if the bark is loose or falling off; if it has noticeable cracks or splinters in the grain; and if when you tap it, the sound is deeper and more full-bodied than the short, dull thud you'd hear from a green log.

Once you've got what you think is a good piece of seasoned wood, I recommend you burn it alongside a green piece, either in your smoker or just in your fireplace. Take note of the difference in rate of burn, amount of smoke, and the nature of the smoke.

One of the goals of the pitmaster is to control as many variables as possible during your cooks, which is why many of you might be tempted to start with fresh-cut wood and season it yourself. But be forewarned, seasoning takes time—from months to years, depending on your conditions (temperature, humidity, and the like).

Some general tips on seasoning? Don't start with very long logs. The path by which water works itself out of the grain of the wood is the same as the one the live tree used to transport fluids up and down its trunk and branches—by the grain of the wood. So chop them down to manageable lengths, and the wood will dry out

faster. Surface area is also important, so if you leave logs in full rounds, seasoning will take longer. Best to split them into the very smallest size of wood you eventually want to use (see below). Stack the wood loosely enough to get airflow between the logs and make sure the ends of the logs are exposed to the air.

Warmer temperatures have a big impact on drying. If we get a load of green wood in the spring, I can stack it in a sunny place in the yard, and due to Central Texas heat, it can be dry enough to use in just a few weeks. But because we are in the middle of a city, we don't have the space to do this to any reasonable degree. That stack of wood that I just spent three months drying will get used in less than a week.

If you've got a backyard, I recommend you start your own pile of wood, just to make sure that you've always got some well-seasoned logs on hand. Cover it loosely with a tarp to keep the rain off (covering it too tightly can result in trapped moisture, which can rot the wood), though occasional rains will generally just run off the wood rather than into it. If you're in a wet place like Seattle, consider keeping the wood in a shed or in the basement. High humidity will slow the drying process.

## HOW TO SPLIT WOOD

At Franklin Barbecue, we buy wood that has already been split for us. But depending on your wood source at home, you may need to do it yourself someday. And we often still have to split larger logs down into more manageable sizes. I suppose the first question to answer in this section is, why split wood in the first place? Well, for one thing, it makes it easier to fit it in our smokers and to carry and stack.

But one of the most important reasons to split wood is because, as I mentioned above, it facilitates proper drying and seasoning.

After wood is cut from a tree, moisture trapped in the wood will begin to drip away, moving parallel to the grain, or toward the cut ends of the round log. The longer the log, the farther this water has to travel, so chopping logs into shorter lengths means the water will leave the wood more quickly. Once we have chopped the logs into shorter lengths, we also split them through the diameter into smaller pieces, to expose more surface area and further speed up the drying process.

### HOW MUCH WOOD DO YOU NEED?

You might wonder how much wood you should have on hand to cook a brisket. I wish I could tell you. Unfortunately, so much of barbecue is dependent on context, equipment, wood, and conditions that to give you any sort of estimate would possibly be to lead you astray. The best I can suggest is that you should have more than you think you'll need. Having too much wood is never a problem. Running out of wood is a huge one. So make space and get a good woodpile going in your yard, garage, shed, wherever. Keep 100 to 150 logs on hand. You won't use that many on a single cook. But if that cook goes well, there will certainly be another. And another.

This may seem like an elementary topic, but at the restaurant I make sure anyone who's going to be tending the pits and feeding wood into the fire knows how to properly split wood. Failure to know this can result in injury, which is bad for the individual and bad for the restaurant. As I've explained, our wood is delivered to us already split into sizes that we can use, but sometimes one of the logs is too big and needs to be split into more manageably sized pieces.

The first thing to remember is that the process is called *splitting wood* for a reason. We're not chopping it and we're not cutting it. We're splitting it—splintering it along its grain. That's why we don't use an axe, which is best for chopping, but a maul, which is best for splitting. Anyone with a barbecue and a woodpile should own a maul.

A maul is sort of the love child of a sledge-hammer and an axe. On one end of the head, it's blunt like a hammer; on the other, it's wedge shaped like an axe though lacking a sharpened blade. A maul, which typically comes in 6-, 8-, 10-, and 12-pound weights, is also much heavier than an axe and uses that weight to splinter the wood apart as opposed to slicing it. One of the advantages of mauls is that they don't need to be sharpened. Because of that, they're safer than axes. You generally don't need a particularly heavy maul to split the kinds of smaller pieces you'll be using for barbecue. The heaviest ones are more difficult to control and will tire you out if you've got a lot of logs to do. So for spot work, it is best to choose a lighter maul.

The rest is pretty simple. You probably should have a chopping block, though at the restaurant we just prop logs up on the ground. We're not splitting heavy, full rounds that much, but rather just halving splits that are too big for the size of the fire we've got going. Make sure you've got your feet spread apart enough to provide a stable anchor for your body. Always remember to focus your eyes on exactly the spot you want to hit and never take them off that spot as you raise the maul overhead and prepare to bring it down. When swinging it down, don't swing it in a long arc, as if you were tracing the edge of a circle, but rather bring it straight down to the contact point. You don't have to put a lot of force into it; the idea is to let gravity and the weight of the head do most of the work. Your job is to guide it and not hurt yourself. But I've seen people hurt themselves by being off balance and incautious, so take splitting wood seriously.

FIRE + SMOKE

## • *Chapter Four*

It's hardly glamorous, but the tool I probably use the most at the restaurant is not a carving knife or a boning knife or a fancy digital thermometer. The tool you'll find most often in my hands when doing a cooking shift is a shovel. At all times, there's one shovel propped outside the firebox of each of our six cookers. It's an essential tool. I don't like the heavy shovels that last forever; I like the light ones you can throw around real easy. That's because, let's face it, I'm using it nearly constantly, and the heavier the shovel, the harder it is on the old body.

Shovels are our high-precision, state-of-the-art tools for tending our fires—the implements we use to constantly groom and tune our fires to optimally produce the smoke we want. The fire and smoke are what set barbecue apart from other forms of cooking. And cooking solely on wood fires is what sets great barbecue apart from the bad or the merely good.

Managing a fire is the most important aspect of the pitmaster's job. It's the crucial factor that determines the success or failure of your endeavor (not to mention hours and hours of time and hundreds or thousands of dollars' worth of meat). We pitmasters are more thermal engineers than we are cooks. Igniting, coaxing,

cajoling, molding, suppressing, and enabling fire is the essence of our work. You hardly need to be a scientist to be good at this, but it does help to have some of the characteristics of a good scientist: observational acuity, and an analytical sensibility. But you also need some of the qualities of an outdoorsman: experience, patience, calm, an ability to listen and intuit. And, of course, some of a chef's talents come in handy: an understanding of how meats absorb heat and smoke to gain flavor and color.

But ultimately it all comes down to the fire. Anyone can light a fire and burn wood and cook meat. But doing it well, on demand, over and over again in whatever conditions are present—this is what truly able pitmasters do. It's fine to know how to burn a fire, but knowing why it's working or not and being able to sense what's going on inside the firebox are what makes the process all the more successful and repeatable. As the authors of *Modernist Cuisine* (another of my favorite books) write, "creating and controlling smoke may be a lost art these days . . . a return to first principles can help recover that primeval understanding of why and when wood smolders and burns. You need that knowledge to create quality smoke. And if you also understand some of the basic chemistry of smoke, you gain control over its effect on flavor and appearance."

## HOW WOOD BURNS

But before you get that sought-after smoke, you need fire. And in order to get a fire, you need fuel. In general, barbecue, as practiced today, can use many forms of fuel. Gas, electricity, and charcoal are popular in most modern barbecue restaurants because they run with timers and computers and are more convenient and efficient. But in my mind there is no substitute for good, old-fashioned wood.

The negatives of using wood? Well, it's hard to control. Getting and sustaining the temperature needed to properly smoke a brisket is not easy and requires technique, experience, and stamina. Once you've managed to achieve the optimal temperature, level of smoke, and airflow, keeping it there for the 12 or so hours needed to cook a brisket is another challenge completely. The positives of using wood lie almost entirely in the quality of the smoke it produces, which imparts beautifully complex and savory flavor to the meat, something not really replicable with any other

method. But to get the wood to produce that really fine smoke, you need a high-quality fire.

So you probably remember from elementary school the model of the fire triangle, which illustrates the three elements that a fire requires: heat, fuel, and oxygen. Fire, as we know it, with crackling flames and a homey warm glow, is basically the molecular unraveling of wood caused by heat in the presence of oxygen. Once it gets going, a chain reaction forms that sustains the release of heat through combustion. But when wood burns, several things are going on simultaneously.

When a heat source is applied to wood, the first thing that happens is drying. Even wood we consider really dry still has about 20 percent moisture. Drying happens as the wood's surface temperature approaches 212°F and water contained inside starts to boil and evaporate. Evaporation also creates a cooling effect, which is why it's so hard to burn green (wet) wood. But once that liquid has largely disappeared, the wood heats much more rapidly.

When wood is heated enough so that all of its moisture has evaporated and it is effectively dried, the heat turns its attention to the structure of the wood itself. At 500°F to 600°F, the heat starts dissolving the bonds between the molecules of cellulose and hemicellulose cells. This releases water vapor, then organic gases (the beginning of smoke).

Finally, as the temperature continues to rise, combustion occurs. The dancing blue, orange, yellow, or red flame you can see (what many of us commonly think of as "fire") is actually the ignition of oxygen and the gases (smoke) released by the wood, a process known as secondary combustion. (Primary combustion, in case you're curious, is the name we give to the direct burning of the solid material—so, the smoldering embers of the wood itself.) As these gases depart, the wood is being reduced to solid fuel—charcoal and, ultimately, ash. Along this journey, at various temperatures, different compounds—among them carbon monoxide ($CO$), methane ($CH_4$), and about a hundred others—are released and create the complex mixture we call smoke.

So if wood plus heat yields smoke plus charcoal, you can suddenly see why I'm not so keen on cooking over just charcoal. When you do that, you get plenty of heat, sure, but since the charcoal is already in its elemental state, you don't get smoke (which is a by-product of the process of converting heat, wood, and oxygen *into* charcoal). With only charcoal in an offset cooker, what you're basically creating is an oven—great for roasts but not for smoked brisket. Any healthy fire in your smoker needs to have a good bed of coals (glowing embers from the already-burnt wood—that is to say, primary combustion), which supplies heat and helps burn any new wood you add to the chamber, and live fire (secondary combustion), which releases the smoke.

To create the kind of smoke you want, you must keep the fire within an optimal range of combustion temperatures, which is done by regulating both the release of heat and the release of smoke. You are able to manage the fire because you have control over all three components of the fire triangle—heat, fuel, and oxygen—though the tools available are rustic. You can manipulate oxygen with the firebox door and/or a smokestack damper (if you have one). Fuel and heat are controlled by the choice of logs put on the fire and management of the coal bed that you've created from burning logs (as well as airflow).

What's important to remember is that not all fires are created equal and that the manner

## THE REALITIES OF YOUR BACKYARD SMOKER

If you're working with a little backyard one-brisket smoker like I started on, you probably won't have room in your firebox to build the necessary-size wood structure completely out of logs. If your heart is set on starting your fire *just* with wood, then I suggest cutting your logs into even smaller pieces (perhaps 9 to 12 inches long and 4 to 6 inches wide, or whatever fits comfortably inside your firebox) and stacking them in a miniature structure with tinder and kindling.

But to be honest, it can be frustrating to start a roaring fire in such a small space with so few logs. So I propose a little cheat: use a "chimney" charcoal starter (one of those metal cylinders with an attached handle and a charcoal grate inside) to get fifteen to twenty charcoal briquettes rip-roaring hot and then dump them into the firebox. You will have created a quick and easy coal bed to give you the temperatures needed to get wood burning. Just lay your logs down on the bed of charcoal, then you can get the honest-to-goodness, smoke-producing wood fire going. Keep adding wood, as needed, to get your cook chamber up to the desired temperature. (For more on that, see page 95.)

in which your wood burns is just as important as the fact that it's simply burning. Next, I will address some of the key factors in starting and maintaining the kind of fire that will give you the heat and smoke to cook successfully.

## HOW TO BUILD A FIRE

At the restaurant, our smokers are fired up pretty much all of the time, so we have plenty of glowing beds of hot coals that we can shovel into a smoker that's been taken out of service briefly (for cleaning, modification, or the like). That's the easy way to start a fire: we just shovel in a glowing-hot base of coals and throw a few logs on top of that. But starting one from scratch isn't so hard either. When lighting up a cold smoker, I want the fire to start quickly and vigorously, because when cooking something that will take hours and hours, there's never any time to waste.

First, start with well-seasoned dry wood (see page 80) that's going to catch quickly. I choose slim, straight pieces of wood that are noticeably light and dry and split them into skinny pieces like kindling. As with so many aspects of handling a smoker, the primary concern is airflow. Inside the firebox, I build a little crosshatched structure with them, almost as if I were building a cabin with Lincoln Logs. I start with two wedge-shaped larger pieces on either side to create a base, and then I put three smaller pieces, about 2 inches in diameter, on top of the those, and then one more layer of three small pieces or three logs, spaced about 2 inches apart and positioned crosswise in the firebox. Next, I place two logs perpendicular to the first two logs, creating a square. Then I stack one more layer of two logs directly over and parallel to the first ones I laid down. In the structure, the curved shape of my preferred firebox comes into play. Because the logs on the base stretch across the arc of the circle, they allow airflow underneath them too. (If I were forced to work with a flat firebox, I would do the same.)

Now you need some tinder and possibly kindling. For tinder (dry, flammable things to help get a fire going), I usually employ a used piece of butcher paper in which we had wrapped a brisket. It's saturated with fat and grease and goes up like a torch. If I don't have a brisket wrapping, I'll take butcher paper (newspaper will work too) and coat it with vegetable oil. The point is that I've only ever put organic substances in my firebox—no lighter fluid or any other chemical. Splinter a few thin, dry slivers off of a dry log for kindling (larger pieces of tinder to catch from the paper and continue to grow the fire). Now simply crumple up the butcher paper and place it in the middle of your little structure. Place the kindling inside the structure atop the tinder and give it a light.

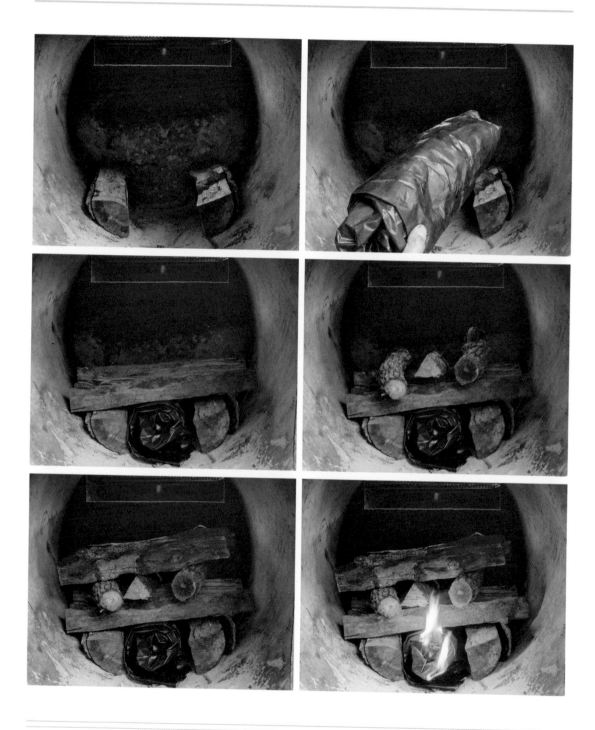

## MY BASIC PHILOSOPHY OF FIRES

My general philosophy of fires may sound a little hippie-dippie or like some sort of flaky cop-out. But it's really not. It works. It's simple, but I find myself having to remind my cooks of this all the time: Let wood burn at its natural pace. You don't want to force it do something that it doesn't naturally want to do. You don't need to pump air into it, you don't need to choke it off, you don't need anything but the wood, heat, and air that nature provides you. Your job as a pitmaster is to find the size and shape of the fire you need to sustain your temperatures with good smoke and then do your best to keep it there. This usually doesn't require anything more than adding wood in the right manner and making sure that there's plenty of air.

## SMOKE

There have been few moments during the last five or six years when I have not smelled like smoke. Even if I'm away from the restaurant for a day or two and have taken multiple showers, that smoky smell can still creep up. The scent of burning wood has been with me so long and so pervasively that I can't even really smell it anymore.

That ability of smoke to coat and penetrate almost anything, and then to persist there for a while, is almost magical. Magical too is smoke's value to us as an ancient tool for preserving food (besides its drying qualities, it imparts antimicrobials and antioxidants to meat that prevent spoilage; this method has been used for thousands of years) and its ability to make things taste good.

How can something without a form have such a powerful impact on everything it comes into contact with? That question has long fascinated me. And although people love the taste of smoked foods, few who aren't avid barbecuers give much thought to the fact that not all smoke is created equal. You can have good smoke, bad smoke, and too much smoke. This point should be obvious, of course, since whenever you see dark, nasty smoke billowing from something that shouldn't be burning, such as a building or a tire, you are reminded that there are lots of kinds of smoke that you don't want anywhere near your mouth. Much of the craft of barbecue depends on making sure that only good smoke in the correct amount comes in contact with the meat. So what is good smoke?

> ### TROUBLESHOOTING
> ### FOR TRICKY CONDITIONS
>
> Weather can present two big challenges to getting a good fire going: cold and wet. The solution to the latter is to start with well-seasoned wood. If it is raining outside, and thus extremely humid, logs that are especially dry can be helpful in getting a fire started. Windy conditions can likewise cause problems. If you can move your cooker, shield the firebox door from the predominant wind and keep it mostly shut while you get the fire going. Once you get it going, you can anchor it with a couple of big logs, which will bring up the heat and get you started on creating that big, deep coal bed that will ensure a good fire.

Well, just like everything else in barbecue, it's simple and complicated. Smoke itself is a complicated thing, containing, as *Modernist Cuisine* handily explains, all three states of matter: solid particles of soot and droplets of liquid suspended in a vapor of air and chemicals. Two of these three forms are visible, the book says, with soot turning smoke dark gray and black, and droplets of tars, oils, water, and other condensates appearing as a gentle blue. Those parts are important, but it's the other part that concerns me even more. "The components of smoke that are in the vapor state, on the other hand," the book notes, "cannot be seen at all—yet it's the vapor that does all the heavy lifting of smoking. Contrary to what you might have heard, the invisible gases in smoke contain nearly all the compounds that color, preserve, and flavor smoked food. Although they're typically just 10% of the volume of smoke, these gases do more than 90% of the work."

The particles of smoke—solids and liquids— that might attach themselves to the surface of the food can contribute some flavor and texture to the meat's exterior. But it's the gaseous elements of smoke that actually penetrate into the interior of the meat itself, giving it the deep, rich flavor that you want to be integrated into every bite.

Getting your fire to the state in which it's producing good smoke most of the time is one of the most crucial aspects of barbecuing with wood. But because we lack the technical instruments and clinical environments that the scientists who analyze the components of smoke use to do their research, we've got to rely on our eyes and nose to determine when our fire is a good one.

## Good Smoke/Bad Smoke

People who don't pay close attention or who don't eat smoked foods very often might not notice the distinction between good and bad smoke. They are probably hardwired, as we all are, to respond positively to the generic flavor of smoke—that little caveman or cavewoman in all of us that over hundreds of thousands of years associates the smell and flavor of wood smoke with sustenance, home, and well-being.

But if you're attuned to it, you can easily tell the difference between meat that has absorbed good smoke and meat that has absorbed bad smoke. And once you get it, there's no going back.

Something with bad smoke might taste good the instant you put it in your mouth, but then you'll notice that there is an acrid taste to it that verges on a bitter aftertaste. You may notice a sneaky, biting acidity that jangles on your tongue and that the smoke sits more on the exterior of the meat than inside it. There's no sweetness. Once you get past your initial inherent programming to feel pleasure from smoked meat, you find a caustic, corrosive harshness. And it lingers bitingly in your mouth long after you've finished it.

Good smoke is the opposite. It's lighter and finer. Whereas the bad smoke has an ashy monotone, good smoke offers complexity. The impact is powerful yet strangely delicate at the same time. There's an ineffable sweetness and a level of finesse that penetrates every bite. That's good smoke.

## Good Smoke

Getting good flavors out of smoke depends on two things: the wood being burned and the temperature at which it's created. It's very easy to cook meat with bad smoke. In fact, that's what most people do. Not only at home but also at restaurants all over. We get chefs coming through all the time on research trips for the barbecue place they plan to open in their own cities. They want to know our methods, our ingredients, our recipes. And, for the most part, we share that stuff.

What they don't know is that the secret they were looking for by coming to Franklin Barbecue was right there in front of them and wasn't a secret at all. It's all about good smoke. But good smoke requires real wood fires, and real wood fires require space and a level of mindfulness and commitment.

We've already talked about the compounds and flavors of different woods that give slightly different flavors in different smokes. But the difference in character between the smoke that comes from apple versus pecan versus hickory is minuscule compared to the differences between good and bad smoke. So let's concentrate on that.

At the most basic level, good smoke has to do with the efficiency of your fire—the more efficient it is, and the more complete its combustion, the better the quality of your smoke. But what do I mean by "complete" combustion? Here's where things get a bit technical again. Complete combustion happens when there is enough oxygen present to convert *all* of the fuel (specifically, those hydrocarbons I mentioned earlier) into just two by-products: carbon dioxide ($CO_2$) and water ($H_2O$). For our purposes, complete combustion

is more of a theoretical aspiration. For one thing, it is impossible to achieve complete combustion outside of a laboratory setting, because there is never enough oxygen present in the air to convert the fuel completely. But this is actually good news for us pitmasters, since in complete combustion, there isn't *any* smoke at all—just water vapor and carbon dioxide gas. So really, our goal is to get something *close* to complete combustion, so that our smoke is clean with few by-products, but not all the way there.

On the other end of the spectrum, if you have very *incomplete* combustion, then you'll end up with tons of unwanted by-products in your smoke, such as creosote and impure carbon in the form of soot. Soot in your brisket—not so tasty.

So now the question is, how do we control the level of combustion? The short answer is we need to control the temperature, which in turn is affected by the amount of fuel, the moisture content of the fuel, and the amount of oxygen.

Remember, moisture content directly affects the temperature of the fire. Greener, wetter wood will cool a fire, resulting in lower temperatures and incomplete combustion. That's why the burning of wet wood issues nasty smoke. A fire composed primarily of well-seasoned wood is of prime importance.

Likewise, insufficient oxygen to the fire causes incomplete combustion, which results in that thick, dark smoke. When this is happening, some of the more noxious components in wood are being formed or released without being burned off or broken down into smaller, less offensive particles. You will note that you don't need to have flames to have this kind of poor combustion. Some of the nastiest smoke comes from wood that's smoldering—burning without

flame. This is a sign of low oxygen levels (since, as you'll recall, secondary combustion—those dancing flames—is a result of oxygen igniting gases released from the wood).

As you increase the airflow to the fire, though, it becomes happier and perkier. When the fire starts to burn more efficiently, more heat is produced. With the rise in temperature, production of the more off-putting compounds wanes and the more desirable gases start to emerge. At these temperatures, the hemicellulose and cellulose are breaking down, releasing compounds (carbonyls, phenols, cresols, vanillin, and many more) that start to flavor and color the meat. As the temperature continues to rise, the lignin starts to break down and even more flavorful by-products are released, including the ones that produce flavors of vanilla, peat smoke, caramel, nuts, and spice— the complex mixture of flavors and aromas that we know as good smoke. A hot fire likewise incinerates many of the nasty volatile compounds that were being released at lower temperatures. Books like *Modernist Cuisine* and McGee's *On Food and Cooking* agree that, to get the sweetest smoke, the best temperature for your fire is between 570°F and 750°F. Above that, the wood is releasing only the lightest and most subtle elements of the smoke, with the heavier particles being incinerated. Good flavor can come in this stage too, but with less impact. Truth told, I don't measure the temperature of the fire itself. I'm more concerned with the temperature of the smoke chamber at the level where the meat sits. Having active flame at all times is important, though. The temperatures at which burning wood instigates visible flames are also the temperatures at which desirable smoke is issued. Another indication is the color of the smoke itself.

It takes some work and practice to produce and maintain a fire that undergoes near-complete combustion. But it's really important to do so, because if you're subjecting a piece of meat to hours and hours of smoke exposure, you want it to be the good stuff. This is why, in my opinion, classic Central Texas–style barbecue is so good. The whole art is predicated on making a fire with near-complete combustion and generating hours and hours of the pure, sweet good smoke. The gas and electric smokers that so many restaurants use these days don't rely on wood to create their heat. Rather, the wood is there only to supply smoke, and it's often smoldering or choked off. Obviously this is not a strategy based around good fires, and thus these cookers and any others that inhibit airflow end up producing a lesser, more acrid smoke, which is why I don't care for them. We've seen these kinds of cookers take over mainstream barbecue, especially as enthusiasm for it has bloomed in major metropolitan areas where it's not as easy (for practical and legal reasons) to burn so much wood. But in recent years, it's also been heartening to see a small trend back to the original, purist form that I practice.

## The Color of Smoke

I love to watch smokestacks—not only to see the energy with which the smoke is pumping out the stack but also to gauge the color of the smoke. Simply observing what kind of smoke is coming out of your stack can tell you a lot about the kind of fire you've got and how the meat's cooking.

You'll note that a fresh fire will produce a range of different qualities of smoke as it gets going. At first, the smoke will be thick and gray for a while. Then it becomes white, as the growing combustion reaction craves more oxygen and heat. After a little more time, the fire will hit a groove, and you'll notice that the smoke turns a thin, light gray with even a bluish tint. Then it might even be so faint that it's clear, only noticeable by the rippling in the air. It's kind of like getting up in the morning: you start off dense, slow, and foggy, and as you wake up, you become clearheaded and quick.

The color of smoke is determined by the size of the particles that compose it, and the size of the particles appear to be directly related to the fullness of combustion. So the more incomplete the combustion, the bigger the size of the particles. Large particles actually absorb light and appear black to gray. Slightly smaller ones look white. And even smaller ones reflect only the blue wavelengths of the spectrum and create blue smoke. You can witness blue smoke erupting from such other places as the tailpipe of a motorcycle, but when it comes from a barbecue chimney, it's a thing of beauty, considered the most desirable of smoke phases and the key indicator that your fire is burning properly. Then again, sometimes the smoke that issues from my stacks has no color at all, just clear ripples in the air. This is that step beyond blue—that light, clean, delicate smoke. Given our long cook times, I'm happy to have a certain amount of that to go along with the various other smokes that are perpetually hitting the meat.

## GROWING THE FIRE AND GETTING GOOD SMOKE

While all of this technical talk about smoke and fire is interesting, actually accomplishing it isn't as hard as it sounds. As I said before, once you introduce fire to wood, it's just a matter of the fire finding its own rhythm and burning the way it wants to burn. For beginners, the best thing you can do at your early stages of barbecue is watch your fires and become familiar with the way they go.

### Burn Seasoned Wood

You can eventually get good smoke with green wood, but you'll have to go through a lot of dirtier smoke to get there. The best smoke comes from well-seasoned dry wood that will burn vigorously and fairly quickly. You go through more wood this way (and have to keep a watchful eye on the smoker), but the results are worth it.

### Heat That Cooker Up

Cold surfaces keep the temperature of the fire down, which results in dirtier smoke. So once you get your fire going, give your cooker time to absorb the heat thoroughly throughout the firebox and the cook chamber. I build a new fire in a cold smoker and let it go for anywhere from 30 minutes to an hour before I throw any meat on. You want everything to be solidly in its proper temperature zone before you upset the conditions by adding a mass of cold meat.

## Don't Rush the Fire

Remember, always let the fire burn at its natural pace. And that means letting it find its groove. I've seen the analogy of a truck used for a smoker. The firebox is the engine for a big heavy truck. If you stomp on the gas and get it revved up, it will gradually accrue more and more speed and force. You do it too quickly and suddenly you find yourself barreling down the road at breakneck pace, which forces you to crush the brake to slow down or stop. The result is a very unsmooth ride and a great waste of energy. The same thing goes for a fire. Instead of piling on wood and building a huge, raging fire that you then have to choke back, I prefer to gradually grow a fire to ease into where you want it to be. It may take a little longer, but it's ultimately a much more graceful and sustainable ride.

## Have a Strong Coal Bed

Once the fire gets going and has broken down a few logs into a nice bed of glowing embers, you've got your foundation. This goes part and parcel with warming up your smoker properly, but developing that foundation of coals is key to holding a stable temperature, which is a key to a successful cook. Having a nice, deep bed of coals will also allow new logs to start combusting quickly, minimizing the release of bad smoke.

## Preheat the Wood

This is a technique that I use in cold weather. In warm weather, there's no need. But cold wood—and especially cold, green wood—can take a while to get going and might pump out volumes of dirty smoke before it really takes off. You can reduce this time by warming the wood before you add it to the fire. Once you have that primary fire started, before you've added your meat to the smoker, just stack a few pieces of wood on top of the firebox and let them hang out there for a while warming up their little toesies before they jump in. Then, when the meat's on and you need to add more wood, the logs will be ready to combust much more rapidly.

## Cook with the Fire Door Open

To say "cook with the fire door open" is like saying "look both ways before crossing the street"—almost a cliché and such a basic truism that it almost doesn't need to be said. Then again, lots of pedestrians are hit by cars every year, and lots of firebox doors are left closed. If the conditions are good, there's no reason not to allow the maximum airflow your fire needs. Adjust its temperature by the amount of fuel you put in it, but let that fuel burn as cleanly as possible. A healthy fire will gulp that air up and turn it into thorough combustion and the kind of smoke you want on your meat. Of course, there are times when you might want to close that door a little bit, however. For instance, in rain, cold, or really windy weather, the elements might affect your fire in a negative way.

Many people think that if your fire has gotten too big and hot, closing the fire door is a way to suppress it, at the cost of producing some dirtier smoke. It would have to be DEFCON 1 ("Nuclear war is imminent") for me to consider closing the door. Sure, sometimes you get too much of a rager, with dangerously spiking temperatures. But in those instances it's much better to just open up the cook chamber doors and let the heat out quickly and completely (or shovel some coal towards the back of the cooker, or both) than to slowly choke down the fire.

## TUNING THE FIRE

Now that your fire is built, your coal bed is full and self-sustaining, your smoker has warmed to the right temperature, and wispy blue smoke is swirling from the stack, you're ready to put the meat on. We'll talk more about the meat in chapter five. But once you've put it on, you're not going to do much with it for a long time. What you will be doing is constantly checking your temperatures and maintaining the fire. The most important pieces of equipment during this stage are your handy shovel, a thermometer to follow the temperatures in the cooker, and an ice chest full of cold beer.

Yes, this part is the long slog of barbecue, but it's also the time to pull up a lawn chair, pop a beer, chat with friends, or, if you're alone (as I often am on long cooks), simply reflect on life. You'll learn to keep a near-constant eye on the fire, smokestack, and cooker temperature gauges. Generally, just looking at one of those will give you an indication of what's going on. And periodically, you'll get up to throw a log on or adjust the fire.

The goal at this stage is consistency. You want to keep your temperatures within the zone in which you've decided to cook (see chapter six for more on that). Inevitably they will rise and fall a bit, but get too far off course, and you can either damage your meat or you'll find that it's

taking hours longer than you planned, which can be a problem if you have people waiting to eat.

It's also important to remember that you have more control than you think. Even a chef in a modern kitchen will see a lag in time between when he or she turns up the dial in an oven versus when the food actually sees that heat. You will see that happen in a good smoker much more quickly. Smokers look clunky, heavy, and dull, but a well-built one will respond quickly to your adjustments. When I rummage through the woodpile looking for a piece that might give me another 10 degrees of heat and then I throw that small, dry piece on the fire, it might catch instantly. And when it does, thanks to that good airflow, that heat that the wood has just created will be whisked into the cook chamber within seconds. Because of that, I do feel I have the ability to control the temperature in the cook chamber almost in increments of degrees. (It's just holding them there that's the challenge.)

Skill at this part of managing a cook comes largely from experience. You have to know your wood, your smoker, and the weather conditions. Below I'm going to offer some of my techniques for managing the fire, but the best advice is to develop your own methods depending on your equipment.

## CHOOSING WOOD AND MAINTAINING THE FIRE

Wood choice depends on what you want at any given time. And my favored techniques tend to change and evolve over time. Lately, I've preferred to use smaller pieces of wood. These offer more precision, more consistency, and a tighter control of the fire. Using smaller pieces means that I have to put more individual pieces in the firebox, of course, but I avoid the problem of really big spikes. The choir of smaller voices keeps a steady chatter going, maintaining the desired temperature, instead of the up-and-down, up-and-down bellowing that comes from larger pieces. The trade-off is that it's higher-maintenance cooking, which means you'll have to keep up with the fire more frequently instead of just setting a large piece of wood and walking away.

## FIRE AS CHESS

Your fire is always evolving. So while it's good to take stock of it at any given moment, you also have to look at where it's heading. Think of it like a game of chess. Your opponent is inconsistent temperatures. Your pieces are your logs and your shovel. The board is the fire itself. You study the board, think about where you want to get, consider what the opposition is likely to do, and then plot your moves.

Here's an example: The temperature gauge may show that the cooker's humming along at a nice 275°F. But you see that the main log that's been burning is about to break down. It needs to be replaced. But if you put another big one in there, you're going to lose heat and smoke as the log heats up and starts to burn. So instead of that one, you might opt to put in two smaller ones. Or you might decide to use a small piece that's going to catch quickly and give a bump of heat, then follow that immediately with a larger, denser piece that's going to anchor the fire for another 30 minutes.

Here's another situation: I might stoke the fire a little bit with the shovel because I need about 5 degrees of temperature, but I don't want to put a new piece on because I'm about to open up the smoke chamber to flip the ribs, and I don't want to inhale a bunch of smoke. So I'm creating clean heat (poking at the embers, stimulating primary combustion) instead of smoky heat.

Of course, there are an infinite number of scenarios, and your plans and plays will be evolving constantly.

The key is to be both analytical and prepared for where your fire is heading. There are many different paths to get to the same end. But it's good to have the flexibility that's offered by a decent-size wood supply. Having a number of logs of various shapes, sizes, densities, and dryness gives you a lot of options for keeping your fire on track.

## THE MAGICAL SHOVEL

An arsenal of different wood sizes is helpful, but even easier is just altering the structure of the fire itself. For this, never forget your trusty shovel. It's the number one way to keep air flowing over and into the fire. Use the shovel to slide logs or coals forward toward the cooker if you need more heat, or to pull them back toward the door if you want to slow down the fire by letting heat escape through the backside. When I put a new log on, I'll often use the edge of the head of the shovel to carve out a little channel in the coal bed, creating a pathway for the air under the log so that it lights faster. On a cold day, I'll spread coals toward the back to preheat the air hitting the fire.

## USING GREEN WOOD

It's been well documented that I use a fair bit of green wood when I cook. For the record: that's because of necessity, not design. If I had a big lot stacked high with perfectly seasoned wood, I'd use that all of the time. But instead I have to take what I can get, which sometimes includes a delivery of green wood. So here's how I use it.

Greener wood offers heavier smoke. And I cook with so much light smoke that every now and then I want to get a dose of some of the denser, low-temperature smoke that comes from green wood.

However, for the most part this is not the smoke I'm after. Thus, the most common way I'd use green wood is for heat, not for smoke. If I had a stack of really green wood, and I needed to step away from the cooker to run some errands, I'd consider using it *after* I'd wrapped the meats (see page 154), at which point the briskets continue cooking without absorbing tons of smoke flavor. At that stage I might put on the green wood and close the firebox door a bit. It would smolder but provide enough temperature to keep the meats cooking, and the wrapping would prevent them from taking on the smoke.

• • •

Good smoke is an indispensable element of great-tasting barbecue. In this chapter, I presented some key techniques and the thinking behind them, but there's really no substitute for just getting in there with your own fires. Remember to be mindful at all times—of your wood, of the fire, of the airflow—and you should come out fine.

MEAT

## • *Chapter Five*

As someone who makes his living selling enormous quantities of cooked meat—we're talking 2,000 pounds on our busiest days—meat quality is something I care deeply about. High-quality meat is by far our number one expense. Unfortunately, by far my number one headache is also the work it takes to secure the consistent supply of meat at the quality level we require. When things are going well, our supply of well-butchered, ethically raised meat is something I don't have to think about too much. But when things go wrong, they can make for the worst times in this line of work. I'll never forget our one epic month of brisket drama.

In 2013, the meat plant that supplies our briskets caught on fire and had to shut down for about a month. Luckily, we had just taken delivery of a couple of pallets—about three hundred briskets. But we saw the trouble on the horizon and tried to ration our meat accordingly. We were slightly stingy for a couple of weeks, cutting it close as to how much we cooked to get through a day, and more careful than ever about how we cut our meat and what we might throw away. But our stocks on hand dwindled and dwindled and eventually our supply ran out.

Within about two days of having used up the last of the meat in our own walk-in, I exhausted the entire supply of all-natural (hormone- and antibiotic-free) brisket in the state of Texas. For a few days, we had to dip down and use an entirely different grade of brisket, the crappy commodity stuff that's widely available everywhere (and that most barbecue joints use). This truly was the last resort, because our commitment to high-quality, ethically raised meat is something I never want to compromise. Indeed, before we even took this step, the idea of closing the restaurant until we got our beef back did enter my mind, but that was impossible. We have customers who may have organized their trips and planned months ahead to eat at our restaurant, not to mention employees who need to work. The show, as they say, must go on, so we had to figure out a way to cook the second-rate briskets.

And it was tough. Yes, the meat, but also those few days! It was probably the hardest period we've ever had. Trying to nurse that meat into something our customers would still rave about was almost impossible. The briskets were so incredibly lean and tough. We resorted to techniques we never do: mopping with oil, butter, onions, and garlic to add moisture, richness, and fat; wrapping them with foil (the dreaded so-called Texas crutch) to try to seal in what little juiciness they had. It felt as if I were running a different restaurant for those days. And unfortunately, a food writer happened to come in at the time, resulting in the only bad review we've ever received. All of this was the result of some guy at the meat processing plant leaving a tool on a conveyor belt and burning down part of the factory.

The whole time I was feeling pretty crappy about the quality of our product, not to mention the welfare of the animals the meat came from. I worked maniacally to source more, better brisket. The benefit of having one source for all of my briskets is the convenience of dealing with one vendor who knows exactly what I want. The risk—well, the risk is obvious. If something breaks down, there's nowhere else to go to pick up the slack. You can't just order one hundred cases of brisket (five hundred to six hundred pieces) from a purveyor you don't normally use, because they don't keep that much extra product in their supply chain.

We were scrambling. Within a day, calling in every favor I had, I exhausted all of the briskets in Austin. We were working every meat supplier we could find. I went through San Antonio. I went

through Dallas. Trucks were showing up at 2 in the morning with briskets from Oklahoma. One day, I had to drive two hours out of town to meet a semi on the side of a highway behind a truck stop to pick up meat, because the driver couldn't go any farther off of his scheduled route to meet me. After that strange transaction, I hauled ass back to the restaurant, rubbed the briskets down, and threw them on the smoker. I barely got them cooked on time.

Finally, our usual supplier came back online, just in time for the *Texas Monthly* barbecue festival—an annual festival showcasing the magazine's Top 50 barbecue joints—at which we were scheduled to cook for thousands of people. It was a huge honor, since the magazine had just named us the number one barbecue joint in the state, but I'll admit I was *stressed*. Our deliveries had only just started arriving again, which meant the meat was completely fresh because we were starting from scratch. When the briskets arrived, I discovered that they had been butchered so quickly and carelessly that only two of them looked what I'd call acceptable, and we needed eighty. Normally, we like some postmortem wet aging on the briskets (see page 111) because it tenderizes them and deepens the flavor. These were from animals that had been alive a mere three days before we were preparing them. Thus, we unfortunately appeared with brisket that was clearly not on top of its game.

That's what happens when you run a place that deals with as much volume as we do. Supply will no doubt never stop being an issue. If I was shopping every couple of weekends for a brisket or a few racks of ribs, as the average home barbecue cook does, it would be much different. I'm sure I'd enjoy the process of procuring meat. But we go through so much meat and have such rigid standards about it that simply getting as much meat of as high a quality as I want is a constant challenge.

Some people get all excited about their brines, rubs, injections, and all of the other various treatments they subject meat to. We don't have that option, because at Franklin, we don't do much. We keep things simple, secure in the knowledge that it's the smoke and the cooking methods that are the keys to our success. And meat quality is at the heart of that.

We serve brisket, pork ribs, sausage, pulled pork, and turkey breasts on a daily basis. And once a week, on Saturdays, we also sell beef ribs. Now, just as with wood and fire, I do think it's important to have some understanding of what you're cooking and where it comes from.

## BRISKET

It's true that a bumper sticker on my truck reads, BRISKET IS MY SPIRIT ANIMAL. If Texas barbecue has one emblematic cut, it's the brisket. It's the longest to cook, the hardest to perfect, and the one meat by which every Texas pitmaster is ultimately judged. If your brisket is tough, dry, or flavorless, you're going to hear about it.

As long-standing and venerable as the tradition of Texas barbecue is, brisket, surprisingly, wasn't always the main attraction it is today. It's a relatively recent phenomenon, which probably hit its stride in the 1970s. That's when what we call "boxed beef" became widespread. Before the advent of boxed beef, cows were pretty much slaughtered locally or shipped as whole carcasses—what the industry

calls "hanging beef." In those days, Central Texas barbecue joints were really just meat markets where shop owners would break down whole animals and sell the most desirable parts for people to cook at home. The leftovers they would cook up themselves. This would most likely include the brisket—a tough, ornery piece of meat—but was hardly restricted to it.

When IBP (Iowa Beef Processors, now Tyson Fresh Meats) introduced boxed beef and pork in the 1960s, it was the beginning of a revolution. Rather than shipping whole carcasses, IBP started breaking down steers into their constituent cuts at a central processing plant and then vacuum-sealing each cut individually. This accomplished a number of things. Vacuum-packing allowed the meats to remain sanitary for longer (something that was previously accomplished by just shipping the animal carcass whole, which made it slower to decay). Vacuum-packing also reduced the cost of shipping because it meant processors could leave unwanted trimmings, fat, and bones behind. And for customers, boxed beef allowed them to order and receive precisely what they wanted to cook without the hassle of having to break down a huge hunk of meat and figure out what do with the less desirable parts. Most people would consider brisket a less desirable cut. But what it had working in its favor was that it was extremely cheap relative to steaks and loins, and, in the right hands, it could become something magical.

Today, brisket has become Texas's sacred cow, to the point that Texas A&M University's meat science department offers Camp Brisket for the meat and barbecue curious, an intensive two-day investigation into everything having to do with this holy piece of meat. One of the founders of Camp Brisket, Dr. Jeff Savell, has become my go-to guy whenever I have a meat-science question.

## What Is the Brisket?

Brisket is the pectoral muscle of a steer and is roughly comparable to a human's pectorals, which gird the chest. (It's a bit larger, though—okay, a lot larger. A brisket used in Texas barbecue might weigh anywhere from 8 to 16 pounds.) If you imagine the cow standing on its hind legs, it's the big muscle stretching across the chest and right under the neck. A steer has two briskets, one on each side. Large, dense muscles, briskets are worked heavily in their role supporting a majority of the animal's enormous weight. Although briskets often come with a robust fat cap, inside they are fairly lean and sinewy, dense with connective tissue that enables the muscle to do heavy lifting.

"You've heard that phrase *eating high on the hog*?" says Dr. Savell. "Well that saying comes from the fact that meat from higher on a standing hog or steer is softer. Anything that is on the back is the most tender, anything down on the front end is tougher, and on the legs even tougher. It's not that the muscles are any different in the way they function from other muscles in the body; it's that they have more connective tissue to help harness that movement." In other words, the more work a given part of the cow has to do to walk, run, or just support its weight standing, the tougher the meat. It makes sense then that the cow's legs (shanks) are toughest and its back (tenderloin) is most tender, with brisket falling in between.

A single brisket is actually comprised of two distinct muscles, the deep pectoral (pectoralis profundus) and the superficial pectoral (pectoralis superficialis). Colloquially, these are called the "flat" and the "point." The flat is the lean, broad, rectangular thinner muscle that is the major part of the brisket. The point, or supraspinatus muscle (commonly known as the rotator cuff on humans), is an almost pyramid-shaped mound of muscle connected to one end of the flat. The point has more marbling and connective tissue than the flat and becomes very tender and juicy with long cooking. One of the challenges of brisket is that the point rides right on top of the flat, but its meat is of vastly different consistency and has a completely different grain. They're separate but connected.

Brisket would be an even greater challenge to eat if not for the massive layer of fat, called the fat cap, that covers one entire side of it. Its gradual rendering over long cooking times adds flavor and keeps the meat moist. Try to grill, sauté, or otherwise flash-cook and you'll be unhappy—left with tough, sinewy muscle and a pretty much impermeable layer of fat. But cook it slowly, at perfect fat-melting temperature, and that fat cap liquefies and imbues the muscle with its delicious flavor and texture.

"We did a study of the tenderness of forty major muscles of the cow when cooked in the same manner, over direct heat like a steak," notes Dr. Savell. "And the brisket was thirty-ninth in tenderness. But the fact that in Texas barbecue, you're taking one of the worst pieces of the animal and converting it into one of the best is a miracle itself." Amen.

## How to Buy a Brisket

There are many things to look out for when buying a brisket, and knowing the difference between different grades and breeds will help you choose the right meat for your cook.

### Grades

In my early days of cooking brisket, I could occasionally buy very low grades of meat on sale for $0.99 a pound. Those days are long gone, but brisket is still one of the cheaper cuts you'll find. For a long time, cheap, low-grade brisket was probably what everyone was cooking. But, over the years, with the increased attention that brisket is getting, the grade of the meat has come into sharper focus and can affect the way you buy meat, the way you should cook it, and what you can expect of it when done.

When you get beef from a USDA-inspected facility, it usually comes with one of three grades: Prime, Choice, or Select. Prime is the best grade, Choice and Select a little lower down the ladder. There are lower grades still, but we won't mess with those. The grades are composite scores issued by highly trained meat inspectors based largely on degree of marbling—tenderness, juiciness, and flavor. Marbling, or intramuscular fat, by definition from Dr. Savell, is "the intermingling or dispersion of fat within the lean." It's easy to see the marbling—little wavy strands of white within the lean, red meat. Marbling is very, very important for brisket.

Prime beef is defined as being from young (nine to thirty months in age), well-fed beef with abundant marbling. Choice is considered good

### THE FLUCTUATING PRICE OF MEAT

In the barbecue business we deal with many vagaries—temperature, humidity, and wood quality, to name a few. But one of the most inconsistent factors we deal with is also one of the most important: meat. Barbecue is supposed to be a relatively inexpensive food, but these days it's hard to keep meat costs down. Meat has always been a luxury item for mankind, but now many, many factors affect our costs. For one, meat is in greater demand worldwide than it ever has been. This point has been made a lot in the news, but as growing populations like that of China attain new affluence, they want to enjoy more meat, just as we all do. Of course, with limited production, this means a much more competitive global marketplace and escalating beef prices. There are, of course, other factors too. For instance, drought in Texas and other southern and midwestern states has taken its toll on cattle farming, as the price of grain and water has gone up. Escalating fuel prices also affect meat prices, as the meat has to be shipped to me everyday across several states. Yet despite these rising costs, barbecue seems to be steadily rising in popularity. This is a good thing for me, but (hey!) it also means more competition and higher prices for meat.

quality but lower in marbling than Prime. And Select beef, according to the USDA, is very uniform in quality and normally leaner than the higher grades. "It is fairly tender," the USDA says, "but, because it has less marbling, it may lack some of the juiciness and flavor of the higher grades."

All grades of brisket are used in the professional barbecue world; everyone has his or her preferred grade. The most popular around the state of Texas is probably Choice, because it's relatively affordable and in the hands of an able pitmaster can still produce fairly juicy brisket. I use Prime grade, which is by far the most expensive, but its marbling is important to the style of brisket I'm going for, which pushes tenderness and moistness to the extreme. In many grocery stores, you'll be fortunate to find Choice or Prime, but it's worth putting in some effort to try to track one of them down. This is especially true if you're just beginning, as there's a larger margin for error with fattier grades. Then again, the errors are more painful with more expensive beef.

What's most important to me is that the beef we use comes from ethically treated cattle who are raised and slaughtered in a peaceful, comfortable environment. I have visited the plant and talk frequently with the company that supplies our meat, so I do have confidence that we're getting what we pay for. And we pay a lot for it: it's more expensive to raise cattle in an ethical way, and that cost is reflected in the price of beef. Looking at what goes into industrial-farmed cattle and how they're treated, our decision to spend more on better quality and better treatment is an easy one to make. But the supply for this kind of beef is much smaller than the market for conventionally raised animals, which is why we occasionally run into issues.

## Breeds and Brands

The breed we use is Angus, which is well respected but also quite common in American beef. You may see packages labeled "Certified Angus Beef." But if your meat doesn't have that stamp, that doesn't mean it's not Angus beef. It still might be Angus, so that's a distinction that you really needn't worry about. The CAB (Certified Angus Beef) brand was started by the American Angus Association in 1978 and is just one—admittedly very big—seller of Angus beef. It has stringent standards, in that the beef CAB sells must bear a grade of either Prime or top-tier Choice. That makes it pretty reliable and popular among chefs. But there are other brands that both raise Angus breed cattle and maintain high standards, even though they don't have the CAB seal, including Niman Ranch (California), Creekstone (Kansas), and Meyer Natural Angus (Montana). If you're going to be doing a lot of barbecuing, I suggest that you take a little time to research the brands available in your area to find one or two that work well for you and then stick with them. You don't have to own a restaurant to value things like consistency and reliability. If you're investing 12 hours into cooking a brisket, you want some assurances that the product is something that you're comfortable cooking.

Another beef breed you might see occasionally is Wagyu. Its name when translated from Japanese is much less exciting than when you don't know what it means—*wa* means "Japanese" and *gyu* means "cow." Japanese cow, that's all it is. But you probably know that Japan is known for its ultra-marbled beef, such as the famous cows from Kobe. Kobe beef is not produced in the United States, only Japan. But we do have beef that comes from cows bearing Japanese bloodlines, though most of these animals have been interbred with American breeds to help them adapt to local climates and conditions. Still, American Wagyu tends to be extremely well marbled and is a popular brisket on the competitive barbecue scene for its sheer decadence. I've cooked many Wagyus for various special events and always find them extremely moist and tender, if not always delivering the deepest, beefiest flavor that I prefer. Still, they are magically textured, with all of that intramuscular fat melting slowly and turning that piece of beef into a buttery, smooth, melt-in-your-mouth kind of experience. Naturally, Wagyu beef is really expensive, but I've always had great success with the product from Snake River Farms in Idaho.

### Choosing the Package

Sometimes at the store you'll find a brisket already broken down into the point and flat cuts to make for smaller, more easily workable pieces for the home cook. Brisket is also one of the premier foods in Jewish cuisine, where it might get turned into corned beef, pastrami, or braised brisket with horseradish and onions. No doubt it became popular in Jewish cooking, as in barbecue, because of its low cost. But this is also in part because brisket is from the forequarters, the only part of the cow that is certified kosher in the United States. Pastrami is yummy, but don't buy your barbecue brisket preseparated. You want the entire thing, untrimmed. It will probably come whole, sealed in a Cryovac package, which is called a "packer-cut" brisket.

You'll likely find briskets that weigh anywhere from 10 to 20 pounds. Deciding on size is just a matter of preference. But don't forget to take into account that larger briskets will take longer to cook, 1 to 1$\frac{1}{2}$ hours per pound, depending on the temperature at which you cook. Consider the size of your smoker and what else, if anything, you might want to cook at the same time. Big honkers of briskets take up a lot of space on a small grate.

### Pack Dates and Aging

If you go to buy a single brisket at the store and see that they're all individually Cryovac packaged, you're going to have trouble determining the date the brisket was packed. It's not that the processors are trying to keep it a secret from you. It's just that they put the pack date on the whole case, not on each individual brisket. Your best bet is to ask your grocer about the pack date. (And in case you're curious, the slaughter date will likely be no more than two days prior to the pack date.)

Of course, if the brisket has been flash frozen, the pack date doesn't really matter, since meat won't age when frozen. All the brisket we use has never been frozen. Freezing breaks down the fibers in the meat somewhat, and you'll end up with a mushier product. Always look for fresh meat, though you might not be able to avoid frozen at big-box stores. If you see a lot of blood in the Cryovac-packed brisket, or if it feels overly floppy, it's likely been frozen. If in question, it never hurts to ask the grocer.

The question on aging and briskets is an open one. According to Dr. Savell, the research is conclusive that aging tenderizes and boosts flavor in ribs and loins (steaks). But he says that official research has not been conducted on brisket. Yet unofficial research is being

## DRY AGING VERSUS WET AGING

Dry aging refers to beef that has been hung or placed on a rack to dry, whereas wet aging refers to beef that is aged in a vacuum-sealed bag (which helps it retain moisture). If you encounter someone trying to sell you a brisket that's been dry aged, avoid it, if your intent is barbecue. I had to cook dry-aged briskets once, and they were very unpleasant. They've lost so much moisture by the time you cook them that it's already a dicey proposition. Then you have to cut off all of the outside meat and fat that is crusty and dry. By the time you're finished, the cut is so small that it looks like a squirrel brisket. Then a long cook in the smoker further removes so much fat and moisture that you end up with a dried piece of driftwood. Don't ever waste your money on dry-aged brisket.

conducted all of the time. Even though the USDA doesn't suggest there's any benefit to aging briskets, I think there is. In competition barbecue, I've heard of people holding on to a brisket for forty days or so from the packing date, pushing it as far as they possibly can. I wouldn't take it quite that far, but I do keep my briskets anywhere from fourteen to twenty-one days after the packing date before cooking them.

### Flexibility

If you've got a number of vacuum-sealed, packer-cut briskets in front of you at the store, how do you choose which one to buy? Some people will start enthusiastically telling you about the importance of a brisket's flexibility. But we're not talking about Mary Lou Retton on the uneven bars here. So instead of talking about meat's *flexibility*, I tend to use the more fun word *floppiness*.

The idea is that a brisket with more marbling and softer fat will have more give. So if you press on it gently, pick it up, and sort of toss it around in your hands for a few seconds, you might find one brisket that's floppier than the others, and that's the one that you'll want to buy.

I give some credence to this idea. If the briskets are not frozen yet still hard as a rock, that stiffness may not disappear entirely during cooking. Stiffness may be due to the hardness of the fat. Huge amounts of hard fat are undesirable, though some is unavoidable. Plus, vacuum-packing is snug and the plastic these briskets are wrapped in is tough, so it's not always easy to get a sense of flop value just by handling a brisket at the store. But if you're about to drop anywhere from $40 to $100 on a piece of meat, it doesn't hurt to be thorough.

### Fat and Grass

Speaking of fat, I really do try to avoid briskets that sport heavy, compacted layers of rock-hard fat on the outside. In my experience, this kind of fat is a hallmark of a cow that's been raised industrially on grain and fed all kinds of growth hormones and antibiotics to be brought quickly and unhealthily up to a slaughtering weight. I find much less of this fat on briskets from cows that have been more humanely raised. Tender, white fat is something I really like to see.

If that fat is not white but has a yellowish tint, that might be a sign that the animal was grass-fed. Grass-fed beef is a growing movement, and in general I support it, but not for brisket meant for the barbecue. An animal that's been raised entirely in the pasture will have a much more diverse diet than one raised primarily on grain. That diet will be reflected in the diverse organic compounds found in the meat and fat, resulting in a stronger flavor and aroma when the meat is cooked. A grass-fed steak can be an interesting and rewarding eating experience. A grass-fed brisket cannot. Trust me, I've done it. The long, slow cooking of a huge, fatty piece of grass-fed muscle brings out too much of that funky, herbaceous, beastly flavor. It's not an enjoyable meal.

A lot of the animals we use are pasture raised for the first part of their lives and then transitioned onto a grain and corn diet for the last part. That seems to produce healthy animals with good flavor and fine, soft fat.

## Meat on the Flat

The thinnest strip of meat on the brisket is going to be at the end of the flat, where the muscle starts to taper down. You can see this part through the packaging, and it is a good indicator of the level of marbling and general evenness of the meat. One side of the end of the flat tends to be thicker than the other, so I always look for a flat that has a fairly consistent thickness across the end because it will cook more evenly and slice better. If I don't have a choice and have to use a brisket that tapers off wildly, I'm going to end up trimming that back anyway until I get a more even shape. So if you do have a choice, look for a consistent thickness across the end of the flat.

## BEEF RIBS

Almost as iconic in Texas as the brisket, beef ribs are spectacular for both cooking and eating. Incredibly rich, tasty, and delightful, they're also really expensive and take pit space away from our staples like brisket and pork ribs. But they're delicious, so we cook them only on Saturdays. People love them and it's not hard to understand why: they are truly impressive cuts. At Louie Mueller in Taylor, the spot that's probably most

### LEFT-SIDED BRISKETS

Some people in Texas say that they like to cook only a left-sided brisket—that is, the brisket from the left side of the steer. Their reasoning is that most steers sit on their left side when they're lying down to ruminate or rest. That suggests that they'll have to push harder on their right side to raise the majority of their mass. Therefore, these people contend, the left-sided brisket is less worked and more tender than the brisket on the other side.

For the record, I think this is a joke. In all the thousands of briskets I've cooked, I've found no evidence that the meat from one side of the cow is noticeably more tender than the other. I guess I slightly prefer the shape of left-sided briskets because it's easier to wrap, but it's not really something I pay much attention to and I recommend that you don't worry about it either.

famous for them in Texas, the beef ribs are served as a giant hunk of meat with an enormous, caveman-style bone sticking out one end. The meat is succulent, juicy, and thickly coated in black pepper.

The cuts of ribs on a steer and on a pig have both similarities and differences. Of course, they come from either the top or the bottom of the animal. One major difference is that a steer is much, much bigger than a typical pig, meaning that there are much greater differences between the ribs on one end versus the other. Another difference is in the nature of the meat that attaches to the ribs on the top and bottom of the animal.

The rib cage and shoulder area of the steer is so big that it's divided into three main sections called primals: the chuck, the rib, and the plate. The chuck and rib primals are on the top of the animal and the plate primal is underneath. The division between the chuck and rib is made with a cut between the fifth and sixth ribs. Ribs 1–5, which are on the head end, go with the chuck primal, and ribs 6–12 go with the rib primal. Chuck meat, which is the hardworking shoulders of the steer, is best cut up for braises and stews. Those few ribs on the chuck side are often found cut very thinly and horizontally (with each piece of meat containing multiple round pieces of bone) as flanken- or Korean-style short ribs. Not too many people barbecue chuck ribs.

Back ribs come from the top of the animal, much as baby backs do on pigs. The difference is that the meat that beef back ribs are cut away from is the rib-eye, the most desirable cut on the whole animal. Therefore, butchers cut as close to the bone as possible to preserve as much on the boneless rib-eyes as they can, which can almost always be relied on to leave shiners (see page 116) on the ribs. Obviously, not a lot of meat is left, and it's generally found between the bones, not on top of them. It's tasty though not hugely popular at a lot of barbecue joints.

The real showstopper, the kind of ribs we use, comes from the plate primal. (To situate you, the plate primal sits on the underside of the cow just behind the brisket and in front of the flank.) The plate short ribs are the meatiest, with the meat on top of the bones layered with fat. The meat on these is heavily marbled and also dense with connective tissue, making them richly flavored and ideal for long, slow cooking. Shorter cuts of these are often sold as short ribs. We go for plate ribs 6, 7, and 8—right in the middle of the rib cage—which have the longest, widest, meatiest bones, like brontosaurus ribs. They make spectacular barbecue. Although beef plate ribs are perhaps not the easiest thing for the professional to cook every day, they are fantastic for the home cook.

## PORK RIBS

The conventional wisdom has it that Texas barbecue means beef, and the barbecue from most other places is mainly pork. In this case, the conventional wisdom has it wrong. Although there is a strong beef tradition here, Texans have also been smoking pork for a long time. And visiting various barbecue joints across the state will show you that all manner of pork is widely available on menus, from shoulder to ribs to chops. At Franklin Barbecue, we offer pulled pork (not a Texas specialty), but we're even better known for our ribs.

## SHINERS

As a beer from Texas, Shiner can be quite desirable. But as a quality on a rack of ribs you're buying, it's something to look out for. On ribs, a *shiner* is the term for a bit of the bone that's showing through on the top of the rack where there should be meat. This happens when overzealous butchers rob the rib of meat in order to give it to another cut (or when a piggy was just too skinny).

Shiners are more likely to be found on spare ribs than on baby backs for the simple reason of the cut spareribs sit next to. Baby back ribs are next to the loin, which is not a highly desirable cut of pork and usually sells for less than the baby back ribs. Therefore, when separating the back ribs from the loin, it actually behooves the butcher to leave a little more meat on the ribs because he's getting more per pound for ribs than for loin. Spare ribs, on the other hand, are taken from the belly. The belly fetches some of the highest prices on the pig. So it tempts butchers to leave as much on the belly as possible when removing it from the rib. And if they remove too much and cut too close to the bone to where you can see the bone on top, that's a shiner. Avoid them and look for meaty ribs.

It wasn't too long ago that baby back ribs blasted into the American consciousness, but even though most people are familiar with the term, they have no idea what it means. Baby backs come from the top of the rib cage. So, if you visualize the ribs of a pig being long and rounded (like us humans' ribs), you can imagine that the baby backs are taken from up near the spine, which is where they get their signature curve. They might just as easily be called back ribs; instead, they get their name not because they come from baby pigs, but because they are smaller than the spare ribs (the longer, bottom half of the rib cage). Attached to the loin, which is a lean cut of meat, baby backs are typically leaner than spares. But their meat is still juicier and fattier than the loin, which is one reason for their popularity. Another reason is a certain boppy commercial jingle for a national restaurant that never seemed to go away.

Baby backs are nice, but for the kind of smoking I do, I prefer spare ribs. Spare ribs—also spelled *spareribs*—come, as noted above, from the bottom of the rib cage. They're not called spare because they're thin or left over or not as good as strike ribs or kept in the trunk in case your main ribs get a flat. According to *Merriam-Webster*, the word *sparerib* is "from Low German *ribbesper*—pickled pork ribs roasted on a spit." More important, they're the opposite end of the rib cage from baby backs. That places them down at the belly, to which they're connected. (I shouldn't need to remind anyone of the glorious fattiness of the pork belly—just remember that that's where bacon comes from.) Spare ribs also connect to the breastbone. Usually coming thirteen to a rack, spare ribs are straighter, have more bone, and have more fat and connective tissue than the baby backs. It's that last reason that makes them particularly appealing for long, slow smoking. The meat is juicier and richer down on the belly, which translates to robust flavor and fall-away tender meat.

I use a bone-off spare ribs, which I'll explain more in the section about trimming ribs in the next chapter (see page 161). Put simply, the ribs are separated from the breastbone, and the rib tips are not cut off, giving the rack a vaguely rectangular shape with fairly even consistency, which makes the ribs good for cooking in large numbers every day, which we do, starting at 2 a.m.

## How to Choose Spare Ribs

When buying pork spare ribs, I look for as much marbling as possible. Like briskets, the ribs may come prepackaged, but you can always get a good look at the meat, which should show lots of wispy threads of marbling throughout the pinkish red meat. You should be able to see the square ends of the bones, where they've been sawn from the baby backs on one side. The other side ends in soft cartilage where the breastbone was. Sometimes you'll see this section of the slab taken off in the "St. Louis cut." That section, composed of meat and cartilage and connective tissue, can be cooked up into rib tips, which make tasty little snacks. Or you can leave this delicious end on the rack itself, as I do, because it provides good eating and actually cooks better when it's part of the whole.

## The Solution Problem

Most of the prepackaged ribs you'll find at the major store chains and in big grocery stores will have been what they call "enhanced." Always be suspicious of words like that, which are designed to make you think you're getting something better without telling you exactly what has been done to it. In this case, they're not trumpeting the word *enhanced* but rather printing it in very small letters, if at all. The enhancement in question is the common practice of big meat packers to inject solutions consisting mainly of water and salt into the pork and poultry they sell. Other components of the brine might include sodium phosphates and sugar. They might offer all sorts of reasons for this, but they all pretty much mean that it's an industrial solution to the industrial problem of mass-producing and mass-distributing pork. "Enhancement" adds artificial moisture to pork that's otherwise dried out, extends its shelf life, reduces the amount of liquid that seeps from meat that's been sitting around for a while, and, most insidiously, makes meat more profitable by adding weight to something you're buying by the pound. I never buy solution-injected products.

Now it can be tricky to identify these products, as that's exactly what packers don't want to happen. It's also possible that your local supermarket won't carry anything but solution-injected pork. Look for terms like *enhanced, improved, injected, marinated,* or *basted,* then, as with any food product, look at the list of ingredients. If it includes more than one thing, you're holding a piece of meat that's been "enhanced."

If you do find yourself unavoidably trapped into cooking with some of this stuff, be aware that it's going to have unnaturally large amounts of water already in it, making it more likely to steam than roast or fry. And also be careful about oversalting, as these cuts are basically prebrined. But my best advice is to find a meat market that will sell you pork that has not been messed with.

## Breed

Breed has much more of an impact on pork than it does on beef, and you've probably heard a lot about heritage pork over the last few years. There are dozens of different heritage breeds available these days. As the term suggests, these were pigs raised in different places (and thus different conditions), but always outdoors. Heritage pork comes from farm animals who often forage and dig for their own food. Because they live outdoors, they exercise and develop a healthy layer of fat to combat the cold. In addition, their meat tends to be darker and more flavorful.

Heritage breeds were once the standard, but after World War II, things began to change. Consolidation and vertical integration led to more industrial pig farming, which also meant focusing on a few breeds designed to live indoors and on muscle rather than fat. As we all know, fat usually means flavor. Purveyors decided to develop a strategy to market pork as a health-conscious, lean alternative to poultry. Remember "the other white meat" days? Eventually people started to notice the declining genetic diversity in American pigs, and a movement began to popularize heritage breeds.

The pork ribs we use are from pigs of a hybrid heritage breed, a combination of the Chester White and Duroc breeds. The mix yields great marbling, tenderness, and juiciness—perfect for smoked ribs. Plenty of information about heritage breeds exists online, but my major recommendation is to look for ribs from heritage breeds. That's where you'll find that beautiful, richly colored, heavily marbled meat that is a bit more delicate but has so much flavor.

## PORK BUTT

Pulled pork is something that you hardly ever used to find in Texas, but these days it is becoming more and more popular. Why? I'd hazard that Texans have traveled more and experienced the wonders of pulled pork from Tennessee and the Southeast, and they have been inspired. We've also had a lot of people move to Texas from other parts of the country, and they may have brought their pulled pork skills with them.

My inspiration came from a really good meal I had in Memphis once when I was on tour. I'd never had pulled pork before, and it really just struck me. In hindsight, maybe this place wasn't so great. I've been back several times since then and it didn't seem as good. But at the time it blew my mind. When we got back from the tour, I went right home and bought some pork butts to cook.

The pork butt is the most misleading of food names (along with Rocky Mountain oysters, headcheese, and geoduck). At least the *pork* part of the name is legit. It has nothing to do with the rear end of the pig and everything to do with the shoulder, which, in fact, it is.

A whole pork shoulder may come divided into two parts. These are the lower and the upper cuts, which are almost always divided. The top is known as the Boston butt or simply pork butt, while the lower is known as the picnic or the picnic ham. (Just to make matters even more confusing, picnic ham does not refer to the ham you know and love. That ham comes from the butt—well, the hind leg, or haunch, of the pig.) In pulled pork circles, there is always debate about whether the butt or the picnic makes for the better preparation. The pork butt, coming from higher up, has more connective tissue and less bone, thus is more tender and meaty. Some say the picnic is more flavorful, and it definitely has more bone and is prone to larger pockets of fat that won't dissolve with long cooking. I always use the pork butt.

Whichever cut you use, make sure to take the skin off, if that's how it's presented at the store. While pig skin is edible, it's tough as a football when barbecued and will absolutely block both smoke and rub from flavoring the meat. There will be a shoulder blade bone in the pork butt, which I advise leaving in. Taking it out can cause the meat to cook more unevenly, and it is much, much easier to remove when the meat's done cooking.

## SAUSAGE

Sausage is a work in progress at Franklin Barbecue. Don't get me wrong: I love sausage and eat a sausage wrap practically every day. But a critic once dinged us (her only complaint) because we don't make our sausage in-house. Instead, we've had someone else make it for us to our recipe. There's a reason for this. Primarily, it's that sausage making is very labor-intensive, and we've had our hands full dealing with just the day-to-day running of an insanely busy restaurant. But making our own sausage in-house is something I've always planned on getting around to (in fact, I've been working on it while writing this book).

Sausage doesn't have the glamour that brisket and ribs do. But here in Central Texas, which was settled early on by German and Czech settlers with rich sausage-making traditions, it's taken very seriously. A lot of people really pride themselves on their sausage, and rightly

so. I don't care how good your brisket and ribs are, when you nail sausage, it's a thing of beauty. But nailing it isn't easy, and that's why it's been an evolution here at Franklin. That said, I've done lots of research, and performed plenty of sausage-making experiments, so I can talk about it a little.

Generally speaking, sausage is an excellent and efficient product of whole-animal butchery—a way to use up the bits and scraps that wouldn't otherwise get cooked and served (I'm looking at you, intestines). In its purer forms, sausage is just meat and fat that is ground together, seasoned, and stuffed into casings. So why do people get so squeamish about it? Commercial sausage manufacturers—the ones who throw salivary glands, nostrils, and eyeballs into the mix—are the ones to blame. Buy a random hot dog or chorizo and who knows what's in it? But I digress.

At Franklin Barbecue we take a more old-school approach, which means we treat our sausage as an efficient use of all of our brisket and rib trimmings. We trim quite severely, and to toss that stuff in the trash is basically to throw money away, especially since we use Prime brisket and all-natural heritage pork. Even so, sausage making is a labor-intensive (and consequently costly) endeavor. The trimmings themselves have to be trimmed (separating the lean from the fat), then there's the tricky task (craft, really) of stuffing and tying off the individual sausages.

Coming up with a sausage recipe isn't terribly difficult—it's hard to get wrong, really—but variations in the meats you're working with can make following an exact recipe a difficult proposition. And because sausage is largely

composed of scraps, what you have available to put in it might vary. Having a restaurant that produces a consistent volume of scrap meat makes it easier for me to have a consistent mix. But for home cooks, feel free to play around with your own mixtures and to discover what works best for you. The main things to remember are to include enough fat to ensure that the sausage is juicy inside and not to be bashful with seasonings, as you want the flavors to really pop.

Generally speaking, a good rule to follow for sausage is 70 percent lean, 30 percent fat. At Franklin we get there by mixing about 60 percent Prime-grade brisket, about 10 percent pork (mostly from the pork butt), about 27 percent raw brisket fat, and around 3 percent all-natural beef hearts for depth of meaty flavor. When coming up with your recipe, you must consider both the amount of fat you want to grind into your stuffing and the fat content of your meat. For instance, because we use Prime-grade brisket, I add less pure fat than someone who is using Select. Meat from a heritage pig like a Duroc or Berkshire is going to have more fat than meat from a conventional pig. It's something you have to judge for yourself.

Seasoning a sausage is a measure of balance. The spices are there to enhance the meat and the savory appeal of each bite. It's important not to overspice, as you don't want to drown out the flavor of the meat. When you're tweaking your recipe at home, season, then break off a small nub of the filling mixture, shape it into a patty, and grill it. Taste the cooked sample for seasoning and add more if you need to.

## Sausage Casings

The biggest challenge when it comes to making sausage is finding the perfect casing. I'm a perfectionist, and perfect sausage is an elusive thing. A perfect sausage is one that's been cooked and looks smooth and glistening on the outside. When you bite into it, your teeth meet a little resistance before the casing breaks with a snappy pop and all that delicious flavor bursts onto your tongue. A great bite of sausage is a textural, flavor, and even aural experience.

How do you get the perfect casing? It's incredibly hard, because the casing is the one variable in sausage production that we at Franklin Barbecue don't have full control over. Casings, which are made from hog intestines, are never uniform and tend to have varying dimensions, textures, and lengths. (Note that you *can* buy synthetic sausage casings—they're more prevalent, actually—but I always say you should go for the real thing.)

We use a 30- to 32-millimeter-diameter casing made from pretty young hogs. For small batches, you can buy them packed in salt, then rehydrate and clean them in water to get the salt off. (When bought in bulk, sausage casings usually come in a bucket of solution.)

But the real issue is that all of the casings come from commodity pigs. It's seemingly impossible to get casings that are all natural, made from animals that were well treated and raised cleanly and sustainably. Here, we are filling the casings with all-natural pork, really high-grade beef, and all-natural beef hearts from ethically raised cows, and they could be coming from anywhere—China, Mexico—where we have no inkling of how they were produced. This means that we can't claim all-natural sausage, because we aren't at all sure. Almost all pork casings are supplied by DeWied, a big corporation that describes itself on its website as "one of the largest selectors of hog casings worldwide." That alone suggests that the casings can and probably do come from anywhere, and that DeWied does not have much control over the original animal. It's a problem for which I still don't have a solution.

## TURKEY

Honestly, I don't have much to say on the subject of turkey. But I do have a recipe for smoked turkey breasts in this book, and chances are if you own a smoker, you'll cook a bird in it at some point in your life. So my advice is simple: don't buy turkeys that come prebrined or preinjected, because you'll have no control over the saltiness or moisture content of the meat (not to mention the random chemicals manufacturers might decide to squirt up in it). As I suggest earlier in this chapter with regard to pork, read the packaging or consult with your local meat purveyor to find unadulterated, natural, or organic birds if possible. Heritage breeds are cool, but they're usually very expensive and more unpredictable to cook than the conventional, untreated turkeys we cook here at the restaurant. They're delicious, however, and turkey on a smoker is always a good thing.

# THE COOK

## • *Chapter Six*

At long last, it's finally time to get cooking. You've gotten to know your smoker and you've sourced or seasoned the best wood you can possibly find. You've considered building and tending a fire, generating the good smoke that makes food tasty, and you went to the store and bought some nice meat, whose quality you can really stand behind.

Now it's time to put all of this information to use. Now it's time to put the meat in the cooker!

In this chapter, I'm going to walk you through four separate cooks: brisket, pork ribs, beef ribs, and turkey. You'll notice that the steps for each are quite similar—nearly identical, in fact. And now I've got a confession for you: almost everything we cook in the smoker is done in a comparable way. There's really no secret. Let your meat—whatever it is—smoke at a consistent temperature until it has absorbed enough smoke. Determine this by the color it has turned and by the quality of the bark that has formed on the outside. When it's reached this condition, wrap it and let it keep cooking. It's that simple.

You might balk when you see that there are only four recipes in this chapter. But I swear it's not because I'm being lazy, secretive, or anything like that. I don't include tons and tons of "recipes" here because at the end of the day, the method for smoking pretty much any meat is the same. I can give you rough guidelines for the time it takes to cook things, but, as always with barbecue, it's done when it's done. You can't rush it; you can't cut corners. The trickiest parts are knowing when to wrap and when something's done. Although I can do my best to describe how and under what conditions you should make these decisions, ultimately you just have to cook a few times and learn from your mistakes. So read through this chapter carefully, practice, and take note of what went right and what went wrong. In the end, you'll be able to cook incredible meat with great consistency in all conditions.

## AN IMPORTANT BARBECUE FABLE

But before I send you off on your brisket- or rib-cooking way, I want to share one more story—an important one, I think, for anyone who is nervous about screwing up their first brisket cook. Let me preface this by saying that this story has a happy ending. It also touches on many of the topics I've discussed in the preceding chapters, making it a good summation leading into the all-important cook. And there's a moral at the end: even when everything is going against you, never quit and never stop trying!

Braun, our kitchen manager and one of our longest and most trusted pitmasters (and Stacy's cousin), and I were in New York to cook at a big event. There were bands, cooking demos, and renowned chefs from all over the country. This was going to be a big event, so we had to be on top of our game.

We showed up at noon the day before the event to meet the wood supplier, to receive our meat, and to see the cooker arrive. Turns out the cooker they had arranged for us was actually a grill—not gonna work. So I reached out to a buddy of mine on Long Island—we like to call him Long Island Phil—who found us an actual smoker so we could cook all of the meat.

The festival was on an island, so there we were, on the island, waiting for the trucks to bring our stuff. We're waiting and waiting, and they keep telling us the trucks are on their way with our stuff, so we stick around to receive the goods. Eventually the cooker arrives from Long Island Phil. It was a reverse-flow Lang; I think it was a dual 84, a huge cooker. Supposedly this thing was big enough to cook all of the meat they wanted us to prepare, but, alas, it was not. And it was reverse flow, which, you will recall, I do not like because it has this plate running through it to redirect the smoke and heat. It's also got more baffles and levers than I know what to do with.

It's a sunny day, just beautiful, except for the fact that our meat never shows up. We were expecting all of these great briskets to arrive and they do . . . super-duper late. Late and brisket is never a great combination. And then the firewood was supposed to be there. We were supposed to be getting oak that was not kiln dried, which was going to be a feat, because in New York it all has to be kiln dried. Supposedly we were getting some under-the-radar oak, more like what we were accustomed to using at home.

The meat finally shows up at about 7 p.m. We were supposed to start cooking at 6, because we had planned to cook them most of the way, go to bed, and finally finish them off in the morning. By the way, the festival organizers' initial emails said they were expecting us to feed thirty-five hundred people. That's so impossible, I don't even know what to say. But I promised to cook as much of the meat they gave us as I could.

So it's starting to get dark now, well past the time we wanted to begin our work. I'm wandering around looking for the hand-washing facilities (clean hands and sanitary conditions are of extreme importance to me). No luck. No water. No hand-washing facilities. And it turns out . . . no lights! The crew had turned off all the lights and left because no one was cooking overnight except for us and a couple of other guys. So our meat shows up late and by the time we start trimming, it was dark. We're trimming it as fast as we can by moonlight, just hacking the briskets up in the middle of a field in the dark on an island.

Finally at 10 p.m. our firewood shows up. And it's nothing like what we wanted. It is kiln dried, no life to it, and it's also not even close to the amount I'd asked for. It's going to burn fast, hot, and with absolutely no smoke at all. And that's to say nothing about the quantity. We have to do a 15-hour cook and then keep stuff warm. We're looking to burn this pit for 20 to 24 hours. And they bring us a single wheelbarrow full of wood.

So we finally start cooking 4 to 5 hours too late. I spent much of the night playing the part of the barbecue panhandler—calling everyone I knew, bugging them to please bring us more wood. We beg drinking water and even more wood from some other cooks who had turned up. Compared to us, they're like wealthy aristocrats. I remember one group shows up with ten or twelve people to cook a single pig. They have a huge cooler full of beer. They have cars because they live around here. Another team shows up with a car service—a driver in a black van just waiting around for them.

By about 3 a.m., more wood shows up. Braun's getting a little worried because we haven't opened up the lid once (trying to retain every degree of heat due to our limited wood supply). So we open up the lid, and these briskets look horrible. They're splotchy from weird airflow. They've got no color. They're yellowed, and their fat hasn't even started to render. They look as if we'd put them on an hour ago.

Then, of course, a huge storm blows through. Turns out there's a tornado warning; we get word that one has just touched down not far from us in Queens. When the lightning starts, we're standing in water up to our ankles, with water also submerging electrical outlets that are hooked up to a generator. I start thinking this will be the cook that breaks us.

As I stand in a puddle of water, I smell something distinctive that sets off an alarm in my head. "Oh, no," I yell. "Grease fire!"

This Lang cooker is not really meant for this kind of use because of that reverse-flow plate onto which our brisket fat, finally rendering, is dripping. I crack the lid and spy a little tiny flame about the size of a quarter on the plate over the firebox. It's not really much at all. But as soon as I open the lid, it becomes a scene from *Backdraft*. A sheet of fire erupts across the whole cooker. I try to shut the fire down by closing every vent and pipe on the cooker, but it doesn't work. So I just start pulling out briskets in the rain, throwing them to soaking-wet Braun who puts them down, steaming, on our little soaking-wet table. In the back of the cooker a couple of briskets have caught on fire.

Then my buddy and super chef Adam Perry Lang comes running over. Not actually running—I remember it being more like in the movie *Crouching Tiger, Hidden Dragon*: he came skipping over the tops of the tents like a ninja. He pulls this giant knife out of its sheath and uses it to stab and toss each burning brisket from the cooker. The grease fire is out of control now and flames are licking at his arms, which I'm trying to cover with wet towels as he heroically helps pull the briskets off.

Finally we get the last brisket out and shut the lid. The fire goes out. The briskets and the three of us are just sitting there in the rain, thinking about how awful things are. But we still have to serve these fatty, hard-as-a-rock, nowhere-near-done briskets . . . and now the whole place smells like burned arm hair.

We get the meat back on and the fire under control about 4 hours before service. Braun takes a piece of cardboard and goes and sleeps under a tree for about 30 minutes. Then it starts raining again. The only good thing is that it's wetting our balsa wood, which at least slowed down the burn rate and ironically may have helped us not run out.

We're pushing the briskets really hard, just trying to get them done. It's light outside, and I've cranked the cooker to push these briskets through. I can smell that they're cooking too fast, but I have no choice. At last, around 11 a.m., we get some color and wrap them. About a half hour before service, I pull off one brisket that feels about right. I set it on the table. About 20 minutes later I pull another three, then all of the briskets right before the gates are opened.

I unwrap the meat, which has just started to get tender. I can feel from the briskets' form that they just might be okay, despite coming off too soon and not having nearly enough rest time. I slice one end and show it to Braun, as a wave of irrepressible joy shoots through us—it's rendered, it's tender, it actually looks pretty good. There was maybe a bit of a crispy char on the bottoms, but it was definitely better than we ever could have hoped for. Then the gate opens and the hordes of people bum-rush from the gate directly to our tent. There are TV cameras, and they record a literal stampede heading toward the Franklin tent. For the next three hours, we have a long, snaking line to the counter until we run out of meat. Somehow we've pulled it off. Worst. Cook. Ever.

A moral of this incredibly long story of brisket woe? Is it that brisket is more forgiving than you think? Is it to plan even further in advance than you think is more than enough?

No. The moral of the story—and for every cook you ever do—is this: never give up.

Brisket can test you, but you just have to persevere. The other moral is that there are many paths to cooking a good brisket. Things can go wrong—hopelessly, horribly wrong—but at the end of the day, there are multiple ways to pull it together. Also, have a portable espresso maker, which, luckily, I did.

## GETTING READY FOR THE ACTUAL COOK

It seems somewhat artificial to divide the book into all of these chapters, as I have, since smoking meat is in many ways inseparable from choosing wood and tending a fire. People ask me what the secret to my success with brisket is, and I always tell them the same thing: attention to detail. In this case, attention to detail means sweating the little things that others may not even notice. It means being vigilant and present throughout a cook that can last 10 to 15 hours or longer. It means paying individual attention to each piece of meat you're cooking and giving it the specific care that it needs.

So on the one hand, barbecue appears relaxing and simple—the kind of cooking that allows you to pull up a lawn chair and prop your feet on your cooler full of beer and settle in for a long, easygoing afternoon. On the other hand, you have to pay regular, if not constant, attention to the fire and to your temperature gauges. So, I guess you could call the required state of the pitmaster a stance of relaxed focus. Enjoy your beers, but don't have so many that your concentration lapses.

## SAFETY CONCERNS

I'm a real stickler when it comes to food safety, not only at the restaurant but also wherever it is that I'm cooking. Of course, at the restaurant, one mistake on this front could mean the end of everything we've worked so hard to build. So we don't mess around or cut corners. But at home too, it's just as vital. The last thing you want is anyone getting sick or worse because you were simply lazy about the handling of meats.

Here, I won't go into the science of meat safety. Instead, I'd recommend you go over the information offered at www.foodsafety.gov, which includes a thorough discussion of grilling and barbecuing safety issues. The most common and serious issue is cross contamination, which is what happens when germs from raw meats or tainted items spread to foods that are ready-to-eat. Proper cooking will kill dangerous microbes, but carelessness can allow them to spread onto foods that we're going to put directly into our bodies.

The number one thing you can do to prevent cross contamination is to wash your hands. A lot. When I work a shift, I probably wash my hands twenty-five times or more. And this is thorough washing: with soap under a full stream of warm water for at least twenty seconds. We also put on sterile, disposable, nitrile food-service gloves every time we handle meat (I don't like vinyl). We keep boxes of these in the kitchen and a box at every smoker. Before I open the smoker and handle the meat, I always put on a new sterile glove. This is as ingrained a habit as throwing another piece of wood on the fire.

At home, wearing sterile gloves may seem a bit excessive to you. At the very least you need to train yourself to handle raw meats with only one hand. Your clean hand holds the knife when trimming and holds the shaker when applying rub. It never touches the meat. Your gloved hand flips the meats and turns them as needed. That way you'll never get the knife handle or the spice shaker dirty. And then, of course, wash your hands every time you handle raw meat.

We also thoroughly wash down every knife and cutting board we use to trim and rub the meats, as cutting boards are one of the prime culprits when contamination breaks out. In food safety courses, you're instructed to keep cold foods cold and hot foods hot. We follow that to the letter, never letting cold meats warm up until they're about to be cooked. And after they've been cooked, we hold them at 140°F until they're going to be served.

Lastly, there's one other safety issue I care deeply about: the pitmaster's. If you work around smoke as often as I do, you are going to be smelling a lot of smoke. If you're smelling it, you're inhaling it on some level. So, it's of prime importance to minimize smoke inhalation as much as possible. For me, this means turning my head and holding my breath every time I have to go into a cooker. This is not hard to do, since all you get when you open a smoker is a big face full of smoke anyway, but think about it every time you open the chamber door and consciously try to form this good habit.

And while the cooking itself is easy, there are several steps along the way that need to be done right. Now, these are steps that all good pitmasters will take, but I have particular methods that I follow every time I cook and that I teach to all of the people who come and work at Franklin Barbecue. On pages 147 to 158, I share precisely how I do it, but you are more than welcome to come up with your own methods too. There are many ways to get to the same, delicious end, but as I said, you've got to have a way and follow it precisely each time.

## PRINCIPLES OF SMOKING MEAT

The art of long-smoking meat is about cooking it to an extreme form of tenderness while capturing smoke for flavor. To that end, we want to expose the meat to a constant supply of fresh, good smoke and also keep it at a consistent temperature that will allow it to cook slowly, gradually, without drying out. At the same time we want to generate a flavorful crust or "bark," which is the result of regulating the surface temperature and texture of the meat to facilitate smoke adhesion. Luckily, in a properly controlled cooking environment, all of these processes happen in a well-choreographed procession.

As always, I believe a rudimentary understanding of what's actually happening is a key to success. The more you understand *why* a brisket cooks the way it does, the better you'll be able to control the finished product.

Many of our favorite meats are in fact muscles, which are in turn made up of bundles of fibers that are interwoven with thin wrappers of connective

tissue. This connective tissue is largely composed of collagen, a very tough substance. The toughness of muscles is determined by the woven fabric of muscle fiber and collagen. Muscles like brisket, pork shoulder, and ribs have plenty of collagen, making them ornery and tough.

Lucky for us, collagen can be broken down into gelatin, that soft and silky substance that makes sauces thick and glossy. In its melted form, gelatin provides the meat with texture and richness. Our goal, then, is to break down that collagen into supple goodness, which will render the meat tender and flavorful. But the fascinating thing about collagen is that it requires specific conditions to break down in the way we want it to.

At the most basic level, all you need to break down collagen is heat and water, a process called hydrolysis. There's ample water in the meat to fuel this reaction. We supply the heat, which starts to be adequate when the internal temperature of the meat gets above 122°F and happens faster as the temperature increases. The more collagen, the longer a piece of muscle takes to break down (which is why a finer-grained piece of meat is more tender). So that's great, you think to yourself, but then what's the deal with all this "low and slow" stuff? Why not just cook things faster and avoid all of this endless fire tending? That's because of a confounding trait in collagen's nature. Push temperature too hard, and it doesn't break down well. The action is sort of like one of those Chinese finger prisons. You stick a finger from each hand into either end. The faster you try to pull your fingers out, the more it contracts and binds them. Only the very slow and relaxed withdrawal of your fingers allows them to escape the prison. Collagen, when heated quickly, begins to shrink. Just like squeezing out a washcloth, the shrinking of this connective tissue squeezes the moisture right out of the muscle fibers, causing them to be tough and dry. (And if you heat things up *way* too much, all of the moisture will evaporate and hydrolysis will not occur, leaving behind solid collagen and an unfortunate mess of dried-out, chewy muscle fibers—no good.)

This is why even meat submerged in liquid (that is, a braise or stew) can be dry and tough if heated too high and too quickly. But at long, slow cooking temperatures, the collagen slowly melts away, and the fibers of the meat just fall apart. What about all of the moisture that we've lost, you ask? Well, even though the long cooking and shrinking of the collagen has caused the meat to lose water, there is ample gelatin and melted fat to lubricate the meat and make it succulent.

Fat is also important. As Harold McGee explains, "Fat contributes to the apparent tenderness of meat in three ways: fat cells interrupt and weaken the sheet of connective tissue and the mass of muscle fibers; fat melts when heated rather than drying out and stiffening as the fibers do; and it lubricates the tissue, helping to separate fiber from fiber."

Fat is also richness. Fat starts to melt early on in the cooking process, well before the collagen breaks down. Because it's right there, interwoven between strands of collagen and muscle fiber, it brings moistness and a glossy richness, basically basting the meat internally. A good amount of intramuscular fat aids the cooking process immensely, another great argument for using Prime- or Choice-grade beef.

Furthermore, fat contributes flavor. "Meat flavor," McGee writes, "has two aspects: what might be called generic meatiness, and the special aromas that characterize meats from different animals. Meatiness is largely provided by the muscle fibers, character aromas by the fat tissue."

## Meanwhile, Back on the Surface . . .

Now that we have a picture of the internal transformations of the meat, let's briefly talk about what's happening outside. Over the course of the time the meat is in the cooker, its color will evolve from a rosy pink to a crusty golden brown to almost black (in the case of brisket), if you do it right. And while it might initially appear burned, this crust, which is called the bark, is not overcooked at all. Rather, it's deeply, deeply smoked and caramelized.

Two different things are occurring on the surface of the meat. One is that the meat is browning due to classic browning reactions, in particular the very famous (at least in cooking circles) Maillard reaction. My barbecue science friends at Texas A&M describe the Maillard reaction as "when the amino acids in foods react with reducing sugars to form the characteristic brown cooked color of foods." But we laypeople know it as the sweet, irresistible flavors that come from searing steak in a pan, toasting bread in the oven, roasting coffee, or, yes, cooking brisket in a smoker.

But the Maillard reaction flavors are subtle, and of course with brisket we get a great deal of flavor from the smoke (not to mention the rub). For this reason, one of the pitmaster's primary tasks is to expose the meat to smoke and maintain the meat's ability to capture smoke for as long as necessary. This may seem simple: *Just leave the meat on the grate and keep the smoke going, right?* Well, not exactly. If you want the smoke to both adhere to the surface *and* deeply penetrate the meat, the conditions have to be just right.

Smoke is composed of many—as in, hundreds—of chemical compounds, some liquid, some gaseous. As *Modernist Cuisine* describes, "Capturing the flavor of smoke . . . involves two challenges. The first is making sure the flavor compounds you want are gases, not liquid droplets, when they reach the food. That requires keeping tight control of the temperature of the smoke in the chamber. The second challenge is keeping the food just wet enough to allow the volatile organics in those vapors to stick to the food, form a film on the surface, and then diffuse deep inside." In other words, we need to keep the temperature of the cook chamber *just so*, to maximize the amount of gas particles in the smoke. But at the same time, we have to make sure that we don't get things too hot, lest the surface of the meat dry out and the smoke's gas particles have nothing to adhere to. It's a delicate dance.

To achieve the proper bark, we need to have a humid atmosphere inside the smoker. A humid environment both encourages the penetration of smoke and slows the drying of the exterior of the meat, allowing it to smoke for longer. As the meat's exterior dries out, it becomes harder and harder for the smoke to penetrate. Yet it's also difficult for smoke to adhere to the dried crust. That's why it's crucial to keep a water pan in the smoker at all times, which ensures ambient humidity thanks to the slow evaporation of the water.

I also directly moisten the surface of the meat further into the cooking process, using a spray bottle filled with practically anything wet.

Common liquids sprayed onto meats are water, vinegar, and apple juice. But it could be wine, marinade, anything. I often spray the surface of the meats in the last half hour to hour before they get wrapped. Your goal is to keep the surface of the meat from getting hard and dried, but you don't want it to be wet either. The surface needs to have a tacky, glistening sheen. That's when you know you've gotten it right.

At a certain point, the meat will have absorbed enough smoke. You'll know when this is happening by looking at the darkness of the bark. I provide color cues for each of the different meats featured later in this chapter (brisket, ribs, turkey), and as with everything else, you'll get better at figuring out the ideal smoke saturation point the more you practice. If you're unsure about the color, you should observe the drying rate: eventually it will become harder and harder to keep the meat moist, even as you spray it. That's when it's time to wrap.

## THE BASIC STEPS FOR SMOKING MEAT—ANY MEAT

Before we dive into the recipes themselves I want to explain the fundamental steps of pretty much any and every cook. When I talk about "attention to detail," in many ways, these are the details I'm talking about: how you apply the rub, when you wrap, whether or not you recognize and account for the stall, if and how you maintain the temperature of the cook chamber. These are the elements that are at the heart of all barbecue—and how well you master each technique will decide whether your finished product is pretty good or great.

## The Rub

The spice mixtures called rubs are important to barbecue for two reasons. One, they help meat taste and look delicious and they're crucial to the formation of a tasty, crusty bark. Two, they help meat attract and adhere smoke, because smoke is attracted to tacky, uneven surfaces, and rubs typically contain salt, which draws moisture to the surface.

Aside from the presence of salt, what exactly is in the rub is of debatable importance. Although people niggle about their rubs and guard their secret spice mixtures with the zeal of a Colonel Sanders or Coca-Cola, the role of a rub in smoke attraction and bark formation is arguably more important than its composition. Ultimately, the flavor the rub contributes is subtle when compared to all of the other flavors contained in meat and smoke. So, by all means, get a good rub recipe. But even better, come up with a spice mixture that works for you.

Here in Central Texas, the standard issue for German- or Czech-style barbecue is just salt and pepper. On this point, I agree with tradition wholeheartedly! A mixture of salt and pepper is by far the simplest and most magnificent seasoning; it complements the natural flavors of any nice piece of meat. But sometimes you're in the mood for a little something extra. And that's good too. One great thing about Franklin Barbecue is that we haven't been around for a hundred years. We've got no tradition to uphold! No family recipes to stick to for fear of insulting centuries of ancestors. The only thing we've got is the dedication to make the best food we can make and to keep it consistently the same every day (which itself is the biggest challenge). It's that dedication that keeps us evolving as cooks and constantly thinking about new ways to do old things. With a solid foundation of traditional Central Texas barbecue and a desire to keep everything as pure and simple as it should be, we're left with a lot of room to refine our technique and experiment with the five meats we cook every day.

As you build a rub, first think about what it is you are cooking. How do you want it to taste? How long is it going to cook? How big is it? How hot will you cook it? All of these questions play into how I go about making a rub.

Take a brisket, for example: It is large and will take a long time. It will need a good natural bark and will take a lot of flavor from the wood. For that, I like a lot of black pepper. It melts into fat nicely. It provides a coarse surface to promote smoke adhesion and, in my opinion, should be the dominant ingredient for a brisket rub. Next is the salt. Brisket is a huge hunk of meat, so I think it needs a good bit of salt. Since I use good-quality beef, the beef's natural flavors make me want to build a rub that is as transparent as possible, with nothing to conflict with the smoke and confuse the palate. So salt and pepper it is!

That's not to say that playing with seasoning salts, garlic powder, onion powder, or any of the hundreds of other spices and seasonings that are available at most grocery stores would be wrong. I'm just saying that you don't have to have a complicated rub to make great barbecue . . . but sometimes it's fun to add something special.

What follows is a short list of common rub ingredients and some notes on each, where applicable. There are far too many possible ingredients to list, and since each one opens a door to another, I'm just digging in to the more common elements of a basic rub.

## Standard Rub Ingredients

**_Salt_** • I use only Morton brand kosher salt. I like it because all the granules are consistently the same size. The thicker the meat, the more salt you'll use. The amount you'll use will always depend on the size of the brisket, so when it comes to quantity, you should trust your instincts. I use roughly 1/4 cup (which is about 2 ounces with Morton brand) per brisket.

**_Black pepper_** • I like 16 mesh. The mesh number refers to the size of the pepper particles. The pepper has been sifted through a screen that has 1/16 by 1/16-inch openings. It ends up being the right size to mix with its companion, kosher salt. Really coarse pepper would be 10 mesh, where as the finer stuff is more like 20 or 30 mesh. Most people prefer a fresh grind, but I like pepper that's been ground for at least a few days. I want a lot of pepper for texture and appearance, so the fresh stuff is just too strong. The toned-down older version works best for me. (I'm not talking about going into your mother's spice cabinet and pulling out pepper from the 1970s. But I do like it to have been ground for a few days to a few weeks.)

**_Seasoning salt_** • There are many seasoning salts available, and they are typically comprised of all of the usual suspects: salt, sugar, onion, and garlic for flavor and paprika and turmeric mostly for color. You should expect to find countless assortments of ingredients that someone, somewhere thought tasted good on something. Seasoning salt is an easy way to add complex flavors to a rub without having dozens of spices sitting around. Even though I don't think sugar should be involved in a long cook (see "Sugars," right), very small amounts contained in the

finished rub don't seem to have an adverse effect on bark formation.

**_Granulated garlic and granulated onion_** • Both of these are great! Try to use granulated garlic and granulated onion instead of powdered, as the granulated stuff is close in size to the kosher salt and your 16-mesh black pepper, so texturally it just mixes and disperses much better than a fine powder. Do not try to get fancy and use fresh ingredients. Fresh aromatics don't work for rubs; they're too strong and will completely dominate the meat and they will burn.

**_Paprika_** • Big fan! Paprika is made from ground dried chile. It can come from many different countries and in various varieties, such as smoked, sweet, and hot. I like plain ole Hungarian paprika, just to keep it simple. If you cannot find it at your local grocery store, check for it at a gourmet grocery. The more common and cheaper Mexican variety is great for adding color but doesn't add much flavor. The Hungarian is a nice dark red and has a complex flavor that is mild and savory.

**_Chile powders_** • Many ground dried chiles don't end up under the paprika header, and since Texas is so far south, most of the chile powders I use are from Mexican peppers. I don't use them in rubs at the restaurant, but they certainly lend a wonderfully "Texasy" flavor to meat if I'm playing around or cooking something for friends. The generic type of chili powder will have a Texas-chili kind of taste and won't specify which chiles are used to make it, but others can be chile specific. Some of my favorites are made from dried poblanos (ancho powder) smoke-dried jalapeños (chipotle powder), or dried cayennes (cayenne pepper).

***Sugars*** • Almost every commercial rub has a high level of sugar. I like sweets plenty, but not on my barbecue. There, I've said it. Sugary rubs burn and turn bitter when exposed to high heat for too long and are a way to cheat the acquisition of bark over a long cook. There are many sugars to choose from, some more processed than others. Use them *all* with caution.

### Other (More Questionable) Rub Ingredients

***Hickory or mesquite flavor*** • I use real fire to get my smoke and wood notes, so these seem silly to me.

***Beef or chicken flavoring*** • Useful only if you're seeking a high concentration of flavor. Seems like a cheat to me, but I suppose it could help you get an edge in a competition. I'd much rather use flavorful, high-quality meat than some sort of processed flavoring, however.

***Worcestershire powder and soy powder*** • These are good if you want to bolster the umami quotient, the so-called fifth taste, which is best defined as a sense of savory deliciousness. Umami is said to be caused by glutamic acid and is typically in fermented and aged proteins. Its most common application has been in MSG. Yes, soy and Worcestershire taste good, but many commercial rubs just use MSG for that type of flavor enhancement.

### Building the Rub

Every rub I make starts with a base of salt and pepper. Then I add other spices to complement the meat that I am cooking. The goal of any rub is to complement a nice piece of meat, not to obscure a crappy piece of meat. All spices should react well with one another. No one spice should stand out or be too recognizable, so add just enough to taste. It would be a shame to buy a nice piece of meat, spend a ton of time prepping and cooking it, and have it taste like an overzealous mixture of flavors. Restraint is the name of the game when using seasonings other than just salt and pepper.

## RUB RECIPES

### Brisket and Beef Rib Rub

**INGREDIENTS** Equal parts 16-mesh ground black pepper and kosher salt.

**QUANTITY** A rough guideline is that you'll need about ½ cup (4 ounces) of rub, total, for each 12-pound brisket. A 3- to 5-pound rack of beef ribs will require just a bit less rub, maybe ⅓ to ½ cup, total.

### Pork Rib and Turkey Rub

**INGREDIENTS** 2 parts 16-mesh ground black pepper and 1 part kosher salt.

**QUANTITY** A rough guideline is that you'll need about ¼ cup (2 ounces) rub, total, for each rack of ribs or turkey breast.

### Optional Add-ons

**GRANULATED GARLIC**

**GRANULATED ONION**

**PAPRIKA** Add for color and savory aspect.

**SEASONING SALT** However much you add, subtract the same amount of salt from your rub.

I mix my salt and pepper in a large 16-ounce shaker, which is actually a spice container from a restaurant supply store. It's got a top with three openings: one large opening with a sliding lid for pouring and two sets of different-size circular holes for sprinkling. This is the vessel I use to apply the rub. I start by pouring one layer atop the other as a form of measurement, using my eyes to ensure that the thickness of the layers is equal to the proportions I want. Then I shake them all up until thoroughly mixed. (Remember to close off the lid.)

### Applying the Rub

Always apply the rub to meat about 1 hour before cooking and let the meat warm up to room temperature. That will let the seasoning "sweat" into the meat, and the warmer meat will shave off hours of cook time.

The following directions might seem trivial. But again, the devil is in the details. And I'm not joking when I say that every new kitchen employee at Franklin Barbecue gets a lesson in how to properly apply the rub. The goal is to get it evenly distributed with the right concentration over the entire surface of the meat. If you apply the rub more densely or more sparsely in certain areas, patches of the meat will cook unevenly, yielding splotchiness, dry patches, and general mayhem over the course of a multihour cook.

To apply the rub evenly, you've got to keep things loose—in the elbow, in the wrist, and in

the mind, with a relaxed but focused attitude. First, keep the shaker about a foot or two over the surface of the meat, or however high you feel comfortable. (Of course if you're aiming for a specific spot, you can bring the shaker down lower.) Sprinkling it from a height allows it to spread out and apply more evenly than if you're trying to direct it from up close.

Once you start sprinkling the rub, you've got to keep the shaker moving. This is accomplished with two separate but related gestures. With the elbow and forearm, gently get the shaker moving in small circles to get the rub flowing out of it. At the same time, allow the wrist to swivel a bit to keep the granules inside jumping around. Being heavier than pepper, salt tends to quickly congregate at the bottom of the shaker, making for an uneven mix if you don't properly jumble it all up.

## Slathers

Slathers are a liquid or paste applied to the meat before the rub goes on. They act as a kind of glue to help rubs stick to the meat and can be anything from yellow mustard to hot sauce to plain ole water. Slathers are also a neat way to sneak in very subtle flavors and can be quite useful in some situations. Things to remember when using a slather:

- Due to the solubility of certain types of smoke, I prefer to use a water-based rather than an oil-based slather.

- Keep a very low sugar content. Too much sugar will harden and can seal off the surface of the meat, inhibiting flavor penetration.

- Apply a very conservative amount, just enough to create a tacky environment for rub and smoke adhesion. Too much and you run the risk of building an impermeable barrier between the meat and the pending flavors. Too heavy a slather can also give you a premature crust that has the potential for flaking off, taking most of the smoke and seasonings with it.

## Wrapping

Most of what I cook gets wrapped at some point in the cooking process. Ribs and pork butts get wrapped in foil; brisket gets wrapped in butcher paper.

Wrapping a brisket in foil has been derisively referred to as "the Texas crutch," because it helps a long-cooked brisket turn out better and keep from drying out in the last stage of cooking. Strangely, in the serious barbecue community it's looked down upon almost as cheating, despite the fact that it helps many people make better brisket than they would otherwise. Even some pros use it on a regular basis, so I don't exactly see the evil in it.

The idea is that at a certain point, the meat has absorbed all of the smoke it's going to or all of the smoke it needs, but it's not yet done cooking. This is the moment when I wrap. The meat then continues cooking in a sealed environment until it's done internally. Technically, at this point you could remove the meat from the smoker and continue cooking it in a conventional gas or electric oven, but we just throw it back on the smoker, which is already at the proper temperature. (We don't have oven space for sixty briskets anyway—that's cheating!)

How do you know when to wrap? I judge by color. The meat's already to temperature. It's looking fine; I just want to make sure that I get a really dark color on there. Some of the color will actually wash off as the meat steams in its wrapper, which is why you want to make sure that you have a good, authentic dark color before you wrap. Toward the end of the smoking process— particularly if you're using fairly dirty smoke—it's possible that you're just layering ashy smoke on the outside, so I hit brisket and ribs with a spray of water to gauge the true color of the meat or bark. If the color washes off easily, I'll give the meat more time in the smoke. If it seems dark enough, I'll wrap immediately.

Early on in my career, I found that I liked the way a brisket cooked in butcher paper better than in foil. Whereas foil creates a fairly hermetic pocket, the butcher paper still allows a bit of interchange with the outside environment. Because of this breathing, using butcher paper is a blend of using foil and not wrapping at all, a happy compromise that works really well for me.

There's a time and a place for foil, however. If you have to cook something that's really lean or you need to speed something up, use foil with caution. It's a trick to have up your sleeve. I might wrap a brisket in foil if it's an especially lean one. A lesser grade with little marbling needs every bit of its moisture conserved, so I'd wrap that in foil and probably wrap it quite early. For richer cuts, it's not as important to seal it up as soon, as they have ample moisture, thanks to all of the intramuscular fat of the marbling.

## Maintaining Temperature

If I have a favorite temperature—other than 98.6°F and 75°F and sunny—it's got to be 275°F. This is my reference point, my safe place, when it comes to the ideal temperature for a cook.

Now I've said in several places in this book that the pitmaster needs to be flexible, read each situation, and adapt depending on the circumstances. That said, if I'm using equipment other than my own (which I feel very comfortable with), I'll always try to get the temperature of the cook chamber (at grill level, remember—where the meat is actually sitting) to 275°F. It's my default, and you can cook just about everything, from brisket and ribs to sausage and turkey, at this temperature. It's basically right in the middle—not super low, not too high. Some people are more comfortable cooking brisket *really* low and slow, which is around 225°F. But it's not just that that's a little too slow for me (which it is). Keeping things at 275°F is ideal because it allows

### COOKING IN WEATHER

One thing that professional pitmasters and home cooks have in common is that at some point or another, we all have to cook in crappy weather. If you're working at a restaurant, you can't just close down because it looks like rain. And if you've planned a backyard fiesta for weeks and guests are showing up at 3 p.m. no matter what, you can't *not* cook because a cold front blows through.

Every kind of atmospheric condition requires its own set of responses, though no matter what you're doing, you're trying to counter factors you can't control. There are no easy answers, but here are a few things I've found.

High wind High wind can wreak havoc with fires and airflow. Although it's good to keep your firebox door open as much as possible, when it's windy, especially if the wind is blowing into your fire, you've got to close the door to shield the fire. Position your cooker so that the firebox door faces away from a prevailing wind that will whip the fire and stoke things up too wildly. In the case of crosswinds, try pushing your fire up in the box, away from the door.

Rain Nothing is worse than cooking in the rain. Both you and your cooker will inevitably be miserable for having to get soaked while trying to keep your temperatures up. Just make sure to keep your wood dry (cover it with a tarp or move it under shelter) and push through it.

Cold Wood selection changes for different weather. I'll be sure to use drier wood that burns hotter on cold days. I'll also probably cook a little hotter than usual to compensate for the low ambient temperature outside. I'll rake the coal bed too, so that it's a little longer than normal and goes all the way to the firebox door. That way, the air crossing it gets preheated before it hits the fire.

Heat You have to be careful on really hot days not to let your temperatures get away from you. I might cook lower—at, say, 265°F instead of 275°F—knowing that the smoker is not fighting the ambient temperature outside.

brisket to form a good bark while still rendering properly on the inside.

This is yet another reason why when I'm on the road, I always take my handy ThermoWorks probe with me. I'll take an onion or a potato, cut it in half, and turn it into a little stand for the thermometer, which I then prop in the cooker because I don't trust other people's gauges. I even take four Tel-Tru temperature gauges in my travel kit and have been known to unscrew the existing thermometers and substitute these just to get a better sense of the hot and cool spots along the cook surface.

Sometimes I might go up from 275°F but not usually higher than 315°F or so. I know people who start it on 350°F and then slow it down as the cook moves along. I don't agree with that. I find it impractical and risky to pull temperatures back if things start cooking too fast. I'd much rather nudge it forward with gradual temperature increases until I find

---

### THE WATER PAN

Always cook with a water pan. If you don't, you'll dry out the meat and it won't cook at a proper rate. You need a very humid environment, as it slows down the rate of moisture evaporation, collagen breakdown, and fat melt so that they all happen in concert. The slower rate of cooking also allows the interior of the meat to keep pace with the cooking of the exterior. Finally, the humid environment helps preserve the moist, tacky surface of the meat, which is desirable to attract smoke.

---

just the right place. Too hot is more dangerous than too low. You can always cook something longer, but you can't unburn it. Also, the slow progression upward along the temperature scale, I believe, allows me to get the depth of flavor and layers of smoke that I'm looking for. Balance is key. At the end of the day, yes, it should taste like smoke and salt and pepper. But you also want to taste the flavor of the beef. And 275°F is the safest way to get there.

Now, to be clear, 275°F is not the word of God for the temperature for brisket, because every brisket is different. If you showed up at Franklin Barbecue on any given day and took the temperature of our smokers at grill level, odds are you'd get a reading of 285°F. But that's on our cookers, cookers we know well, so we can afford to go a bit hotter and faster. Every cooker is different. Every brisket is different. With briskets containing more marbling, you can cook at a lower temperature and still get the rendering you need. But if it's a low-grade, commodity brisket with a lot of hard, waxy fat, you're going to want to cook higher to break that stuff down. The big takeaway? A temp of 275°F is always a good place to start; just pay attention and go up or down as needed.

## The Stall

I often get emails that all say the same thing: "I cooked a brisket, and it looked great and tasted great, but it was tough. What did I do wrong?" Inevitably, I'll write back, "Let me guess the temperature you pulled it off at. Was it in the 160°F to 165°F range? You pulled it off during the stall!"

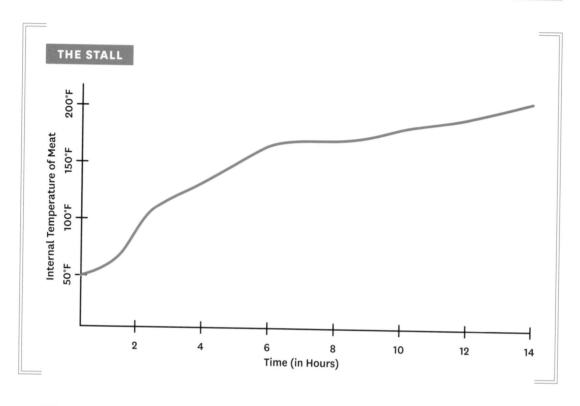

**THE STALL**

Internal Temperature of Meat — Time (in Hours)

What is the stall? Similar somewhat to the way a prop plane might stall before restarting its engine and continuing through the air—and far more heart-stopping—a big piece of meat cooking in the smoker hits a patch in its progress where cooking appears to stop. You can chart it with a meat thermometer. At first, the temperature goes up and up, just as anything we cook always does. And then, gosh darn it, it levels off. This is usually between 160°F and 170°F. And it stays leveled off. And it stays. And it stays at the same temperature until you think it's not going to get any higher. This freaks people out. It sure did me when I first encountered it.

What do freaked-out people do with meat that's been stuck at the same temperature for

hours? They're not stupid—they pull it off. After all, at 160°F or thereabouts, it easily satisfies the FDA guideline for when beef is done (ahem, 145°F). And then they cut into it only to find the brisket is as tough as a sneaker.

Anyone can be forgiven for doing this, because the stall defies logic. Not only does the meat hold the same low temperatures for hours in an ovenlike environment, sometimes it can actually be observed dropping in temperature. So what gives?

The stall happens as a result of something called "evaporative cooling." It's the same mechanism that allows sweat to cool down the body. Sweat works like this: when moisture sits on the surface of the skin, it's evaporated by heat energy given off by the body. So when the water changes from liquid to gas form, it absorbs a significant amount of heat energy from the skin, creating a cooling effect on the surface it's leaving. Basically, your sweat is sucking up radiant heat from your body, getting converted into gas, and then evaporating away. This happens more easily in a dry heat than a humid one, which is why a hot and dry day feels cooler than a hot and humid one. Your sweat evaporates much more easily when there's less moisture already in the air. In high humidity, it doesn't evaporate well or at all and we feel warmer, even if the actual air temperature is not high.

This is why we often refer to "dry bulb" and "wet bulb" temperatures. Dry bulb measures the actual air temperature, whereas wet bulb measures the temperature of the air but adjusts for the cooling that occurs as moisture dries from a surface. Therefore, wet bulb temperature is lower than dry bulb, except in an environment of 100 percent relative humidity, in which case the two temperatures are the same. (In 100 percent humidity, there's no room in the molecules of air to absorb any more moisture, so there can be no cooling from evaporation.)

Inside a cooker, the piece of meat is sort of sweating too. It's losing moisture to the air in the form of evaporation. Interestingly, air turbulence and humidity have a greater impact on evaporation than actual temperature—and since there's a huge amount of air movement in a smoker (thanks, convection), the evaporation is quite significant. This means that a lot of evaporative

cooling is happening, that is, the surface of the meat is cooler than the air around it in the cooker. Therefore a wet bulb thermometer would give a more accurate reading of the temperature than the dry bulb ones everyone uses.

Evaporative cooling of the brisket continues until the humidity inside the cooker rises or until the surface of the meat has no more moisture to give. (This is a big part of the reason why a water pan is so important, as maintaining the humidity means that the stall won't happen too early in the cook.) A stall will happen when the temperature of the meat reaches equilibrium with the wet bulb temperature inside the cooker—to the meat, it can get no hotter in there. Of course, this is not the case. The dry bulb temperature inside the cooker is much warmer. As the humidity inside the smoker decreases because of the vanishing moisture in the meat, so does the wet bulb temperature, and the meat might even experience a temporary reduction in temperature.

Finally, the temperature will resume climbing when the accessible moisture in the meat has evaporated and the meat becomes just a dry hunk. But nobody actually wants that—a sad, dried-out piece of brisket! Here's what you do instead: add some humidity to the equation by wrapping the meat before all of that moisture is gone. And this is what I do: I cook it exposed long enough for it to pick up smoke and lose just the right amount of moisture, then I wrap it to preserve what is left and let the collagen continue to render.

## THE SMOKE RING

If you eat at Franklin Barbecue, you might notice that our barbecue doesn't always have that classic pink "smoke ring" underneath the bark that some people love to hold up as the surefire indication of great barbecue. That's because the smoke ring, in fact, has nothing to do with the way great barbecue tastes, how well it was smoked, and so on. In fact, research has shown that smoke isn't even necessarily required to make a smoke ring. That said, it often will occur in meats smoked under certain conditions.

The first thing that you should know is that the smoke ring—and the red color of your steaks and the juice that comes out of rare-cooked meat—has nothing to do with blood. Instead, it's caused by myoglobin, a red-colored protein that carries and stores oxygen in muscle cells. When it's heated, myoglobin loses its pink color and turns the dull, gray color of well-done meat. So rare steaks aren't red because they're still bloody—they're red because the internal temperature has not gotten high enough to turn that myoglobin brown.

It makes sense then that the interior of meat would stay pink. So how is it that the smoke ring on some briskets is on the outside, which presumably gets even hotter than the interior, which has turned gray? The answer involves complicated chemistry, but let's just say that carbon monoxide and nitrogen monoxide in the smoke react with the myoglobin in meat to keep it pink. The depth of the smoke ring indicates how far the smoke has penetrated the meat before it contacts meat whose internal temperature has already risen enough to turn gray.

Thus it's logical that if you start with cold brisket—say, straight from the freezer—you can get a wider smoke ring, as the smoke can penetrate further before the interior of the meat heats up. And, surprise, that's a popular technique in competition barbecue to get that luscious-looking ring.

But smoke rings don't contribute anything whatsoever to flavor or texture, so we're not too concerned with them. And if we were to make an effort to put especially cold briskets on the smoker, it would take them even longer than the 16 hours they already require to finish.

# BRISKET

Brisket is a big, dumb hunk of meat, but it turns into something heavenly when done just right. Cooking a brisket intimidates a lot of people, probably because it's a big investment in money and time. If something goes wrong, there's not a lot you can do. Well, I have two things to say to that: Don't mess it up, as it's not that hard. And if it's not perfect, don't fret—you've still got smoky meat to serve, and most people are pretty forgiving about that.

There aren't many steps in making a brisket. First, I'll outline the entire process, then I'll go into greater detail about each part.

### Ingredients and Tools

- 1 (12- to 14-pound) brisket, packer cut (see page 110)
- About ½ cup Brisket and Beef Rib Rub (page 137)
- Desired slather ingredients (see page 139), optional
- Spray bottle of water, vinegar, or other liquid
- 2 sheets of 18 by 30-inch unfinished butcher paper
- Seasoned firewood (preferably oak)

### Overview

1 • Trim the brisket.

2 • Apply the slather, if using, and the rub (equal parts salt and pepper), then let the brisket warm up to room temperature (1 hour).

3 • In the meantime, start your fire and check that the water pan is full. Get a feel for the wood you will be using—how quickly it burns, how clean the smoke is, and so on. Build a nice coal bed.

4 • When the smoker is reading at the desired temperature (in the 275°F range, depending on preference), place the brisket on the cooker. I prefer fat side up and the brisket point facing toward the fire. Gently close the lid. Maintain a clean fire at or around 275°F for the duration of the 8- to 10-hour cook (timing depends on brisket size and cooker temperature and efficiency).

5 • Keep the lid closed for the first 3 hours. After 3 hours, start periodically (roughly every 20 to 30 minutes) checking the color. Start spritzing occasionally with water or vinegar if the brisket surface starts looking dry.

6 • At 6 hours, the internal temperature should be getting through the stall. Start paying attention to the bark formation and whether the fat cap is rendering. Think about wrapping soon. If the temperature is stalling but you don't have a sufficiently colored bark, or the fat cap is still very hard and solid, consider bumping up the cooker's temperature to push through the stall. When the bark is getting

nice and crusty and the color is looking even, remove the brisket from the cooker, spritz, and wrap it in butcher paper.

**7** • Return the wrapped brisket to the cooker and maintain the fire.

**8** • About 10 hours in, start "feeling" the brisket with a thin towel. Take note of how it starts to feel soft and pliable under the point and the flat. As the brisket gets closer to doneness, the whole piece will begin to feel tender. If you must, check the internal temperature of the brisket in the middle of the flat. It may read anywhere from 190°F to 203°F when it is done. But keep in mind, feel trumps all. If it's tender, it's done!

**9** • Take the brisket out of the smoker and let it rest fully wrapped until the internal temperature comes down to 140°F to 145°F (1 to 2 hours, depending, of course, on the ambient air temperature).

## *Step 1* TRIM THE BRISKET.

The bad news is that there's an art to trimming a brisket. The good news is that it is not a very hard art to learn. What you should know is that trimming the brisket is really important and does factor in to the way the brisket cooks. Basically, trimming well is an opportunity to set yourself up for an easy, successful cook.

A lot of what I've talked about in this book regards feel. I've said that you should let the fire burn at the rate it wants to. I've talked about

envisioning the way smoke flows through a cooker. Well, trimming a brisket falls into that category too. As you prepare to trim, imagine the way smoke and heat will travel across the brisket's surface, borne by airflow. You want to make the surface of the meat streamlined and smooth so that it cooks evenly and thoroughly, removing any odd bits of fat or flesh that might dry out and burn. Basically, you want one harmonious piece of meat. So here's what I do.

First, I put on my nitrile gloves with the idea of keeping one hand clean and one hand that will touch the meat. I will touch the meat only with the dirty hand, while my clean, right hand will handle the knife. The knife I use is a well-sharpened curved, stiff 8-inch boning knife that cuts through the brisket with grace and ease.

It's good to start with a cold brisket, as it's easier to cut into. The brisket will most likely be wrapped in plastic. I put the brisket down on the cutting board, fat side up, and cut through the center of the plastic with my knife, making sure not to touch the meat. Next, I cut open the bag at the end, lift the end of the brisket with my left hand, and use my knife to pull the bag out from under from the brisket. I'll then toss the bag into the trash can that I've conveniently located under or to the side of the table.

Now let's orient ourselves around the brisket. I'm going to call the fat cap side the top of the brisket, because I cook that side up (even though technically it faces downward on the animal). This is the side where the point protrudes upward with a knobby shape. The underside of the brisket, the bottom, is flat.

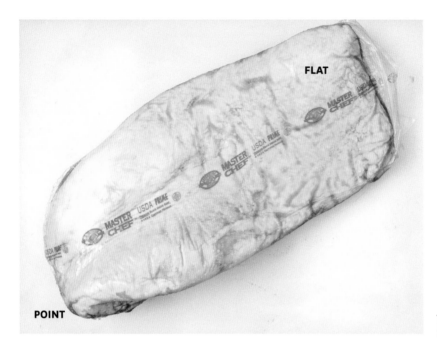

**FLAT**

**POINT**

Top of brisket
(fat cap side)

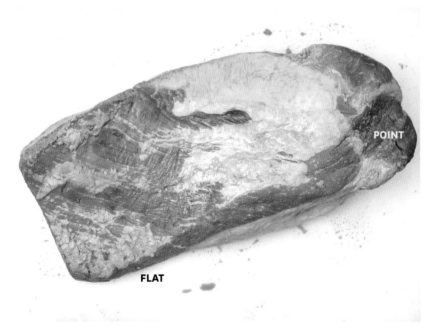

**POINT**

**FLAT**

Bottom of brisket

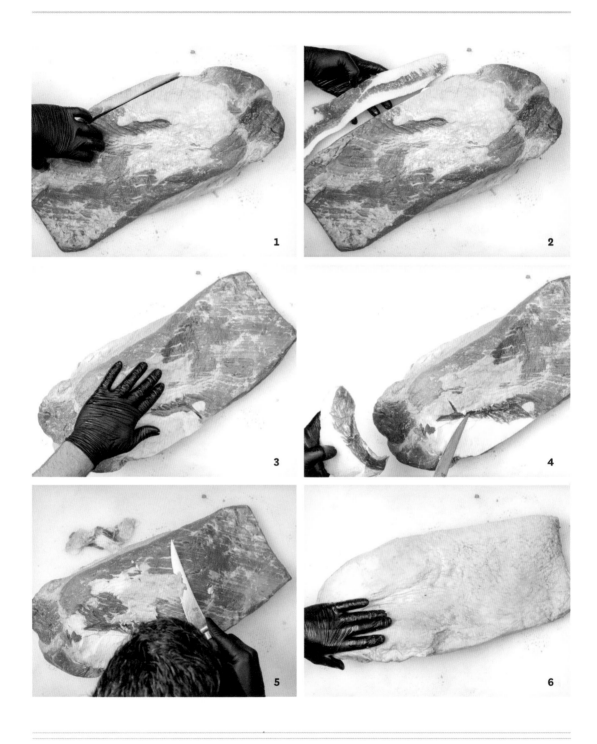

Place the brisket before you on the table, with the point facing down. I first look at the long sides of the brisket, where I like to make smooth, graceful edges. I'll usually trim off a thin strip from the edge, all the way from the top of the point to the end of the flat (see **PHOTO 1**, left). Make a clean, consistent cut, following the line where the seam fat terminates, and you'll have nice sides to the brisket, with meat showing underneath and fat on top.

One thing to understand about my trimming method is that I cut a lot away (see **PHOTO 2**)—more than most, I've been told. That means I'm pretty ruthless, and whereas a lot of people will trim away only fatty bits, I'll cut away both fat and some meat in order to get the shape I want. How do I know what shape I want? I envision the final product after cooking. When looking at the raw hunk of brisket in front of you, try to imagine how it's going to cook down—how the fat cap will reduce into the bark, and how each outward-facing side will render. When you imagine how you're going to slice the cooked brisket, you'll start to see how to trim it. You'll take certain edges and points off, even if they contain some meat, because that surface that you've just revealed will ultimately cook better and offer a better slice of meat.

Take a look at the bottom of the brisket: you'll note a big hunk of fat right where the point and the flat connect. I always think of this big nub almost like a handle you can grip, a fist-size piece that I cut off, because it won't render and won't add anything to the final product. If you make a few entry cuts on one side of it, it's really easy to pull the whole thing back (while cutting it away with the knife) until you can remove the entire chunk and throw it away (see **PHOTOS 3 AND 4**).

Now trim off bigger pieces of fatty membrane that are inevitably clinging to this side (see **PHOTO 5**). This is just a superficial trim, but those thin strands of fat will only disrupt the bark formation as it cooks. Now you're done with the underside. Flip the brisket over so you can get to work on the fat-cap side (see **PHOTO 6**).

Your next step is to trim the fat cap to 1/4- to 1/2-inch thickness. The general goal is to trim it and then to excise any pieces that will burn or cook unevenly. Note where the brisket flops down over the side of the point. Trim this down a bit so that the point will cook more thoroughly (see **PHOTOS 7 AND 8**, page 152). If you don't, the fat that's under the fold won't render and turn to bark.

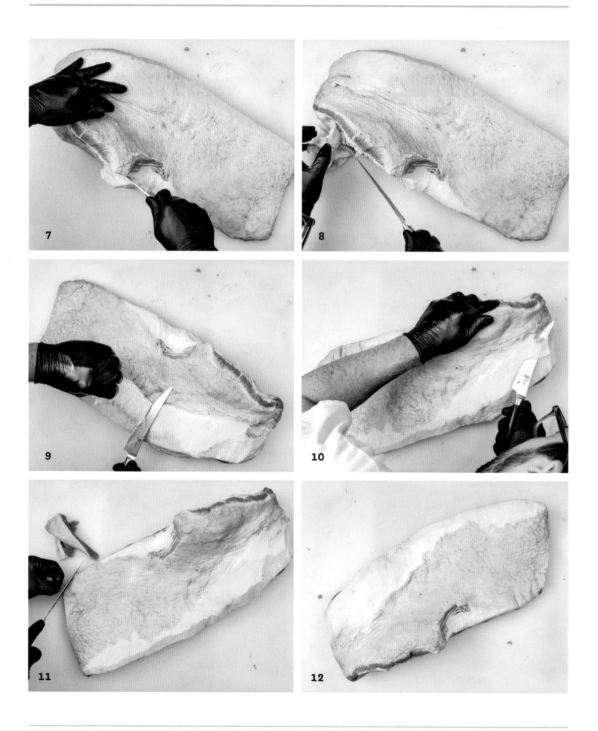

I also like to strip away hard or bad-looking fat that sort of hardens in sheets (affectionately called "Ally Sheety" at the restaurant). I use two general cuts for this. One is a thin horizontal slice up near the point, which I then continue as I peel the slice back while gently cutting underneath it with the knife (see **PHOTOS 9 AND 10**, left). This allows you to cut a long, thin strip off the top. Then I'll go in with shorter slices to get the height I want and a generally smooth surface. You may have to cut away some pretty gnarly chunks of fat. Don't be afraid to do that.

The last step is to round off the edges because corners that stick out might have a tendency to burn and dry out before the rest of the meat (see **PHOTO 11**). You want to remove any little pieces of fat or flesh protruding from the mass, as they can dry out and burn.

Although all of this sounds complicated and precise, it really isn't. Don't get too OCD over this, or you'll find yourself spending 30 minutes doing something that should take no more than 10, and your brisket will warm up and you'll find that your back aches from hunching over it. As I said, turn the brisket into a nice, clean shape with a 1/4-inch fat cap and no bits hanging off the edges (see **PHOTO 12**).

### *Step 2* APPLY THE SLATHER AND THE RUB.

If you wish to apply a slather, do so before adding the rub. Again, it's your choice whether or not to slather. It can help the rub stick to the surface of the meat, but usually the meat's tacky enough that it's not necessary. Feel free to use water, hot sauce, mustard, whatever you want. I've seen it all.

As I said on page 134, you can get as complicated with the rub as you want—chile powder, cumin, granulated garlic, all the classic spices can be good in there. But in Central Texas the classic formulation is just salt and pepper: equal parts of each. A lot of people tend to go pretty heavy with the rub. I think that's a mistake. I like a fairly light, even coating, so the flavor of the rub doesn't detract from the flavor of the meat.

Mix the salt and pepper in a large shaker. (Use the quantity in the ingredients list on page 147 only as a rough guideline; every brisket is different and you may find you need a little more or less. When in doubt, I think it's better to under- than overseason.) Your goal is to get an even coating of rub on the entire exposed surface of the meat. Then, with the shaker high enough over the brisket to get a good, even mix (1 to 2 feet), get the hand moving and gently shower the rub down on the brisket. To get the rub on the vertical sides of the brisket, I hold my open, flat hand just to the side and use it to deflect the rub onto the meat, gently patting it in every few seconds to get every facet of the brisket covered. Make sure you do both sides and all of the edges: the fat cap and the underside. Now you're ready to throw it in the cooker.

### Step 3 START THE FIRE.

Following the instructions beginning on page 88, start your fire and get your smoker preheated to the desired temperature. Again, 275°F is a good starting point. The smoker should also contain a full water pan (see page 66).

### Step 4 PLACE THE BRISKET IN THE SMOKER.

Open the door and place your brisket inside. There are two kinds of people in the world: those who cook brisket fat side up and those who cook it fat side down. I'm very much a member of the former group. This is not necessarily because of any sort of orthodox philosophy; it's just my judgment call for the way briskets cook on my smokers. I cook fat side up because I have more top heat than bottom heat. If it were the opposite, I might cook fat side down, as you need to make sure that the fat renders before the bottom gets overdone. Remember this one very important point: every cooker is different, and you need to understand intimately the particulars of your own device.

Find a good place in the middle of your smoker and position the brisket on the grill with the point facing toward the firebox. I orient the brisket this way because the point is covered in a big fat cap and is the most marbled part of the brisket. All that fat will help protect the meat from the brunt of the heat coming directly out of the firebox. I like the middle of the grill because that's where I'm getting the most even temperature. You don't want to put it too close to the firebox opening, as it will likely be too

hot there. But you should know what your temp reads up and down your cook surface (if it's long enough) because you've installed gauges to take the temp at grate level (see "Modifying a Cheap Store-Bought Smoker," page 62). With your hands, firm up the brisket and sort of nestle it into its shape, then close the door. Now you're ready to settle in and watch the fire for a long time. This is a good time to open a beer.

### Step 5 CHECK . . . OCCASIONALLY.

There's a saying in barbecue that "If you're looking, you ain't cooking." This is very true. Avoid opening the lid to check on the progress of the meat, especially during the first 3 hours of cooking. Every time you open the lid, you're releasing smoke and heat and adding time to your cook. It takes a smoker a while to regain that heat, so it's best just to trust that your meat is cooking. As the meat starts to dry out and darken (around hour 3 or 4), spritz it with your spray bottle once or twice an hour, just to help the bark stay moist and continue to attract smoke.

### Step 6 WATCH FOR THE STALL, THEN WRAP.

If you surmise that a brisket will cook in 8 to 10 hours, you can gauge that after about 4 hours, you'll be in the stall (depending on how hot you're cooking), and after about 6 hours, the brisket will be pushing through the stall and starting its eventual climb to doneness. One thing to remember is this: don't wrap during the stall. You'll lose all the momentum if you open

the lid and take out and wrap the brisket while it's trying to sweat off the last of its moisture. Just like an athlete might find it difficult to cool down and then get back up to full speed in a game, so too with a brisket. Better to let it come out of the stall and then wrap.

Conventionally, at home, if you're just cooking one or two briskets, this may be around 6 hours into a cook. But again, this decision should be based on color and bark formation more than any sort of time parameters. I can't really offer an exact accounting for time in a brisket recipe because every smoker, every piece of wood, and every piece of meat is different. Not to mention weather conditions vary. All I can say

is that as the crust of the meat starts to darken into a deep mahogany, almost blackish color, I'll open the lid briefly to spray the meat with a spray bottle. You can fill it with water, marinade, vinegar, apple juice, or whatever you want. I don't think it adds a ton of flavor, but it allows me to spray off any dark, clinging smoke to assess the true color of the meat and also wets the surface to prevent burning. I use the spray bottle to stretch out the smoke gathering and bark formation as long as I need to before I wrap.

When the color is right—that is, when I spray the bark to remove any ash and see that the true color of the bark is dark, nearly black—I pull the meat out and wrap it.

To wrap the brisket, I prepare two sheets of my pink butcher paper. It's 18 inches wide and "unfinished," meaning that it has no wax coating. I tear off two sheets each about 30 inches long and place one vertically on the table and the other just overlapping it and veering off at a slight oblique angle. Then I hit the spot where I'm going to lay the brisket on the papers with a quick spray from the bottle.

Next, using towels, I pick up the brisket and lay it down at the bottom of the two sheets of paper, 3 to 4 inches from the base of the sheets. The point is facing up and on the left side. I simply fold the edges of the paper over the brisket, as you'd wrap anything in paper, and then roll the brisket over once, keeping the pocket really nice and neat and as tight as I possibly can. Next, I take the wings of the paper, fold them over again, and once more roll the brisket over, keeping the wrap nice and tight. Now, just a little edge of paper is left, which I fold in a bit and leave. The brisket is in the same position it was when I took it off the smoker, only wrapped tightly in butcher paper.

## Step 7 CONTINUE COOKING THE WRAPPED BRISKET.

Put the brisket back in the smoker or even in an oven (set to the same temperature as your cook chamber) to finish cooking. I have to say that I think using an oven is cheating. But realistically, once you wrap the brisket, it's really absorbed all the smoke it's going to. If you want to save wood, or just head inside, finishing the brisket in the oven is a possibility . . . even if I don't really condone it.

## Step 8 CHECK FOR DONENESS.

How do you know when the brisket's done? It's a great question, because every brisket is different. Taking the internal temperature is a good indicator of how the cook is going, but is unreliable for calculating doneness. The only true way to know is to use your hands. If the fibers pull apart with the slightest force, it's tender! Too tough to pull? Keep cooking. Crumbly? Overdone.

Of course, I don't want to cut into briskets before we serve them, so I determine doneness by feel. To do this, I pick it up off the grill and test it for pliability. (Yes, hot! I've long since killed all the nerve endings in my fingers. If you can still feel with your fingers, consider wearing gloves.) I'm looking for looseness and some flexibility. If it's pliable and soft in my hands, it's done.

You can also unwrap it a little bit (do so carefully, as the sticky rendered fat can sometimes stick to the paper) and give the brisket a feel. If it's soft and jiggly, you've cooked it perfectly, and you'll find tender, beautifully moist meat inside. Pull it off at this time, because it's done. If you keep cooking it because you're unsure, you're just going to dry it out and make it tough.

Now, if you really have no idea if it's done or not, you can check the temperature. A brisket may be finished cooking in the wide range of 200°F to 210°F. Although I don't recommend using this specific temperature as your guide, I often find that briskets are done at 203°F. Why 203°F? Only because after smoking many thousands of briskets, that temperature seems to come up more often than not. So, if you're really flying blind, that would be my magic number. But, remember, a brisket's done when it's done.

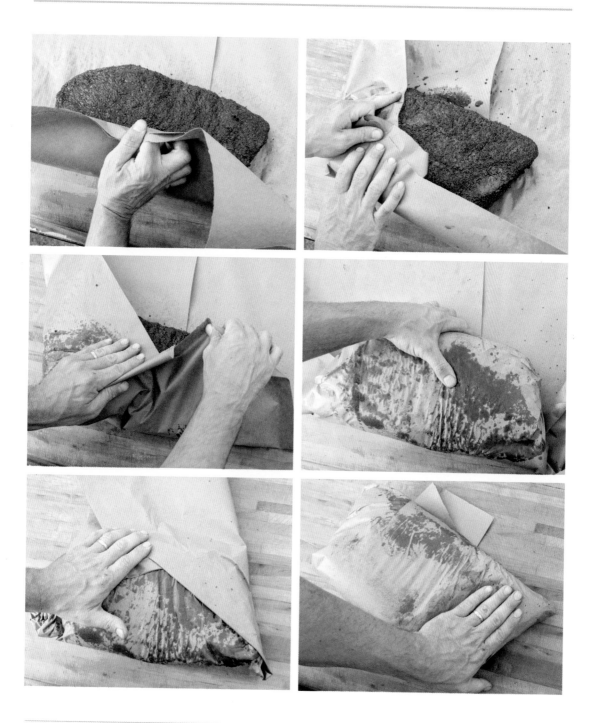

## *Step 9* REST THE BRISKET, THEN SERVE.

When a piece of meat is cooking, it goes through many changes: it starts as a cool, well-seasoned piece of meat (that can absorb characteristics from its heat source), then its moisture evaporates and it forms a nice crusty bark, and finally it becomes the tender, buttery, glistening end product we've been waiting for. But there's still one last step before we are ready to hunker down and enjoy a meal with our little edible slow-cooked morsel of delightfulness: letting it rest.

You'll probably notice the internal temperate of your brisket will continue to climb after you remove the meat from the cooker—that's called "carry-over." It occurs because of conductive heat. If the outside of the meat is cooked by the heat carried in the air and smoke of the cooker, the inside of the meat is cooked by the heat contained in those outer layers. It takes time for that heat to penetrate to the inside of the meat and do its work there (hence, the long cooking time of brisket). The deep internal temperature of any piece of meat can continue to rise even after it's been removed from the heat source because of this simple effect.

Yet resting after cooking is also incredibly important. It allows meat muscles to relax and reabsorb some of the juices that were squeezed out. If you cut it open right after it's been pulled, you will lose a lot of important liquid, and you will see a great brisket dry up in no time after hours of meticulous cooking.

Judging carry-over and resting times is like trying to predict the future. Carry-over can be tricky on a large piece of meat, as you don't want it to continue cooking so much that it becomes overdone as it rests. The idea is to think about how much momentum the meat has. Did you cook it hot and fast? If you did, carry-over will go further than it will if you were cooking low and slow, in which case there may be very little continuation.

Important to consider is where the meat will rest. On a hot table out in the sun on a Central Texas summer day? Or on a cool marble countertop inside an air-conditioned kitchen with an overachieving ceiling fan? If it's the former, you may not want to cook the meat as long, given the resting conditions. Many factors play into calculating resting time and carry-over. So use your best judgment and remember, just because you pull something at 203°F doesn't mean that that's your actual finished temperature.

Let a brisket rest until the internal temperature is between 140°F and 145°F. At this point you can serve the brisket or continue to let it rest for a couple of hours without losing any of its character. Indeed, a good, solid rest for a couple of hours may actually improve the meat.

After that, it's time to cut and serve the meat. I'm of the mind that cutting brisket properly is of the utmost importance, which is why I've devoted several pages to it (see pages 183 to 188). I suggest you read them before sinking your knife into that beautiful piece of meat you just spent hours preparing.

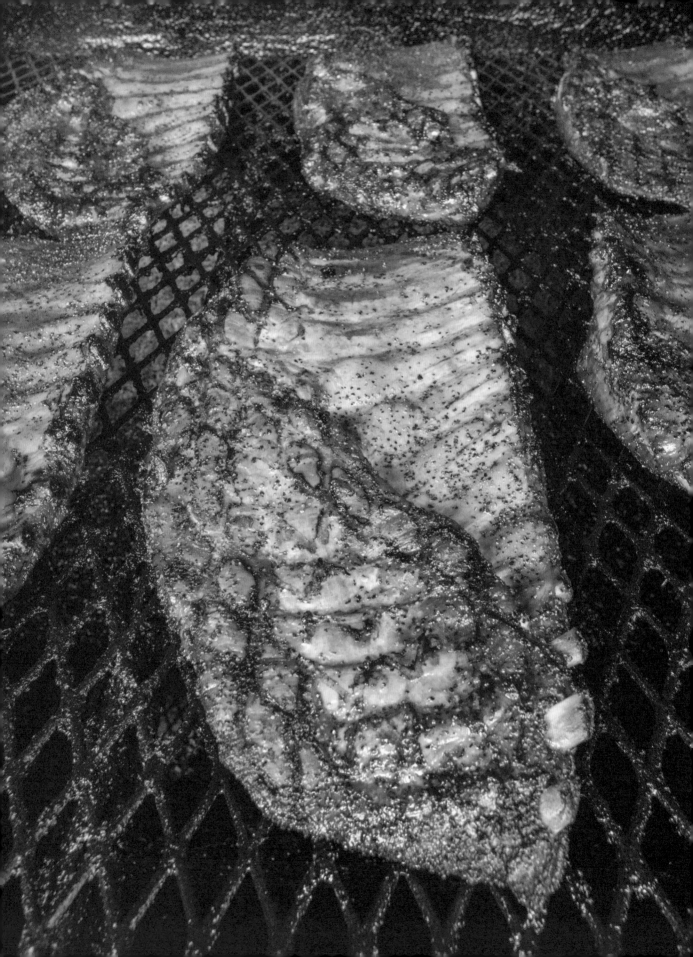

# SPARE RIBS

At the restaurant, a rib shift starts at about 1 a.m. That's mighty early. But what's nice about the ribs, unlike briskets, is that one person can see them all the way through. It starts with trimming and rubbing the ribs, and ends with them coming off somewhere between 8:30 and 10 a.m. Then they'll rest and be ready for service when we open the doors at 11.

Ribs are delicate and have a small window of doneness, but once you figure out when to wrap and when they're done, you've basically mastered the art of cooking them.

### Ingredients and Tools

- 1 full rack of pork spare ribs
- Oil, fat, water, vinegar, or other liquid, for slather, optional
- About ¼ cup Pork Rib and Turkey Rub (page 137)
- Whatever other rub ingredients you choose (see pages 136–137)
- Spray bottle of water, vinegar, or other liquid
- About ⅓ cup barbecue sauce
- Heavy-duty aluminum foil
- Seasoned firewood (preferably oak or hickory)

### Overview

1 • Trim the ribs of excess fat, breastbone, and skirt.

2 • Apply the slather, if using, and the rub (2 parts black pepper to 1 part salt, plus whatever other rub ingredients you choose).

3 • Start the fire and bring the smoker to 275°F.

4 • Cook the ribs, meat side up, at 275°F.

5 • Occasionally check the color and spritz.

6 • When the ribs get to the desired color (after about 3 hours), spray them with vinegar, then coat them lightly on both sides with the sauce.

7 • Tear off enough aluminum foil to comfortably wrap the ribs. Spritz the foil, then lightly coat it with the sauce. Place the ribs meat side down on the foil and wrap tightly.

8 • Return the ribs, meat side down, to the cooker and cook until tender. (Start checking after about 2 hours.)

9 • Let the ribs rest, then serve.

### Step 1 TRIM THE RIBS.

If you get a "full spare" of pork ribs, which is what we serve at the restaurant, there's a little trimming to do to get them into optimal cooking shape. It's also possible that you'll see pretrimmed ribs at your store or your butcher.

They might be advertised as St. Louis cut, which means they've already been trimmed and are ready to cook. I like the full spare because we leave more meat on the rack than the St. Louis cut, which is squared off and looks real nice but is a bit smaller than what I prefer.

The good news is that trimming the ribs is easier and requires less time than trimming a brisket. There are just a few simple, automatic cuts that I make on every rack and a few quick snips. At 2 a.m. when I'm trimming the sixty or so racks we cook a day, it takes me only about 20 seconds to trim each rack.

As usual, as a right-hander, I use my left hand to handle the meat and my right hand to hold the knife, which is a German-made chef's knife with a 10-inch blade. I use this heavier knife instead of the lighter boning knife I use for brisket because I usually have to cut through some cartilage when trimming ribs, whereas with the brisket I'm cutting only fat and meat.

Each rack of ribs has two flat faces, one showing the meat and the other showing the bones, which are covered in a thin membrane. And then there are two long edges. One edge is the straight edge of the bones where the processor sawed off the ribs. The other is a slightly arcing, rounded edge where the ribs were connected to the breastbone. One end of the ribs narrows down into a point. This is the small end. The opposite end is much broader. This is where the rack was connected to the breast plate. These are important references for trimming the ribs (see PHOTO 1, right).

To begin, I place the ribs meat side down, with the straight edge of the bone side facing me. The narrow, small end will be on my left, and the broad end on my right. With my left hand,

I smooth and spread out the whole piece so all of its little imperfect edges are easy to see.

My first cut is to remove the breastbone fragment, if it's still attached. (The ribs we get always have this little bit of the breastbone, connected by cartilage to the rack, but pre-trimmed ones from the store probably won't.) Across from the longest bones is the section that needs to be removed; it's a cartilaginous piece where the rib connects to the breastbone. If your ribs are already trimmed into a St. Louis cut, this part has been removed. But if not, you can see this section, as it's usually covered in a little fat and membrane and separated by an exposed section of meat from the main part of the rack. At about the fourth rib, feel with your hand where the hardness of the rib bones give way to a soft bit of cartilage. Grip the breastbone section with your left hand (if you're right-handed) and, cutting toward yourself with the knife, slide in the knife (see PHOTO 2). You'll quickly hit something harder than the meat. This is the cartilage. Find the line it takes in connecting to ribs 1–3 and simply cut through this with a chop by applying pressure to the knife (see PHOTO 3). I usually press down on the top of the blade with my left hand to cut through the cartilage. It should sound (and feel) like chopping through fingers in a grisly action movie. Once you've chopped off this section, you can throw it away, use it in stock or beans, or cut the meat off it for sausage making.

The next cut I make is down at that narrow end of the rack. If you feel the end with your hand, you'll notice at the very edge a little baby rib bone surrounded by a thin portion of meat. Using a nice, quick slice, cut out all of this bone, squaring off the end of the rack (see PHOTO 4).

rounded end where ribs connected to breastbone

This bone is unattached and you'll end up losing it anyway after the rack is cooked. Plus, the meat it's attached to is so thin that it will burn and might get crusty enough to tear the aluminum foil in which the whole rack will be wrapped. So it's better just to lose this bone now.

We're almost done. With the ribs still meat side down, locate the skirt—a flap of meat hanging off the right side of the rack toward the narrow end. Sometimes butchers will remove the skirt, but often it, or a part of it, is there. Simply slice through it close to the rack to remove it (see PHOTO 5, page 163). It's a nice piece of meat and should be used for something, but for the purposes of barbecued ribs, it's likely to burn up when you're cooking it anyway. It will also pull up and away from the rest of the rack when cooking and create a bald patch underneath it, which won't cook as evenly as the rest.

Now I flip the entire rack over to the other face—meat side up, bone side down. Once again I spread or fan out all of the edges flat onto the board so that I can see what the thin, curved edge of the meat looks like. It's always uneven with little shaggy bits sticking out, so I just cut cleanly around the edge, preserving as much meat as possible to create a neat, consistent line on the meat side for even cooking (see PHOTO 6, page 163).

Lastly, I feel around on the ribs for any bits of hard or stringy fat that might be hanging off. This is easily removed with a quick slice of the knife (see PHOTO 7, left). I also run my fingers across the straight edge of the bones to feel for any sharp or jagged bone ends (see PHOTO 8). This is where the processor has used a band saw to separate the ribs, but sometimes it splinters or makes for a prickly edge, which I smooth up with the knife.

You'll notice that a fine, shiny membrane covers the entire bone face side of the rack. There's a debate about whether to remove this or not. Most competition barbecuers do, but most restaurateurs don't. Members of the membrane-off camp say that it hinders smoke absorption into the meat, but I've found that it doesn't make a lick of difference as to how the meat cooks or tastes and, by the end, is barely noticeable at the level of tenderness to which we cook the ribs. So I leave it on, as removing it is both time-consuming and a little bit tricky because the membrane is slick and hard to grip. But if you want to remove it, the technique is to grip it with a paper towel and then slowly peel it off the ribs. You can use the knife to gently loosen it as you peel it back in one long piece. But, again, I don't bother with it. And now you're ready to cook!

## Step 2 APPLY THE SLATHER AND THE RUB.

Salt and pepper make a great rub for ribs, but typically we augment this to include "something red." That redness could come from any number of conventional spices, such as paprika, chile powder, or cayenne pepper. My only real goal here is to bring a little bit of reddish hue to the already pink color of the ribs. Once again, you should use the salt and pepper quantities listed in the ingredients list only as rough guidelines; I generally shoot for 1/4 cup of rub for each rack of ribs.

Once you've made your rub, you may want to coat the ribs with something to help it stick, though it is not necessary. People slather on oil, fat, water, mustard—anything that will make the surface of the meat tacky so that the rub will adhere to it.

Now, sprinkle on the rub much the same way you would for a brisket or any hunk of meat. Get that wrist and elbow moving and, anywhere from 1 to 2 feet above the ribs, gently shake the rub onto both sides, lightly covering the surface. Again, remember to keep the shaker itself moving in a nice rotation, as the heavier salt crystals tend to sink to the bottom of the mix, making the whole thing uneven when you put it on.

Also remember that it's really easy to apply too much rub, a mistake that a lot of people make. They feel they haven't gotten enough on one section, so they go over that part twice, which then inevitably appears to have a denser layering of rub than the rest of the meat. So they go over the rest again, and suddenly they have too much rub over the entire rack. There are worse things that can happen, but if you're using good meat (which I hope you are), you want the taste of it to be central, with the other flavors of rub and smoke supporting it. So, apply your rub with restraint and consistency the first time, and you're sure to get it right.

## Step 3 START THE FIRE.

The process here is the same as for brisket, so turn to page 88 for tips on getting a good fire going. The smoker should contain a full water pan.

## Step 4 PLACE THE RIBS IN THE SMOKER.

Now it's time to throw your ribs in the smoker. Ribs are the most finicky things to cook, and temperature matters a lot. They're just really sensitive. As always, use trial and error to find the best temperature for your cooker. But a good place to start is 275°F, which often seems to cook them neither too fast nor too slow. Some recommend cooking them as low as 225°F, but I think that's too cool, and it will take forever for them to be ready. I generally prefer to cook between 275°F and 300°F, depending on the quality of the meat's marbling (leaner meat I cook at a higher temperature). With ribs, temperature matters a lot. Too hot, and you might crisp the edges and dry the ribs out. Too low, and they'll never get tender.

People debate on how to position them on the grate: meat side up or down. I'm a meat-side-up guy because, just as with the briskets, the heat in my smokers is greater above the cook surface than below, so I want to have the part of the ribs with the most fat and meat exposed to that heat so they'll cook evenly. But if your heat is greater below the grate, by all means, cook the ribs meat side down.

The ribs can go for several hours without you needing to open the lid to check on them. Rather, keep track of your fire and your temperature gauge, which is placed to read the temperature of the smoker at grill height.

## Step 5 CHECK THE COLOR AND SPRITZ.

About 2 hours in, I take a look to see how the ribs are doing. Hopefully, they're getting the deep color I'm looking for. I cook sixty racks at a time and inspect every one of them to determine how it's cooking. To do this, I take a spray bottle filled with cider vinegar and liberally spray the top of the meat. I don't do this to add flavor but rather to gauge the true color of the ribs and apply moisture. The spray washes off any of the heavier smoke particles that make the ribs look darker than they actually are. Use whatever liquid you want—vinegar, apple juice, orange juice, or water. Or you can dilute a liquid half and half with water.

The color I'm looking for is a deep reddish brown, and I want it to cover the surface fully. The enemy here is splotchiness, which can result from any number of things, but is generally due to some inconsistency in the meat, fat, or rub. This results in the edges becoming dry while the center stays moist, which in turn means there is an uneven surface for smoke penetration. If I see splotches of lighter color on the ribs, I just let them keep going until they've all come to be the same color.

## Step 6 ADD THE SAUCE.

When the ribs have achieved that lovely, burnished red color, it's time to give them a little coating of sauce to prepare them for wrapping. I use our straight-up barbecue sauce for this purpose. Feel free to use whatever kind of sauce you want, though I recommend it not be too thick or sugary, which will result in it clumping as it cooks. If you have a thicker sauce, you can dilute it with water, vinegar, apple juice, or white grape juice to get a good, fluid consistency. I put the sauce in a plastic squeeze bottle for easy application. (Note: If it's cold outside, you'll want to warm your sauce, as cold sauce is also prone to clumping and cooling down the meat.)

Before I add the sauce, I hit the ribs again with another couple of sprays from the spray bottle, just to get them wet. This helps the sauce spread evenly when I apply it. Next, I lightly squirt the sauce from the squeeze bottle onto the ribs, using a back and forth motion. Then I usually spread the sauce out evenly with a (gloved) hand, but you could use a brush. I mist the ribs one more time with the vinegar to help spread out the sauce, and then I close the lid and cook the ribs for about 15 minutes to allow the sauce to set. I flip the ribs over and cook for another 15 minutes to set the sauce on the second side. Now it is time to wrap.

## Step 7 WRAP.

I wrap ribs in aluminum foil, not butcher paper. Each rack gets its own little foil packet. There's nothing special about the technique for wrapping ribs; it's pretty much common sense. You'll need a table or other work surface near your cooker. Cut one piece of foil that's a little longer than twice the length of each rack you're going to wrap and stack it on the table. In preparation for wrapping, hit the foil with a few spritzes from your spray bottle and then give it a quick few streaks of sauce from your squeeze bottle.

Use a towel, not tongs, to pull the ribs off the grill gently with your hands. The last thing you want is hard or jagged metal cutting into and shredding all that nice bark and good color you've worked so hard to get. Gently lay the rack, meat side down, on your spritzed and sauced piece of foil. Then spritz and sauce the backside of the ribs. On the ends of the rack, look for any bones that

might be sticking out, gently wriggle them free of the meat, and discard them. Jagged bones can easily pierce the foil, allowing all the juices and moisture you're aiming to preserve to leak out.

To wrap, simply fold over the sides of the foil horizontally first and then flip the ribs over again until you've created a neat, tight packet. At this point, you can do as we do at the restaurant and put the ribs back on the smoker to finish cooking for another couple of hours. But, as with the brisket, they're not going to absorb any more smoke once they're wrapped. So, if you're doing this at home, you can also stick them into an oven preheated to 275°F for another 2 hours or so, until they're done.

## Step 8 CHECK FOR DONENESS.

The single biggest question mark for a lot of people with regard to cooking ribs is determining when they're done. Unlike briskets, this isn't accomplished with a thermometer for three reasons: the ribs on a rack are of varying thickness and thus will be at different temperatures; the meat is so thin that it's hard to get an accurate reading; and the many bones that are close to the meat will absorb and radiate heat differently from the meat.

The best way to tell when ribs are ready is by feel. This is especially important because these ribs are wrapped in foil, and you don't want to have to go and unwrap every rack to figure out if it's ready or not. It takes practice, but do it a few times, and you'll get the hang of it.

Ribs *can* be overcooked. The meat shouldn't be falling off the bone, which will happen if the ribs cooked too long. The meat will also be dried out. Rather, the meat should be tender and juicy but still require a minimal bit of pull to get it off the bone.

To determine the moment to pull the ribs, I pick up every foil-wrapped rack in my hands with the towel and check its pliability. I grab it with my left hand, placing the tips of my fingers under the ribs in the middle portion. It's these thicker, straighter ribs in the middle that are the last to get done, which is why I check there. Holding a rack in my hand, I let it flex in that hand, allowing it to flop over those fingers with its own weight. If it's too floppy and bendable, it's probably overdone. If it's too stiff, it might need more time. I'm looking for just a nice, easy lever of flexibility that shows that it's perfectly done. There are some ways you can check your work. Some people twist a rib bone in the middle of the rack to see how loose it is. If it starts to break free of the meat, it's ready to eat. Other people might poke into the meat with a toothpick at that midpoint to check the consistency. If it effortlessly punctures the meat with little to no resistance, the meat is done. Generally, you're looking for looseness and a willingness to pull apart without falling apart.

## Step 9 LET IT REST, THEN SERVE.

When you've figured out the ribs are done, leave them in their foil packets to rest. You can do this at room temperature for 20 to 30 minutes, and the ribs will still be nice and warm when it's time to serve.

# BEEF RIBS

If I had to name my own personal favorite cut of barbecue, it would probably be beef ribs. They are the richest and the most decadent, succulent, and flavorful cut of beef you can put on a smoker. That's also why I don't eat them much—too rich, too hedonistic. We only cook beef ribs on Saturdays at the restaurant: they're a special treat, made all the more special because we do them only once a week.

That said, beef ribs are pretty easy to cook. In this recipe, I include a light slather of hot sauce. We don't cook them this way at the restaurant because not everyone likes spicy food, but it's my preference for sure. I rub heavily because there's so much fat, and the extra rub really melts into it well. Beef ribs don't get wrapped. You'll know they're done when they feel jiggly and soft.

### Ingredients and Tools

- 1 (3- to 5-pound) rack of beef short ribs (from the plate, not the chuck)
- 1 tablespoon hot sauce, such as Cajun Chef or Crystal
- About 1/3 cup to 1/2 cup Brisket and Beef Rib Rub (page 137)
- Spray bottle of water, vinegar, or other liquid
- Seasoned firewood (preferably oak or hickory)

### Overview

1 • Heat the smoker to 285°F and check that the water pan is full.

2 • Trim the ribs if needed.

3 • Slather the ribs with a very light coating of hot sauce.

4 • Apply the rub (equal parts salt and black pepper).

5 • Cook the ribs, meat side up, at 285°F, for about 8 to 9 hours.

6 • Spritz during the final 2 to 3 hours.

7 • Check for doneness by poking the ribs; when they feel like melted butter (about 203°F between the bones), serve.

### Step 1 START THE FIRE.

Following the instructions beginning on page 88, get a fire going and heat the smoker so it's about 285°F at grate level.

### Step 2 TRIM THE RIBS.

Beef ribs usually come quite clean and well trimmed, unlike pork ribs and briskets, so there's not much to do. If you see any big chunks or flaps of fat, trim them away. Apart from that, I don't trim beef ribs.

### Step 3 APPLY THE SLATHER.

When I'm cooking for myself, I like to slather the ribs with a bit of hot sauce. Of course, you can slather with anything you like—from water to mustard to vinegar. The slather is mainly there to help the rub adhere to the surface of the meat. I just think a little hint of earthy spiciness from a bottle of hot sauce is a fun addition to beef ribs. You can't really taste it in the final product, but it helps build interior layers of flavor.

### Step 4 APPLY THE RUB.

Using a shaker, and holding it 1 to 2 feet above the ribs, generously apply the rub—a little heavier than you would on a brisket. This is because, as rich as brisket is, beef ribs are even richer. The extra rub ends up forming a bark that balances out that richness just a little bit. I generally use somewhere around 1/3 to 1/2 cup of rub for each rack of beef ribs.

### Step 5 COOK THE RIBS.

Place the ribs, meat side up, in the smoker. As usual, I cook meat side up because I've determined that my smokers have more topside heat and the meat and fat cap can handle that. If you've got more heat coming from below, you might consider going meat side down. Again, it's up to you—the ribs can come out well either way. Cook for 8 to 9 hours, until done.

### Step 6 SPRITZ.

During the final 5 hours or so, spritz pretty frequently with water or other liquid to keep the ends from burning.

### Step 7 FINISH, THEN SERVE.

Check for doneness by gently inserting a toothpick between two membranes: the one outside the bones and the one that separates the bones from the meat. Inside, the meat should be extremely tender. Alternatively, take an internal temperature reading: the ribs should be done when they reach 203°F. Let them rest for at least 30 minutes before serving. Beef ribs are served on the bone, but great for sharing.

# TURKEY BREAST

We're not exactly known for our turkey, but it does come out real nice, and I even know some people for whom it's the favorite of all of the things we cook. That's fine, because it's also the easiest thing to cook. We don't bother with the whole turkey, just as we don't bother with whole cows or pigs. We get nice, plump turkey breasts and try to keep them moist. For this recipe (and in general, in my opinion), it's important to buy turkey breasts that have not been prebrined or injected with any sort of solution. If you're anything like me, you want to be in complete control over what goes into or is sprayed on your bird, and you never know with commercially brined turkey.

### Ingredients and Tools

- 1 (3- to 4-pound) skin-on, nonsolution turkey breast
- 1 cup butter
- Heavy-duty aluminum foil
- Seasoned firewood (preferably oak)
- Generous 1/4 cup Pork Ribs and Turkey Rub (page 137)

### Overview

1 • Start the fire and heat the smoker to 265°F.

2 • Trim the turkey breast and apply the rub (2 parts black pepper to 1 part salt).

3 • Cook the turkey for 2½ to 3 hours, then wrap.

4 • Continue cooking until the internal temperature reaches 160°F (about 1 hour).

5 • Let rest for 30 minutes, then serve.

## Step 1 START THE FIRE.

Following the instructions beginning on page 88, get a fire going and heat the smoker so it's about 265°F at grate level.

## Step 2 TRIM THE BREAST AND APPLY THE RUB.

If the skin is on the turkey breast, remove it. We just tear off the skin and throw it away. I use the same rub for turkey as pork spare ribs, so 2 parts black pepper to 1 part salt. Use your judgement, but I think a bit more than 1/4 cup rub per turkey breast is a good guideline.

### Step 3 COOK THE TURKEY UNTIL GOLDEN, THEN WRAP.

Place the turkey, skin side up (meaning, the side that formerly had skin), in the smoker and cook until golden brown (typically 2½ to 3 hours). Remove the turkey from the smoker, place the butter on top of the turkey, and wrap tightly in two layers of heavy-duty aluminum foil, dull side out. The turkey breast ends up braising in quite a lot of melted butter and its own juices and the double layer of foil ensures against leakage. Return the turkey to the cooker, this time flipping it so it's skin side down.

### Step 4 FINISH THE COOK.

Continue to cook the turkey breast until the internal temperature registers 160°F. This should take about 1 additional hour.

### Step 5 LET REST, THEN SERVE.

Let the turkey rest until the internal temperature drops to 140°F, then slice thinly against the grain and enjoy.

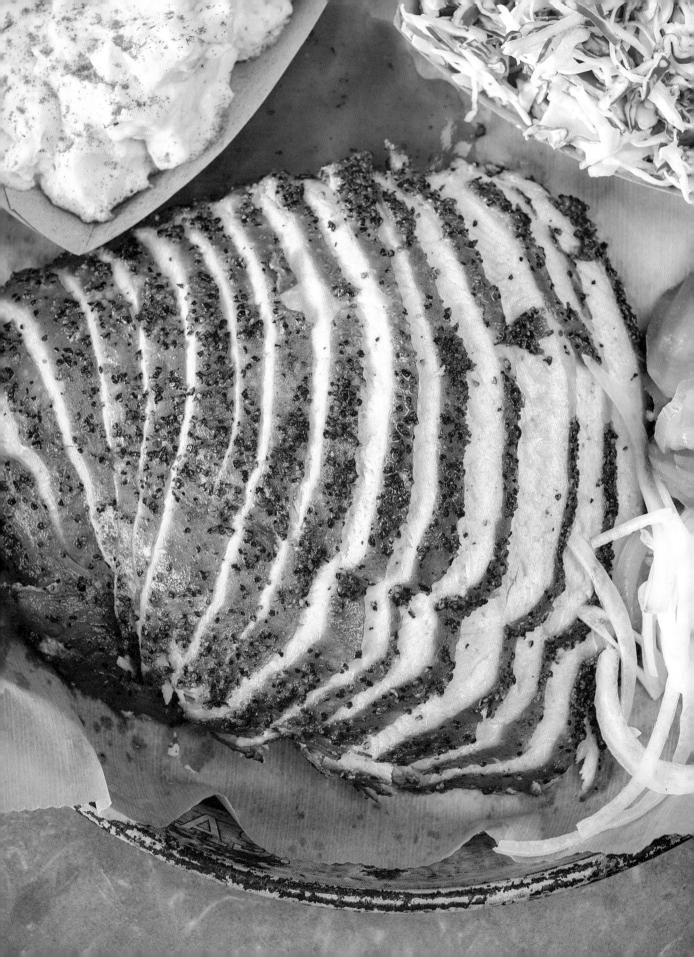

# SERVING + EATING

## • *Chapter Seven*

Here's my little confession: Since I spend most of my life back in the pits, managing fires and cooking meat, I don't actually eat barbecue all that often. However, in the old days before the restaurant opened, I certainly spent my share of time parked in front of an epic barbecue spread—and I know that having delicious barbecue served to you is much more relaxing than cooking it is.

That said, I believe there's as much an art to cutting, serving, and adorning barbecue as there is to cooking it. At Franklin Barbecue, we put a lot of effort into each one of those things, to make sure that all of our hard labor in preparing the food isn't lost at the most important moment: when a diner sits down to eat. And whether you're running a restaurant or just making barbecue for your friends and family, I urge you to pay close attention to the follow-through, right up to the moment when people are digging into the stuff.

In this chapter, I want to give you a little peek into what goes into serving lunch at the restaurant. Cutting brisket properly is practically as important as cooking it well, so I'm going to go into great detail on how to slice it for maximum efficiency and enjoyment. And no matter what you think about barbecue sauce (here in Central

Texas, it's an afterthought), I want you to have the recipes for the sauces we make. The espresso sauce is especially near to my heart, since it combines two of my greatest passions: coffee and barbecue. People tend to have one of two attitudes toward sides, as well. Some have no use for them, believing that all they do is take up room in the stomach that could otherwise be devoted to brisket, ribs, and sausage. Others, however, feel that beans, potato salad, and slaw are an essential part of the barbecue experience. Either way, I offer our humble recipes for those too. Finally, I might rightly be accused of feeling that barbecue is really nothing more than a vehicle to accompany one of my other great passions, beer. At the end, I offer my well-researched conclusions on what styles of beer go best with barbecue.

## CUTTING LUNCH

At the restaurant, the position I care about most—and the one I spend the most time on when it comes to hiring—is the person who stands up at the counter, takes the meat order, and cuts the meat. We call that person "the cutter," and it's the hardest job in the restaurant. That's because slicing, serving, and presenting barbecue takes a fair amount of skill. We own a restaurant that feeds hundreds of people every day, so I take serving barbecue very seriously. How the food is presented and how it looks on the tray are both very important to me. These things might be less important to someone cooking at home, but they shouldn't be. Even when I cook at home, I want the food to look good.

Cutting meat is a simple process, so why is cutting lunch so hard? First of all, it's a long, long shift, three to four hours of a constant barrage of hungry people who have waited for up to five hours to get their lunch. Once we open the doors, the line does not stop, so you have to be ready. You can't run off to the restroom or take a coffee break. You have to slice and slice.

And slice and be nice. You're also the first person to interact with the customer, so you have to be friendly, make them feel welcome and at ease. "So, where're you from? Sheboygan? You don't say . . ." Then you might have to help them with their order, as most people don't necessarily know what they want when you ask them, "fatty or lean?" (we'll get to that later), and they don't really have an idea of how much they want by the pound, which is how barbecue is sold.

To cut lunch, you have to know brisket. Every brisket is different (even at Franklin Barbecue, where we work really hard to ensure consistency), and you have to be able to make quick assessments on how each one is going to slice, which sections might be tender, which are especially lean and crumbly. You have to make good, precise cuts, which is not always easy with the kind of super-tender brisket we serve. We want to get every last edible morsel out of a brisket, and bad slicing can end up meaning lost product. You have to make sure that each slice is what it should be and is consistent, that it has the right amount of bark, the right amount of fat, the right amount of meat. There must be no big glob of seam fat and no big crunchy burnt piece off the back of the point. It's almost like a magic trick, requiring quick, agile hands. You hold up a glisteningly perfect piece of brisket with one hand to show the customer— "Does that look good for you?"—while you slide a chunk of burnt edge into the trash with the other.

You have to make it look good. The customer is standing right in front of you watching your every move. You're the one and only connection between that person and all of the people in the back who have helped cook that meat. If a piece of brisket looks off in some way (God forbid!), our first time to see it is the same as the customer's. It has to look great.

Finally, you have to be able to judge supply, constantly being aware of how much brisket and ribs are left versus the length of the line snaking out the door. Before we even open the doors, our staff has gone out to survey the line for how much food each party is planning on ordering. This is because every day we have more people in line than we have food to serve, and we don't want anyone to wait in line too long and not get fed. So we have a "last man standing" placard that goes

to the last person we guarantee food for. After that person, we leave it up to those people behind him or her to decide if they want to chance it. If you're cutting lunch, you need to be aware of the number of people left waiting to be fed at the end. You have to manage your portions and what parts you might keep, how many bites you are able to give away, and what parts you might be able to stretch depending on the number of people left to feed. (If you mess up either of these things, God help you . . . and the poor folks who waited in line when there was no more brisket.)

The person who cuts lunch must not only have the front-of-the-house skills and charisma of a good bartender or server but also possess the knowledge of how the meat is cooked and the knife skills of a cook. These are not easy people to find. All of this is a way of saying that cutting and serving barbecue is important. Don't concentrate solely on the cooking part of it and let proper service slide once you're almost home. You might have made the best barbecue in the world, but if you screw it up at the slicing table, no one's ever going to know.

## HOW TO ORDER BARBECUE AT A RESTAURANT

When you get up to the front of the line at Franklin Barbecue or any Central Texas joint, if you're a first timer, you may not know what you want to order. At our place, someone has probably already polled you in line on what and how much you're going to get, so it shouldn't be difficult. Also, we try to be friendly.

I'll admit this isn't the case everywhere, but I believe that wherever you go, you should get precisely what you want.

If you say you'd like some brisket, at most Central Texas spots, you'll be asked what kind and how much? You'll have noted that they sell by the pound and you'll be thinking to yourself, *How many pounds can I eat?* With such thinking, many people commit themselves to overordering. So, while it's fine to order a pound or a half pound, it's also acceptable to order one slice or two slices or whatever. In this day and age, everyone has a digital scale that can do the calculations, so it

makes no difference to us whether you order by weight or by amount.

You'll then be asked what kind of brisket you want, lean or moist? At Franklin, that'll be lean or fatty. If you've read the preceding chapters of this book, you'll know that question refers to whether you want a slice off the leaner flat end of the brisket or the fattier point. It's your call. You're also welcome to ask for a piece that's heavy on bark or even something crispy, if they've got it.

Likewise, you needn't feel the pressure to order ribs by the pound. It's fine to order one rib or two ribs or however many you want. Same goes for pretty much anything else on the menu. Just order any way you want and don't let anyone tell you differently.

When I was really getting into barbecue, before I ever dreamed of having my own restaurant, I had a standard order when I went to visit places around Texas: half a pound of moist brisket and ribs, with a side of potato salad. I'd order a sausage only if it was made in-house, and I'd ask for the barky end piece off the flat of the brisket, if they had it.

# HOW TO SLICE A BRISKET

Everybody has his or her own method for slicing brisket, but there's one thing on which we can all agree: never, ever slice with the grain. That one mistake can turn even a beautifully cooked, moist, and jiggly brisket into brutal strands of chewy fiber. Beyond that one, simple truism, though, there are many ways to do it, and many of them work well.

It's important to know that, just like the way a song is performed can determine a lot about your ability to enjoy it, the way a brisket is sliced will have an impact on the way you perceive that meat. For instance, if you go to a not-so-great barbecue joint, you might find yourself getting a plateful of paper-thin slices. That's a time-honored, wily technique for trying to hide brisket that's way too tough. Likewise, if you get really thick slices, the place might be hiding that the brisket was overcooked and is so overly tender that it lacks any structural integrity (or, it might just mean that somebody rushed through the cutting). If the slices weren't thick, they would fall apart before they got to the plate.

But let's start with the knife. At some places you might see the slicer using an electric knife. While I understand why people might resort to an electric knife—ease, comfort, avoiding the risk of carpal tunnel for people who cut brisket for hours and hours—I can't condone its use. First, it's really slow, taking forever to get through a single slice. Second, you can't feel the blade cutting through the meat, which is important. You receive all sorts of sensory information about the brisket—texture, level of doneness and rendering—from the knife. My favorite knife for slicing isn't fancy at all. It's a serrated, 12-inch Dexter-Russell slicing knife, model S140-12SC. It's the kind with a white plastic handle that you can buy at any restaurant supply store. I like it because the serrations are sharp and well defined but not scalloped. That's going to help you get through the softness of the bark without ripping it to shreds, which is a constant risk.

It's the very anatomy of a brisket that makes it such a challenge to slice well. As you know, the whole packer-cut brisket is made up of two muscles, the flat and the point. And the point sits right on top of the flat, separated by a thin layer of fat. The only problem with this arrangement is that the grain of the meat in the flat runs perpendicular to the grain of the point meat. So if you want your brisket to be sliced into nice, tender pieces, you're going to have to cut each section a little bit differently.

## Cutting Brisket, Step by Step

My approach to slicing brisket is based on one simple goal: maximizing the deliciousness of every single piece. To me, the bark holds the most flavor and texture. You can't have a great piece of brisket if it doesn't sport at least a small section of bark, so I try to cut it in a way that ensures every piece a decent bark-to-meat ratio. That's why I don't separate the point from the flat before slicing, the way some people do: the part of the flat sitting directly underneath the point will have no bark. At the restaurant, we may very well not serve some of the meat from this part, as parts of it can be too fat-laden or mushy to be cut into a coherent slice. If it's too fatty, we'll throw it away, and if it's all meat, we may save it to use as chop in the Tipsy Texan sandwich (see page 188), or add it to the beans. Home cooks out there will likely want to save it, even if it doesn't make for great slices.

- You want to wait to cut the brisket until it's cool enough to touch with your hands, maybe an hour or so after you've pulled it from the smoker. Unwrap the brisket and lay it in front of you (see PHOTO 1, right). I'm right-handed, so I like to start with the flat on the right and the point on my left.

- Before I do anything, I imagine the line where the point terminates and where the flat dips underneath it (see PHOTO 2). You'll know where this is because you'll see the seam of fat that runs between them, and you'll be able to see the point begin to rise up from the flat. You can actually feel the point shift around on top of the flat if you gently move it with your hand. This is the place where I'm going to stop slicing the flat. It's not exactly parallel or symmetrical to the end of the flat (on my right), so I also visualize the way my slices will sort of have to fan out across the arc of the meat if I want them to be even and uniform.

- The first cut I make is called the end cut. It's just the little tapered section on the far end of the flat. It's mostly bark and therefore delicious. A perfect end cut is a good indicator of a well-cooked brisket: this is one of the best pieces you can get! I usually slice the end cut in half and offer the two little nubs as a snack for whoever's at the front of the line at the time (see PHOTOS 3 AND 4).

- Now slice the flat. The left hand (for righties) is very important in slicing brisket. If your brisket is really tender, it's your left hand that's going to keep it together as you're running the knife across it. You've got to apply a bit of pressure to hold it together, so don't be shy. I put my left hand very gently on top of the flat to hold it down and hold it together and then I start slicing across the flat. You want to aim for slices that are 1/4 inch thick, the size of a no. 2 pencil, as I like to say. I slice across the flat evenly and gently, cutting it into nice, uniform strips. It's not necessary to be exactly perpendicular to the grain, but rather just cut across it in some way. The flat is never a perfectly even rectangle, so you'll find yourself fanning your angle out a bit. Move the knife smoothly and confidently, sawing gently back and forth. Use the thumb of your nonslicing hand to hold the bark in when necessary, as the serrations of the knife will want to pull some of that bark off (and you don't want this to happen). Stop slicing when you reach the beginning of the point—it's that line you visualized before you started (see PHOTOS 5 AND 6).

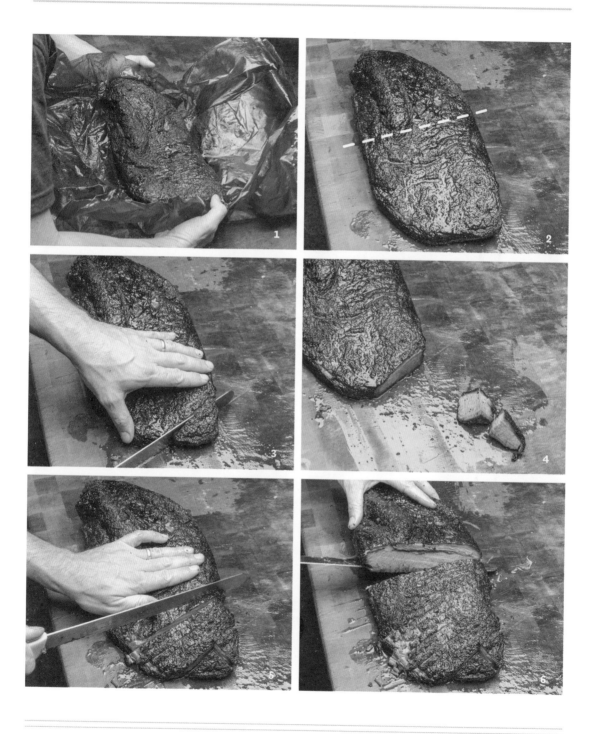

- Now that you've sliced the flat, keeping its slices firmly together (unless you've already served them to a hungry crowd), move the sliced flat out of the way. Sitting in front of you should be the whole, uncut point section of the brisket. Swivel this whole piece 90° (see **PHOTO 7**, left) so its exposed side is now facing you. With your left hand, gently pull back the right side of this piece and you'll find underneath the bark a really jiggly slab of fat with a little meat attached to it. Cut this part away with the knife (see **PHOTOS 8 AND 9**). We throw this slice of mostly fat away.

- Turn the point 180° so that the exposed side where it was connected to the flat is now facing away from you (see **PHOTO 10**). This is where we slice the point in half. It's helpful to cut the whole point in half because it is so soft and moist that it's more manageable to slice this way. After you cut it in half, you can pick up one-half and get that money shot everyone loves of a big chunk of super-tender, moist, dripping brisket (see **PHOTO 11**).

- You'll now be slicing the point against the grain. I like to cut the left half of the point first. Start delicately cutting from the middle out to the edge in slices 3/8 inch thick (the width of a large pencil), or almost twice as thick as you sliced the flat. Place your left hand flat against the bark, gently holding it down as you slice. Keep the slices together as much as possible to prevent the juices from running out across the board (though a lot of juice still will). Also, if you're not going to serve the whole thing at one sitting, the brisket stays juicier and fresher for longer when left intact and unsliced (see **PHOTO 12**).

- If you're going to slice up the whole thing, move the left half of the point (which you have just sliced) out of the way and pick up the right half. Put it in front of you with the sliced side to your right (for righties) and slice it in the same manner as you sliced the other half of the point. When you get to the end, where it's mostly bark, you might find it helpful to push the bark over in front of the knife to make sure that every last possible slice has both some bark and some meat (see **PHOTO 13**, below). It's hard to explain, but when you start cutting it, you'll know what I'm talking about. You'll be left with a thin slice of mostly bark at the end. This is the burnt end, and you can slice it into delicious little snacky-snacks for the hungry hordes who are waiting for you to finish all of this darn slicing!

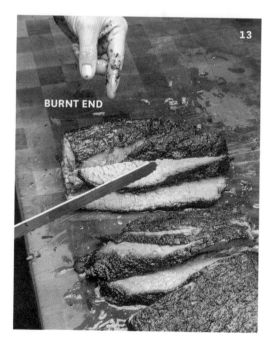

- If you've cooked the brisket well, the point should stay together, but you might encounter some shreds of beef or little scraps coming from the remnants of the flat underneath it. Take those bits that stay behind along with any little crunchy edges and save them for either the chopped beef or the beans.

- You can judge a great slice and the success of the brisket cook by applying the "pull test." Hold up a slice of brisket between the thumb and index finger of both hands. Now gently pull it apart. The brisket slice should easily break, but it shouldn't fall apart. If it crumbles apart or disintegrates, it's overdone. If it stretches out, it hasn't been cooked long enough.

## THE TIPSY TEXAN

At Franklin Barbecue, our menu is mostly traditional Central Texas fare. There is one oddity, however: the Tipsy Texan sandwich, which is essentially a pile of chopped beef, sausage, slaw, and sauce served on a bun. This giant, honking sandwich costs only eight dollars, and considering how much of our prized brisket we use for each one, it's a pretty good deal for the customer (and decidedly *not* cost-effective for the restaurant). I'm not going to lie: I get a little wistful every time I have to chop up some of our beautiful brisket and slap it on a bun. So why do I still keep the Tipsy Texan on the menu? Honestly, I can't really say. But, like the weather or a birthmark, it's just something we have to live with.

The origins of the sandwich date to the earliest days of the Franklin Barbecue trailer. A prominent local bartender, who billed himself as the Tipsy Texan (and still does), would come to eat and, per his request, I'd make him one of these stupid-big sandwiches. In its present-day incarnation, it's a monstrous assemblage of chopped lean brisket mixed with espresso sauce, sausage, slaw, sauce, pickles, and onions, and it probably weighs 1¼ pounds.

In my opinion, the best time to make a Tipsy Texan is when you have extra chips of chopped lean brisket, which we like to mix with Espresso Barbecue Sauce (page 192). But when we don't have chips lying around, our only option is to slice fresh brisket and chop it up—a move that causes many brisket purists to gasp in horror. We top the chopped brisket with a sliced whole sausage, sliced pickles and onions, and finally with about ½ cup of slaw.

What's my final verdict on the Tipsy Texan? Well, it is certainly one of the most delicious and decadent ways to use up leftover brisket—no doubt about it. But it is certainly not the ideal use for pristine brisket. I guess we just keep it around for the sake of tradition. I should also note that *if* you can get your mouth around one and finish it, you might consider a career in professional eating.

# SAUCE

In the rest of the country, sauce is an essential, inseparable component of barbecue. In Central Texas, barbecue sauce is considered optional, at best.

You see, in Central Texas we believe that well-made barbecue has no need for sauce. If the pitmaster has done his or her job, the well-balanced flavors of great beef or pork and sweet oak smoke are complex enough and delicious enough to stand on their own. It's the German-Czech orthodoxy we've inherited, and until recently, there still were places that stayed true to the meat-market origins of the cuisine and didn't offer sauce (or silverware) for their meat. Nowadays, however, pretty much everyone has sauce because diners expect it. And while I truly believe really good barbecue needs no sauce, a little bit can be nice to accentuate the flavors in the meat. But it has to be good sauce.

Bad sauce for me lacks balance—it's too sweet, too thick, too something. And my ultimate hallmark of a bad sauce is a sauce that has liquid smoke in it. Smoke flavoring should come from the meat (and not too much of it, mind you).

Barbecue sauce doesn't make good barbecue, but it can certainly complement good barbecue. There really isn't a Texas-style sauce. Up in the Panhandle, sauce tends to be a bit more midwestern, while in East Texas it tends to have the sweet and ketchupy notes of the Deep South. At Louie Mueller, you get a light, watery sauce with margarine, but if you go to our place, our everyday sauce is a well-balanced ketchup sauce with a little bit of cumin and chile powder going on.

Our sauce is what I'd call Central Texas style in that it's tomato based and balanced between sweet and savory with a bit of acidity. It's really just meant to lubricate already moist meat, to add sweetness that highlights the savory flavor of smoke, and to contribute acidity that helps balance the richness of the fat and protein. I've been working on sauces since the early days of my barbecue cooking endeavor. Stacy ruefully remembers periodically getting home from her restaurant job late at night and me excitedly forcing her to try a spoonful of barbecue sauce the second she walked through the door. That said, I hit on these basic recipes pretty early on and have stuck with them ever since, believing they're the best suited to our style of cooking.

# REGULAR BARBECUE SAUCE

This is what I call sweet sauce, even though it's not terribly sweet on the spectrum of barbecue sauces. It's a good, all-purpose sauce. We bottle it, sell it, and put it on the tables in the restaurant. I also mix it with vinegar to sauce the spare ribs when I cook them.

*Makes about 3 cups*

- 1¾ cups ketchup
- ½ cup plus 2 tablespoons water
- ¼ cup plus 1 tablespoon cider vinegar
- ¼ cup plus 1 tablespoon white vinegar
- ¼ cup plus 1½ teaspoons brown sugar
- 2 tablespoons plus 1½ teaspoons Worcestershire sauce
- 1 tablespoon chile powder
- 1 tablespoon ground cumin
- 1½ teaspoons kosher salt
- 1½ teaspoons coarse black pepper

Combine all of the ingredients in a saucepan and warm gently over medium heat, stirring occasionally. There is no need to bring the mixture to a boil, as the idea is just to warm it enough to melt and integrate the ingredients. Once you have done that, remove from the heat and let cool. Transfer to a jar, bottle, squeeze bottle, or however you want to store it. Store in the refrigerator for up to 1 month.

# ESPRESSO BARBECUE SAUCE

Nowadays various recipes for coffee barbecue sauces are floating around. But when I first came up with mine, it was an original and inspired distillation of my life at the time. I was working at Little City coffee shop, starting to get geeky about coffee and even geekier about barbecue.

An all-nighter on a brisket cook was inevitably accompanied by strong coffee, and it didn't take a genius to notice the affinity that starlight, the sweet roasted aromas of good espresso, and the homey aromas of wood and smoke have for one another. If these smells go so well together in the middle of the night, I thought to myself, their flavors should just as easily merge into a sauce. And the sauce was a way to capture that experience of being awake in the depths of the night watching a fire.

It didn't turn out to be that easy to bring the flavors together. The first time I made the sauce, I used a little Krups espresso machine that a guy I worked with at Little City had given me. And the sauce seemed great to me. Then I tried to refine it, but when I forced a taste of the "improved" version on Stacy, she told me it was nasty and that I needed to hang it up. Then I went back to my original recipe with a few, small tweaks, and it was a go.

It's important to note that there is no substitute for the espresso in this recipe. If you don't have access to an espresso machine, I would take some of the warm sauce to a reputable coffee shop, get them to pull a shot for you, and mix them together there. I know it sounds weird and may even be slightly embarrassing, but the results are worth it. A freshly pulled shot with a good crema brings much more to this recipe than a stale or cold one. I prefer a medium-roast, Central American bean (Guatemala, El Salvador, Costa Rica). The brisket drippings are a matter of taste, but I believe this sauce needs the beefiness to make it taste right.

*Makes about 2 cups*

- 1½ cups ketchup
- ½ cup white vinegar
- ½ cup cider vinegar
- ¼ cup dark soy sauce
- 1 tablespoon garlic powder
- 1 tablespoon onion powder
- ¼ cup brown sugar
- 3 tablespoons (1½ ounces) freshly pulled espresso
- Brisket drippings, for flavoring

Mix the ketchup, both vinegars, the soy sauce, garlic and onion powders, and sugar together in a saucepan and bring to a simmer over medium heat, stirring occasionally. Remove from the heat, stir in the espresso, and then add the brisket drippings to taste. Let cool, then transfer to a jar, bottle, squeeze bottle, or however you want to store it. Store in the refrigerator for up to 2 weeks.

# VINEGAR SAUCE

This is the non-Carolina vinegar sauce that I created to go with my non-Carolina pulled pork. Use whatever hot sauce you like or whatever you've got around. Of course, some are hotter than others, so consider how spicy you want the sauce to be.

*Makes about 3 cups*

- 1 cup white vinegar
- 1 cup cider vinegar
- 1 cup ketchup
- 1 tablespoon brown sugar
- 2 tablespoons hot sauce
- Dash of Worcestershire sauce
- 2 teaspoons Hungarian paprika
- Kosher salt and coarse black pepper

Combine all of the ingredients, including salt and pepper to taste, in a saucepan and warm gently over medium heat, stirring occasionally. There is no need to bring the mixture to a boil, as the idea is just to warm it enough to melt and integrate the ingredients. Transfer to a jar, bottle, squeeze bottle, or however you want to store it. Store in the refrigerator for up to 1 month.

# FIG ANCHO BEER BARBECUE SAUCE

I don't serve this at the restaurant, but I do make fun sauces for some events—and this sauce combines a few of my favorite things.

*Makes about 6 cups*

- 4 ancho chiles, rehydrated in 4$^1$/$_2$ cups hot water and the water reserved
- 12 figs, grilled, stemmed, and quartered
- $^1$/$_2$ yellow onion, sliced
- 4 tablespoons butter
- 1$^1$/$_2$ cups brown sugar
- 1 (12-ounce) bottle (1$^1$/$_2$ cups) stout or porter beer (I prefer Left Hand Brewing's milk stout)
- 1 cup ketchup
- $^1$/$_2$ cup white vinegar
- $^1$/$_2$ cup cider vinegar
- 6 tablespoons fig preserves
- 1 tablespoon honey
- 1 tablespoon kosher salt
- 1 teaspoon coarse black pepper

In a skillet over medium heat, sauté the chiles, figs, and onion in the butter for about 10 minutes, until the figs and chiles are tender and the onion is translucent. Transfer to a blender and add the sugar, stout, ketchup, both vinegars, the preserves, honey, salt, and pepper. Puree until smooth, adding as much of the reserved chile soaking liquid as needed to reach the desired texture. Store in an airtight container in the refrigerator for up to 2 weeks.

## ACCOUTREMENTS: DILL PICKLE SLICES, SLICED ONIONS, AND INDUSTRIAL WHITE BREAD

The German and Czech heritage of Central Texas barbecue is evident not only in the kinds of meats we serve but also in the classic accompaniments for the meats. Not every style of barbecue requires large vats of pickles and sliced onions to be on offer right after you come out of the service line. And although these are add-ons, many people consider them to be highly important to the Texas barbecue experience.

And I don't disagree. The sharpness of dill pickles (sweet pickles or bread-and-butter chips don't work) and of raw white onion is the perfect counter to the unctuousness of good meat (as is beer). Good ole industrial white bread adds a sweet flavor and soft textural touch to the mixture. With brisket, eat these things in combinations and sequences of your own choosing. Some people wrap a slice of brisket in a piece of bread, add a couple of dashes of sauce, and garnish with a few slices of pickle and onion for a delicious sandwich wrap. Others might just pop a couple of pickle morsels and raw onion slivers into their mouth after a particularly good bite of brisket and sausage. Use these tools to your own delight.

# SIDES

In the world of Central Texas barbecue, people treat sides pretty much the same way they treat sauces: they're fine, but you should probably just save the room in your stomach for barbecue. Indeed, the meat-market heritage of Central Texas barbecue doesn't include sides either. But, like sauces, sides have become a staple of the barbecue spread, and today we serve, eat, and enjoy them just the same.

## BEANS

We get a lot of requests for our bean recipe. What makes it so popular? Probably the simple fact that it's another way of delivering brisket, which is its second-most important ingredient (arguably).

*Makes about 8 cups; serves 8 to 10*

- 1 pound dried pinto beans, picked over and rinsed
- ¹/₂ cup diced yellow onion
- ¹/₂ cup bean seasoning (recipe follows)
- 8 cups water
- 1 cup chopped brisket bark and shredded meat

Combine the beans, onion, bean seasoning, and water in a large pot and let soak for 4 to 6 hours, or for up to overnight, which is what we do in the restaurant.

Add the brisket bark and meat to the soaked beans and bring to a boil. Lower the heat to a slow simmer, cover, and cook for 3 to 4 hours, until the beans are tender.

## Bean Seasoning

*Makes about 2 cups*

- 1 cup chile powder
- ¹/₂ cup kosher salt
- ¹/₄ cup coarse black pepper
- 2 tablespoons onion powder
- 2 tablespoons garlic powder
- 1 teaspoon ground cumin

Combine all of the ingredients and mix well. Store in an airtight container.

## POTATO SALAD

I spent hours peeling potatoes, drinking beers, and talking to friends when Stacy and I had our little barbecue trailer. I like flavor, so we engineered this salad to have a nice, mustardy bite and lots of pickles in the German-Czech tradition.

*Makes about 6 cups; serves 12*

- 3 pounds russet potatoes, peeled and cut into 1/2-inch (or smaller) dice
- 1 cup mayonnaise
- 1/2 cup yellow mustard
- 3/4 cup chopped dill pickles
- 1 tablespoon pickle juice
- 1 tablespoon coarse black pepper
- 1 teaspoon kosher salt

Cook the potatoes in a pot of boiling water just until tender. Drain, transfer to a bowl, and let cool. In a small bowl, stir together the mayonnaise, mustard, pickles, pickle juice, pepper, and salt. Add to the cooled potatoes, toss and stir to mix well, cover, and refrigerate immediately. The salad will keep for up to 4 days in the refrigerator. Serve cold.

## COLESLAW

Coleslaw serves an important purpose not just as a side, but also as a condiment for barbecue. It offers a crunchy textural contrast to tender meat, and its vinegary zip is a nice counter to the sweet, fatty, and smoky flavors we serve at Franklin. And of course, it's an important component of the Tipsy Texan sandwich (see page 188). This tangy slaw is great alongside all sorts of barbecued meats.

*Makes about 2 cups*

- 1/2 pound (about 2 cups) shredded cabbage mix
- 1 tablespoon kosher salt
- 1/4 cup sour cream
- 2 tablespoons mayonnaise
- 2 tablespoons cider vinegar
- 2 tablespoons rice vinegar
- 2 1/4 teaspoons coarse black pepper
- 1 1/2 teaspoons dry mustard powder

Place the cabbage in a colander or strainer and sprinkle with the salt. Let the cabbage sit and exude some of its juice while you prepare the dressing. In a large bowl, stir together the sour cream, mayonnaise, cider vinegar, rice vinegar, pepper, and mustard powder. Blot away any excess moisture from the cabbage with a towel, then transfer to the bowl containing the dressing and toss to combine. Cover and refrigerate until ready to serve. Serve cold.

## WHAT TO DRINK
## WITH BARBECUE

I like beer. I like lots of other things too, but I *really* like beer. In fact, it's not at all rare to find one in my hand.

When it comes to pairing beer and barbecue, the first rule is, *yes*! The second rule is, *there are no rules*. That said, I do have my own personal preferences.

Now, I must preface all that's about to follow with the general assertion that I like most beers. But my favorites all share certain characteristics. I'm not into ultra-hoppy beers. They can be exciting for the first half of the beer but end up fatiguing the palate by the end. They also don't pair very well with barbecue—or with a lot of foods, for that matter. I really like more malty beers.

I also really enjoy beers on the lower end of the alcohol scale. This is largely because "sessionability"—a beer's capacity to be consumed comfortably in decent amounts without incurring palate fatigue, slurred speech, motor-skill impairment, and general dufusness—is important to me. I like to drink beer, but I don't like to get drunk, so something not too potent and with a generally balanced and tasteful approach is perfect for me.

Luckily, this seems to be the kind of beer that also turns on lots of Texan brewers, which is one reason I'm so enthusiastic about the brewing scene in this state. Maybe it's only natural that in a hot climate where we drink beer as a form of hydration, mild, sessionable, low-alcohol beers are not hard to find. That doesn't mean that the beers lack flavor or crispness or interest. It just means that it's pleasant to drink more than one of them and to drink them with food.

If I were to name a staple beer for me in life, it would be the Big Bark amber lager from Live Oak Brewing of Austin, one of the best breweries anywhere, if you ask me. Big Bark beer has been on tap at the restaurant since we opened. How perfect is it for barbecue and for me? Well, like Central Texas barbecue, it's has a Czech and German influence—specifically in the form of the Czech and German malts that go into it. It's also got German hops, but not too much—just enough to balance the malt notes. And I like that it has "bark," just like the best part of the brisket, though only in the beer's name. Smooth, balanced, and reddish amber— it's ideal.

But lots of beers are good with barbecue. Even some of the larger-scaled beers like Shiner Bock and Lone Star go real well. Hans' Pils from Real Ale Brewing Company, another Hill Country favorite, is relentlessly refreshing and sessionable. I'm also crazy about the beers from Austin's Hops and Grain brewery. Their Altbier, called Alt-eration, is technically an ale but has a crispness and light hoppiness along with a copper-amber color that makes it not too far off from the style of Big Bark, which is a lager.

Jester King, another local brewery, specializes in sour beers. I'm not always a fan of really tart, sour beers, but a mild sour is delicious, and Jester King makes some good stuff. I think smoke and beer go well together in general, but Ron Extract, one of the founders of Jester King and a serious beer scholar, points out that smoke and sour flavors are a classic combination. "All beer would have originally been smoked," he says, noting that before the days of modern malting techniques, malt was made by drying the grains, after allowing them to steep and start to germinate, over fire, which would have imparted smokiness. He also suggests that most beer in the old days would have been at least slightly sour and funky, since commercial yeast (which is relatively stable and allows for a predictable and notably less funky fermentation taste) had not yet been cultivated. This meant that brewers had to rely on unpredictable wild yeasts to ferment the beer. Wild yeasts are difficult to control and can take fermentations in all sorts of directions, leading to the funky, sour flavors we associate with that style of beer.

If I had to distill my beer-and-barbecue philosophy into a few key points, they'd probably go something like this:

**1** • Excessively hoppy beers, such as West Coast–style IPAs, tend to overwhelm the palate. I don't like to pair them with barbecue very much, as their intense grassy, floral flavors seem to conflict with the mellow, smoky-peppery flavors of the meat.

**2** • Super-boozy beers and barbecue don't really mix. After drinking a few, you're not really going to be able to appreciate the taste of the barbecue (and if you're mid-cook, you risk losing focus). Session beers in the 5% ABV or lower range are my go-to, as I like to be able to drink a lot of beers without getting drunk.

**3** • Czech- and German-style beers are a natural pairing for Central Texas–style barbecue. In warmer weather, I gravitate toward crisp, refreshing styles—think pilsner, Kölsch, or Altbier. In the autumn and winter, I might go for one of the darker styles, like a bock or porter.

**4** • Smoked meat loves sour beer! Try a session-able style like Berliner Weisse, which often clocks in around 3% ABV.

**5** • Smoked meat and smoked beer work well together too. In fact, I like this combination so much, I once teamed up with the folks at Thirsty Planet Brewing Company to create the Franklin Barbecue smoked porter (sadly no longer in production), and with Jester King to create a beer with grilled, smoked figs!

## • *Resources*

### MAIL-ORDER MEAT

**Creekstone Farms**
www.creekstonefarms.com

**Snake River Farms**
www.snakeriverfarms.com

### CENTRAL TEXAS BREWERIES

**Jester King Brewery**
www.jesterkingbrewery.com

**Live Oak Brewing Company**
www.liveoakbrewing.com

**Austin Beerworks**
www.austinbeerworks.com

### WOOD SOURCES

**Craigslist**
www.craigslist.org
* There are many online sources for various types of wood chips and chunks, but your best bet for buying whole logs is to find a local source via Craigslist.

### BOOKS AND WEBSITES

McGee, Harold. *On Food and Cooking: The Science and Lore of the Kitchen.* New York: Scribner, 1984.

Myhrvold, Nathan, Chris Young, and Maxime Bilet. *Modernist Cuisine: The Art and Science of Cooking.* Bellevue, WA: The Cooking Lab, 2011.

www.amazingribs.com
* An amazing compendium of barbecue knowledge, not just in the Central Texas style, but also for all the different styles of cooking meat.

# • *Acknowledgments*

I poured what I know about barbecue into this book, but this tome and even the restaurant itself wouldn't have been possible without all the collaboration, unfettered support, and hard work of so many people over the years.

First and foremost I thank my wife, Stacy Franklin, the real reason any of this ever happened, and the most vital part of everything I am and do.

Hey, Benji Jacob: Those things don't work on water, unless you've got power! Benji is the third pillar on which Franklin Barbecue stands; he has committed almost as much of himself to this project as Stacy and I have, and has always been unimaginably generous with his hard work, time, and creativity.

Ben and Debbie Franklin, my parents, planted the seeds for this in many, many ways (besides the obvious one). Introducing me to barbecue and restaurant ownership at a young age and helping get things off the ground with some early funds are just two of the ways. Thanks so much.

Thanks to Tommy and Anita Howard, my grandparents. I grew up in their music store, and hanging out with them was a huge influence— without them I wouldn't be the person I am today.

Among many other things, they gave me a sense of how to run a family business and an enduring love of music.

Also to my parents-in-law, Helen and Steve Jefferson: Thanks for spending so much time in Austin and always being there to lend a helping hand.

Same to Big Jeff Keyton and Travis Kizer, two guys who believed in me from the get-go, and through gestures big and small have helped me find just a smidge of success in the barbecue world.

Braun Hughes—brisket wizard, workhorse extraordinaire—has been there with me through thick and thin. Braun, besides being part of the family, you keep everything running, and we couldn't do it without you. Thanks, esé. Thanks also to the entire staff at the restaurant and to all the good employees who have ever worked with me. Franklin Barbecue wouldn't be what it is without all the people who have lent a piece of themselves to this project. And that would include

Melissa, the pie woman, often the first person I talk to in a day (when working a rib shift and she comes in at 4 or 5 in the morning to drop off the day's desserts). Also, I thank Rod, the wood guy, for keeping me in the good stuff and saving me from even more headaches. The wood is good. And Dr. Jeff Savell, Meat Science professor of A&M: thanks for bringing barbecue into the academy and giving us all a slight sense of actual sophistication.

When it comes to this book, I've got to recognize David Hale Smith for his hard work and commitment to getting the thing done, as well as for all the other times he's helped me navigate life's pesky fine print. Wyatt McSpadden's photos were totemic for me when I was getting into barbecue, so it was the greatest of honors to have him lend his immense talents to this book. Wyatt's also one of the greatest guys to just hang around and drink a beer with. Thanks to him, his wife, Nancy, and his assistant, Will.

Also, thanks to Jordan Mackay for his words. He somehow managed to make sense of what regularly spills out of my mouth and then spin it into a whole book with things like organization and punctuation. And then Emily Timberlake, our editor at Ten Speed, made sense of his work, while our designer Betsy Stromberg made it all look like a real book. Truly a team effort, so thanks to all the people who made this book a reality.

And, finally, I want to extend my greatest gratitude to all the customers, supporters, and people who've waited hours in line to eat at Franklin Barbecue or at various festivals around the country. I am truly humbled and honored that people consider what we've worked so hard to create to be worthy of their time and energy. Without all of you, honestly, none of this would have ever happened. I hope you'll keep coming back and that you'll enjoy this book.

• *Aaron Franklin*

As work on the book came to a close my wife, Christie Dufault, volunteered that I didn't have to thank her in the acknowledgments because she really doesn't have much to do with barbecue. As someone who sees herself a vegan at heart who is coerced by her husband into all-too-often consuming meat, she sort of had a point. But what she doesn't realize is that she's at the heart of everything I do. It is she that I strive to make proud, and her tolerance of my frequent smoke-tinged trips to Austin, my idiosyncratic work habits, and otherwise self-indulgent way of life allow me to be the sort of writer I want to be. So, sorry, honu, but thanks—for being our anchor and for making me laugh.

I also want to offer gratitude to my mom, Leslie, and to Neal for putting me up all those weeks I was working on the book and for re-arranging their lives so that I could save money by borrowing one of their cars. All that meant a lot. Plus, it was nice to get to spend some time around y'all. Also, I'd be remiss for not mentioning that all that time I was in Austin was likewise made possible by our dear neighbors and great friends Paul and Vanessa Einbund, who looked after Fernie and Thornie.

Thanks also to David Hale Smith for thinking to bring me in on this project and for being there every step of the way. David Black, thanks for getting this deal done; I see great projects in the future. This is my third book at Ten Speed, so I must extend gratitude to Aaron Wehner for continuing to have confidence in me. I also consider myself fortunate to have worked with Emily Timberlake, our wonderful editor. She contributed more than anyone will know. And, of course, muchos gracias to the great Harold McGee, who deigned to look over parts of this book to ensure they made scientific sense.

And, lastly, hail to Aaron Franklin for letting me do this project with him and for squeezing me into his ridiculously busy life (and therefore thanks to Stacy for likewise tolerating my contin-uous presence). Working on this book has been incredible for me—not just in what I've learned about barbecue, wood, welding, meat, and smoke, but in the general confidence I've gained in myself. Aaron, all that comes directly from your own immense knowledge and your own extraordi-nary, unshakable confidence. I just wish you could come see my backyard, because only you can figure out how to get that thing you built into it.

• *Jordan Mackay*

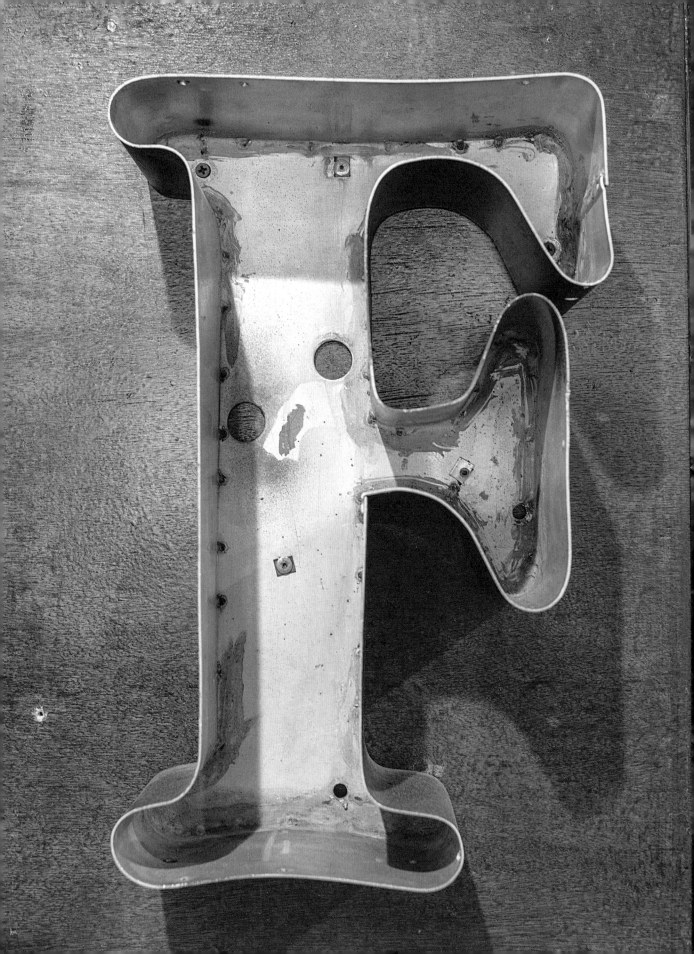

## • *Index*

Copyright © 2015 by Hasenpfeffer LLC
Photographs copyright © 2015 by Wyatt McSpadden

All rights reserved.

Published in the United States by Ten Speed Press,
an imprint of the Crown Publishing Group, a division
of Random House LLC, a Penguin Random House
Company, New York.
www.crownpublishing.com
www.tenspeed.com

Ten Speed Press and the Ten Speed Press colophon are
registered trademarks of Random House LLC.

With the exception of page iv: Photo copyright © Jeff
Stockton, all other photos are by Wyatt McSpadden.

Library of Congress Cataloging-in-Publication Data
Franklin, Aaron.
  Franklin barbecue : a meat-smoking manifesto /
Aaron Franklin and Jordan Mackay ; photography by
Wyatt McSpadden.
    pages cm
  Includes index.
  1.  Barbecuing.  I. Mackay, Jordan. II. Title.
  TX840.B3F698 2015
  641.7'6—dc23
                      2014036177

Hardcover ISBN: 978-1-60774-720-8
eBook ISBN: 978-1-60774-721-5

Printed in China

Design and illustrations by Betsy Stromberg

21

First Edition